The ISDN Literacy Book

Gerald L. Hopkins

 ADDISON-WESLEY PUBLISHING COMPANY
Reading, Massachusetts • Menlo Park, California • New York
Don Mills, Ontario • Wokingham, England • Amsterdam • Bonn
Sydney • Singapore • Tokyo • Madrid • San Juan • Milan • Paris

Figures 5.10 and 5.11 are from the International Telecommunication Union (ITU), and have been adapted with the prior authorization of the Union as a copyright holder. All modifications lie with the author and are in no way to be attributed to the ITU. Complete volumes of ITU material, from which the figures were adapted, can be obtained from: International Telecommunications Union, General Secretariat—Sales Section, Place des Nations, CH-1211, Geneva 20, Switzerland.

The cover logo is used with the permission of the Corporation for Open Systems International. The cover art was created by Roger Williams.
Inside front cover art is based on a concept and design developed by Ray Albers, Jerry Simmons, and Gerry Hopkins and rendered by Mark Heffernan.

Acquisitions Editor: Thomas E. Stone
Sponsoring Editor: Deborah Lafferty
Marketing Manager: Robert Donegan
Production Supervisor: Nancy Fenton
Cover Designer: Eileen Hoff
Text Designer: Ron Kosciak
Text Figures: Peter Whitmer, Editorial Services of New England
Copy Editor: Kathryn Lyon
Senior Manufacturing Manager: Roy Logan
Manufacturing Coordinator: Evelyn Beaton
Project Manager: John Svatek, Editorial Services of New England

Library of Congress Cataloging-in-Publication Data
Hopkins, Gerald.
     The ISDN literacy book / Gerald L. Hopkins.
     p. cm.
     Includes bibliographical references and index.
     ISBN 0-201-62979-8
     1. Integrated services digital networks.
TK5103.75.H67   1994
004.6′2—dc20   94-41198
                                                   CIP

1 2 3 4 5 6 7 8 9 10 — MA — 97 96 95 94

In Love,
To Carole, Fred, and Kate

Contents

Foreword

SDN has been a long time coming, so much so that too many people doubt that ISDN (It Still Does Nothing) will happen. But I have to agree with Gerry Hopkins that ISDN (Information Superhighway Delivered Now) will happen. It is important that we get the word out about ISDN's delayed but inevitable arrival because ISDN offers the major upgrade of our 100-year-old telephone system that will be needed to bring Information Superhighway (Iway) services to small offices and homes. And the current resurgence of ISDN is being taken up by an industry whose importance was previously misunderstood by calling it CPE, namely the personal computer industry. The PC industry (in partnership with telephone companies) is now driving ISDN through its highly competitive product development and distribution processes, all the way through to the development of software and solutions.

Gerry Hopkins and I disagree about ISDN. He's certifiably gung ho about ISDN, and with this book he advances it greatly; but, at the beginning of his unlucky 13th chapter, Gerry admits that ISDN is *not* inevitable. ISDN's long and sad history feeds Gerry's doubts. From up close he's watched telephone companies talk big for a decade about ISDN's potential and then fail to deploy it. All this is true enough, and, if it's any help, I say the trouble has been that the telephone companies have misunderstood ISDN, thinking it was all about various Integrated Services—ISdn—when it's just plain Digital Networks that we need—isDN.

Well, despite ISDN's history, I don't share Gerry's doubts. I'm sure that ISDN's time has come. In short, Vice President Al Gore's vision of an Information Superhighway has captured our nation's imagination. We may not be able to house the homeless, solve world hunger, or contain regional conflicts, but we shall by God build the Iway. When we do, we'll need on-ramps, and the only real, near-term alternative for Iway on-ramps is ISDN.

But even if the Iway takes a wrong turn after the next election, the implacable personal computer industry has recently realized that, to continue its burgeoning growth, it will soon need the next factor-of-ten improvement in communications bandwidth for homes and small offices. So, probably because telephone-company people insist on calling our wonderful PCs customer promises equipment (CPE), PC companies are wrestling control of ISDN away from the telephone companies, and they will make it happen.

If they do, Gerry is wrong—ISDN is inevitable. But of course Gerry is also right. After all, he wrote this book.

Gerry is right that a large number of people will soon have to know a lot about ISDN, will soon have to be ISDN literate. But how many? My estimate, upon which you should base no serious plans, is that about 100,000 people in the United States will need to be ISDN literate to do their jobs. Another 1,000,000 will want to read this book because ISDN is fascinating, especially when you contrast its sad history with its exciting possibilities.

Exciting possibilities? Having myself declared 1982 to be the Year Of The LAN, I am no stranger to hype. On one hand, ISDN has certainly been hyped to death for a long time. The negative reaction to ISDN's early hype and broken promises remains one of the biggest factors slowing its acceptance today. On the other hand, ISDN really *is* a big event. We are talking here about only the second generation of our 100-year-old telephone system. We are talking about taking the telephone from analog to digital— and if these words don't mean anything, don't worry, Gerry is about to explain them to you, even down to what "bit" means.

Digitizing the telephone will make it even more reliable and even less expensive, just for starters. Then it will improve telephone communications for computers, which are themselves digital. (Already a third of U.S. households have computers, and their use is not slowing.) Voice, fax, and computer communications will be unified—making them even easier to use. Or, as Nolan Bushnell, inventor of the video game, regrets he said: ISDN can make your telephone as easy to use as a personal computer. In time, telephones will carry video, so at long last you'll be able to see who your wrong numbers are.

Will the continued use of ever-faster modems suffice for these exciting possibilities? No. Modems are far past their point of diminishing returns. What I like most about the ISDN service I've been using for a year is that my computer calls are completed reliably and silently in under 3 seconds— under 1 second will eventually be the norm from coast to coast. Compare this to the song and dance required when dialing a modem.

This book you're holding is wide-ranging and important. As I've said, it starts with basics, like what a "bit" is. It describes how the current telephone works. And, of course, it lays out what ISDN is technically. But wait, there's more. Gerry thinks that to be ISDN literate you should know about the international standards process that created ISDN and continues its evolution. Then, he talks about ISDN products, their users, and the new applications they are pursuing.

One of Gerry's best chapters describes how to develop an ISDN application. I think it becomes clear at that point how far ISDN must go before it is ready to be purchased by individual consumers. Gerry's most contentious chapter, if you're sure that ISDN is inevitable, is Chapter 13, which tells us what could go wrong with ISDN. Gerry ends with a formidable list of other information sources, as if his book doesn't answer every question you might have about ISDN.

Robert M. Metcalfe

Dr. Robert M. Metcalfe invented Ethernet in 1973, founded 3Com Corporation in 1979, and is now *InfoWorld's* Iway correspondent.

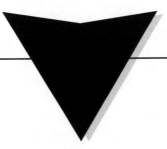

Introduction

I SDN is an enabling technology that provides us access to information from our homes, offices, or wherever else we may happen to be. It is likely to have a major impact on the way we live, learn, and work. We are now at the threshold of ISDN emerging as a household word—being used along with other household words such as telecommuting, videotelephony, electronic mail, and personal computers.

In this book, we introduce ISDN in the context of these real-world considerations and requirements. In addition to defining and surveying key aspects of ISDN, we explore how ISDN fits into the world, and why it is worthwhile. After reading this introductory work, you will be better equipped to read the more technical literature concerning ISDN. The book also provides an additional perspective on ISDN for readers interested in a social, political, or economic view of our society (travelers on the information highway).

By looking at other technologies in their nascent stages, we can glimpse the degree to which ISDN might affect our future. Who would have thought, in 1950, that computers or televisions would so profoundly affect our lives? Or (in 1920) that automobiles would affect the design of our neighborhoods and the style of family living?

Today, ISDN is developmentally where television was in 1950. In that era, shows were broadcast for only a few hours a week; although by then most people had seen television and were beyond the stage of constantly marveling over it, most did not yet have TV sets in their homes. Later in that same decade, TV westerns and situation comedies were the norm, everyone had a large screen TV in their house, and couch-potato behavior had begun to evolve. Television then, like ISDN today, was beginning to change the way we lived, learned, and, to a degree, the way we worked.

During that same era, computers were also emerging. Questions the media often asked about these large, tube-type machines included: "What are we ever going to use these computers for anyway?" and "How many of these do you think we'll eventually have?" (The estimate varied from about 10 to as many as several dozen). Yet by the mid to late 1960s, we accepted the business use of computers; payroll systems routinely used them and computers were beginning to infiltrate other coporate arenas. In fact, it was considered embarassing for a company not to have its own computer, and many companies mortgaged their future to obtain one. Where necessary, organizations connected computers and terminals with data circuits. These early data circuits, like early ISDN, were difficult to install, expensive, and often needed a variety of adjustments.

The introduction of minicomputers and then personal computers brought computing power within the reach of small organizations and individuals. Interconnecting them, however, was economical only within a local area. Wide-area connectivity was much more difficult and generally too expensive for small businesses or individuals. ISDN technology, however, promises wide-area access, connectivity, and flexibility that previously were beyond the reach of most people. In the same manner that spreadsheets for the personal computer rocketed end-user computing into the modern era of high-powered PCs, ISDN services are now encouraging large-scale telecommuting, distance learning, and other uses of distributed computing systems.

In this book, we explore the fundamentals of ISDN in the context of other technologies, trends, and societal changes. ISDN and other information-enabling technologies are on the verge of changing our lives much as automobiles once did. If this were a book about automobiles, it would describe the period just prior to the introduction of the Model T Ford and discuss the basic technology systems of the automobile. It would also examine the need for highway infrastructure, the possibility of the motel industry, the development of auto-repair and parts-supply businesses, and the potential for getting where we wanted to go, when we wanted to go there. It would explore the shift from urban to suburban living and the suburban sprawl that followed.

Like the automobile, ISDN will allow greater freedom of choice. Even considering sticker shock, rush-hour traffic, and ransom-like demands from repair shops, who among us would willingly do without their automobile? Who would be willing to surrender the personal freedom of going where you want, when you want? Who would want to give up the freedom of living somewhere other than in close proximity to work? ISDN (and related technologies) combined with computers hold the promise of giving greater freedom and flexibility to those who use it.

I start by defining ISDN—what it is—and end by describing what it might become. In between, I explore how ISDN can work for us—now and in the near future. The media offer a fragmented view of ISDN and related technologies. In this book, I attempt to provide a unifying view of ISDN and explain how the pieces fit together. I explore various uses of ISDN, generally from the perspective of end-user applications and benefits. I discuss potential pitfalls of ISDN in order to help the user avoid any potholes in the on-ramp to the Information Highway. Finally, I review current work for future ISDN and speculate on its applications.

The book is organized for reading front to back. Each chapter builds on the previous chapters. Nevertheless, I include enough supporting material in each chapter so that if you read chapters out of sequence, they will stand alone. My hope is that you can read through this book and enjoy it, without struggling unduly with the content. To get an overview of ISDN technology, you don't need to completely grasp every detail on the first reading. Instead, first read the book more quickly to get a sense of the whole. Then, you may want to go back and re-examine chapters at the level of detail that suits your needs. Most of all, I hope you enjoy reading this book; we also hope in reading it you become sufficiently "ISDN literate" to participate in a discussion of ISDN when the topic arises. On some occasions, this discussion may be sandwiched between, say, sports and politics. On other occasions, it may be a discussion critical to your personal future or the future of your organization.

* * *

Many people contributed to making this book a reality. At the almost certain risk of omitting someone, I'd like to thank those people here. First, thanks to Ron Aitchison for such a thorough review effort. His insights and comments have helped me think and rethink the contents of the entire book on many occasions. Also, each of the other reviewers has helped in specific areas. They are David Cypher, Jeff Fritz, Harold Zullow, and David LaPier.

Of course, at Addison-Wesley, Debbie Lafferty and Tom Stone have been both encouraging and constructively critical in shaping this book. Others who have been very helpful by encouraging me to write the book are Harvey Deitel, Bill Horst, Shukri Wakid, and Ron Aitchison, among the many.

It has been my good fortune to have worked in Technical Subcommittee T1D1 (later T1S1) writing ISDN standards, at the NIUF promoting the use of those standards and applications of ISDN, and at the Corporation for Open Systems in the ISDN Executive Council. While pursuing the goal of providing an ISDN that end users want and need, I have met and worked with truly interesting and memorable people. Those experiences and acquaintances have shaped this book in a variety of ways. In addition to the people mentioned above, these colleagues include John Seazholtz, Ray Albers, Don Auble, Irwin Waxberg, Jeff Fritz, Bob Downs, Ham Mathews, Randy Sisto, Ronnie Potter, Joan LaBanca, Randy Spusta, Al Vitenas, Al Hood, Laura Izzie, Kaj Tessink, Nick Batis, Earl Anderson, Wayne Felts, Robin Rossow, Ruthy Davis, Anthony Williams, Pat D'Innocenzo, Pat Donovan, Roger Nucho, Dan Sheinbein, Richard Stephenson, Timon Holman, Bill Selmeier, Bob Sherry, Leslie Collica, Leslie (Fraser) Staples, Cheryl Slobodian, Elizabeth Schrock, Rob Williams, Mary Hopkins, Dorothy Mulligan, John Mulligan, Keith Wollman, Stephanie Boyles, Ray Hapeman, Robin Rossow, Art Reilly, Karen Patten, Jim Briggs, Steve Rogers, Dick Aloia, Jake Jacobson, Matt Thompson, Bill Highland, Jim Gaines, Ed Moore, Doug Place, Steve (Oven Stuffer) Wilson, Mike Lipchok, Randy Spusta, Karen Fitzgerald, Zach Gilstein, Kathie Jarosinski, Mike Joyce, H. Gordon Brown, John Kantonides, Dana Shillingburg, Harry Hetz, and Mick Stefanik (and many, many more).

As a final note, this book reflects my own perspectives on ISDN in the context of our society. It does not necessarily reflect the opinions of anyone else or of any organization. To assure this independent view, this manuscript has not been previewed or edited prior to publication by any of the organizations with which I am associated (including the NIUF, COS, and Committee T1) or by my employer (Bell Atlantic). While it would please me to think that members of all these organizations would like this book, the views expressed are my own, and only I am accountable for its contents.

Those wishing to contact me with comments or queries about this book may do so at hopkins@aw.com.

Gerry Hopkins

1

ISDN Concepts and Perspectives

I n this book, we take a guided tour of the often confusing world of telecommunications technologies, practices, policies, and strategies as they relate to the *integrated services digital network (ISDN)*. ISDN is a revolutionary set of new telephone services that has the potential to change the way we live and work. Future technologies, building on the constructs of ISDN, will likely continue to have a dramatic impact on our lives.

Today, everyone seems to be talking about the new concepts in telecommunications: ISDN, *broadband ISDN (BISDN)*, *high-definition TV (HDTV)*, automatic callback, caller ID, and many others. Newspaper articles and trade journals are filled with reports of silicon-chip manufacture, regulatory decisions by some obscure government group, and vague benchmark claims (megabytes, megaflops, megadebt) that imply future change or enhanced capability in telecommunications. But fragmented information such as this can lead to confusion. What is really happening? How do the technological developments relate to one another and what direction are they taking?

This book surveys a wide range of subject matter to put ISDN in a broader context and illuminate why ISDN is a technology whose time has come.

The book places news items and ideas in the context of our changing society in order to explain the nature, motivation, and value of ISDN. Without our present social, cultural, and economic milieu, the role of ISDN might be very different. Unlike the Connecticut Yankee, ISDN would be irrelevant in King Arthur's Court. We explore the current and near-future social, cultural, and economic milieu in some detail to demonstrate why ISDN seems to be the right technology for this time. You will see how ISDN and related telecommunications technologies—if widely deployed—will facilitate trade of information.

1.1   WHO IS AFFECTED BY ISDN?

Ultimately, ISDN will likely transform information exchange just as the wide distribution of the telephone system transformed communications earlier in this century. In other words, we will all have ISDN to consider. Some will consider ISDN an opportunity and, by applying it and other appropriate communications technologies to their advantage, will manage their organizations toward increased success. Others will likely pay an opportunity cost by avoiding it. Executives, managers, working-level engineers, and other staff now have an opportunity to integrate these ISDN opportunities into their planning processes.

Each of us can benefit from an understanding of the changes occurring in telecommunications today, especially changes concerning ISDN. When executives factor in ISDN, they may find themselves reconfiguring entire product lines and rethinking major investment alternatives. Most of us should consider ISDN as a worthwhile technology candidate for use where appropriate. Engineers who design the silicon chips that perform the protocols described in this book can benefit from understanding the impact of their work and may gain insights into new directions for future work. Teachers can use ISDN to instruct students who do not physically attend a class, or distribute homework, or interact with parents. Investment analysts can use ISDN to uncover direct investment opportunities; by understanding ISDN and similar technologies, they can evaluate an organization's ability to communicate effectively and profitably. It would be difficult to find a person who is not able to take advantage of ISDN in some positive way.

1.2 ISDN OVERVIEW

Briefly, ISDN is a forward-looking telecommunication network that has the potential to accommodate both the present and near-future needs of information movement and exchange. The goal of ISDN development is to have one common network to move all possible forms of information (speech, music, images, text, video) so the end user can send and receive information as readily as dialing over the telephone network for voice communications. In addition to connecting voice transmitters and receivers, ISDN can connect computers and other information devices.

ISDN has been over a decade in the making. Developers have had to contend with vast embedded pre-ISDN telephone networks that need additions and replacements to evolve into ISDN. Also, ISDN developers needed to gain industry support to have a credible chance of putting ISDN in place for broad user access. For these and other reasons, it has been a difficult and time-consuming process for the early ISDN concepts to evolve into the present body of standards and networks. As the standards have matured, equipment manufacturers have been able to create products that match the specifications set out in the standards. Many network services providers now purchase these products and deploy them to provide ISDN. These providers have dedicated huge sums of capital and considerable planning to obtain an array of network capabilities with interoperability among equipment manufactured by different companies.

The coming of ISDN is the result of an unprecedented, cooperative effort among a large number of formerly disparate—now interdependent—groups: end users, equipment vendors, service providers, software writers, telephone companies, and even various parts of governments. What these groups are striving for (and achieving) is agreement on exactly what ISDN should be. The next step is for each group to perform its role to make ISDN work. Telephone companies must continue to invest in network capabilities, manufacturers need to develop equipment, end users must be receptive to using ISDN, and government officials need to create rules and regulations to support ISDN development.

These issues seem more complex than they actually are because change is occurring simultaneously along several dimensions. Along the network technology dimension, the idea of ISDN has been unfolding for some years. Even before ISDN development was complete, developers were working on other technology advances for possible future networks. Along the societal-change dimension, the decision to split the Bell System into a group of competing companies paralleled a new interdependency in supplying equipment and completing long-distance calls. These functional changes require other major operational changes within the organizations if we want to have telephony services that are national in scope. Along the organization-management dimension, the recent emphasis on restructuring, reengineering, and downsizing is confusing to people both inside and outside the industry. This book separately introduces the various dimensions of change and development, beginning with the functional concepts of ISDN technology.

1.3   THE FIVE ATTRIBUTES OF ISDN

A common difficulty most people encounter when first introduced to ISDN is getting a good feel for what it really is and what it is not. The ideas and concepts that are the foundation for ISDN are abstractions that indeed can be elusive. A technique to bring our thinking into alignment with IDSN concepts is to define ISDN by its attributes. Understanding its attributes helps us understand ISDN and helps us clarify how it is both different from and similar to today's telephony. Reviewing the attributes is like a test: if each of the attributes is satisfied, then by definition the system must be ISDN. This approach is also fairly intuitive, so most people find it easy to use.

An ISDN network has the following five attributes:

- End-to-end digital connectivity,
- Integrated access,
- Small family of standard interfaces,
- Message-oriented signaling, and
- Customer control.

These attributes mesh with the definition of ISDN in both national and international standards.

End-to-End Digital Connectivity

End-to-end digital connectivity simply means that from the ISDN terminal equipment (or telephone set) at one end to the ISDN telephone set at the other end, the network is entirely digital in nature. This is in contrast to conventional telephony, which is analog in nature. Even though this attribute may at first seem to be a relatively minor consideration, the impact of digital transmission is surprisingly pervasive. In fact, digital connectivity is arguably the single most important attribute of ISDN because so much of our information equipment is inherently digital in nature.

Compared to pre-ISDN analog telephony, signal quality is vastly improved. Digital signals can be reproduced over long distances with far less distortion of the original signal. Because the signal is literally re-created along the way, the signal received can be equal in quality to the signal sent (assuming adequate error-control techniques present in an ISDN environment). Further, digital representation provides a convenient mechanism for message-oriented signaling.

Digital transport is highly desirable because many information signals that travel across the network are natively digital. Much of today's electronic computing equipment operates digitally to perform various logical operations and to store results. Not only do various types of personal computers, minicomputers, and other similar devices operate natively using digital representation, but so do many other devices such as the compact disk player and discphotography devices used to render images.

The notion of digital representation is so fundamental to understanding ISDN that we will discuss it in some depth. A digital signal can take on only certain discrete values whereas an analog signal can take on *any* value in its range.

The conceptual difference between digital and analog is illustrated by comparing Figure 1.1 with Figure 1.2. Figure 1.1 shows that a ball on a ramp can attain any height within the range (between the two walls). Figure 1.2

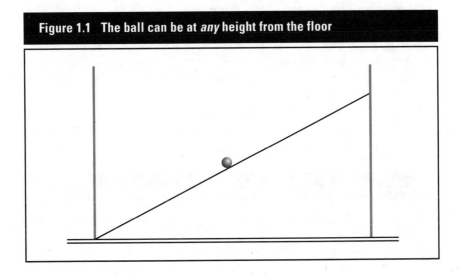

Figure 1.1   The ball can be at *any* height from the floor

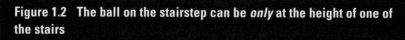

Figure 1.2   The ball on the stairstep can be *only* at the height of one of the stairs

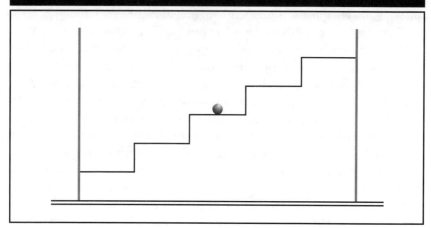

shows stairsteps that span the same range as the ramp. Although the ball can be on any of the steps, the stairsteps do not encompass all the height values that are available on the ramp. (Note: We ignore any heights achieved going from one step to another. In electrical circuitry, such transition states are generally not of interest in digital representation.) As illustrated in Figures 1.3 and 1.4, we can add more and more steps to the staircase to come closer and closer to achieving all the values of the ramp.

In electronic equipment, the basic building block of these discrete values is the *BI*nary digi*T,* or *bit*. A logical bit is either on or off (or up or down, or 1 or 0, or any other yes/no logical construct). Combinations of bits allow us to construct a binary counter, which can count arbitrarily high, one by one. The table below demonstrates the concept for two bits, which are sufficient to count to four (or at least four distinct values).

By increasing the number of bits, we increase the maximum count. (And we all know that by using more fingers we can count higher.) Three bits allows us to count to 8, 4 bits allows us to count to 16, 5 bits to 32, and 6

Binary Representation	Value	Binary Representation	Value
00	Zero	10	Two
01	One	11	Three

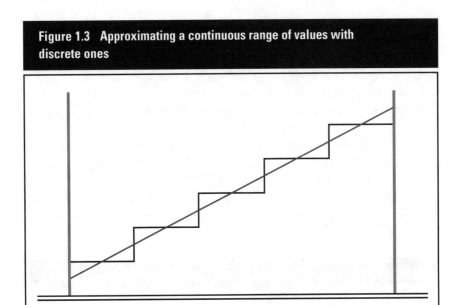

Figure 1.3   Approximating a continuous range of values with discrete ones

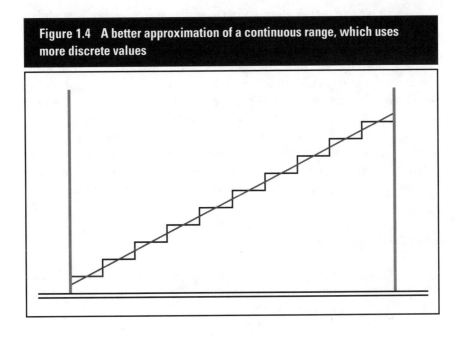

Figure 1.4   A better approximation of a continuous range, which uses more discrete values

bits to 64. A group of eight bits (called a *byte*) is sufficient to count to 128. The key concepts here are that there are discrete or distinct values that we can count one by one and that we can represent by digital values.

But digital representation is not limited to merely indicating numeric values. Our computers and word processors need to represent letters of the alphabet as well as other symbols. For these purposes, strings of bits are mapped to the letters of the alphabet and punctuation symbols. These mapped bits represent a code, and you need to know the rules to encode and decode the message. For example, the Morse code is a mapping of dits and dahs (shorts and longs) to the alphabet. The most popular coding scheme in computing and communications is the *American Standard Code for Information Interchange (ASCII)*. The table below demonstrates ASCII coding for a few letters of the alphabet.

Binary Representation	Letter	Binary Representation	Letter
0100 0001	A	0110 0001	a
0100 0010	B	0111 1010	z

We can represent any information using digital technology. It's simply a matter of encoding the information using a particular set of rules. Of course, the sender and receiver must both apply the same set of rules for a message to have meaning. But for some forms of information, there are so many different encoding/decoding schemes that it is difficult for an end user to know how to interoperate with anyone else. This plethora of methods is one of the most difficult challenges to accommodate in real systems.

You need to use an appropriately complex set of encoding/decoding rules to get the most satisfactory results. If the representation is overly simple, you lose information details. On the other hand, if you work with more complex representations, you need greater amounts of computer and communications power.

Integrated Access

Integrated access means that there is only one passageway allowing the user to access many services. The ultimate ISDN goal is to provide *all* services through one common access line.

If you are not the person who ordinarily orders telephone service for your organization, it may surprise you that in the analog pre-ISDN telephone world, service is bound to the access line itself. That is, a new or additional service (such as a switched data line) generally requires the physical installation of a new or additional access line. Sometimes this requirement is due to the technology (a particular kind of service requires a particular type of access line), and sometimes it is bound to capacity (an additional service requires an additional access line).

If all services could be provided over a common access line, selecting a new or additional service would not necessarily require a new or additional access line. The existing line could be reused—or used alternately—for the new service. The need for additional access lines would be strictly a function of required transmission *capacity*.

This attribute of common access essentially disassociates the service from the access line itself because any service is available over any access line. Consequently, you can request a new or different service and almost instantaneously obtain it because the needed access line already exists. (In contrast, pre-ISDN, you might have to wait several days for simple services and several weeks for special ones.)

Small Family of Standard Interfaces

The family of standard interfaces refers to the user-network interfaces. To be effective, the family must be *small*, and the interfaces must be *stable*, that is, change very little and not very often. You can achieve the small size and stability only by standardizing the interfaces. The need for *standards* cannot be overemphasized; ISDN that is not standardized is an oxymoron.

The fewer the interfaces the easier it is to successfully use ISDN. To effectively select and use terminal equipment, the end user must be able to connect it to the ISDN network. Plugs must fit into jacks. Software must be capable of establishing ISDN connections and supplying digital information to the ISDN network according to the interface specifications so that the network can successfully transport information to its destination. With very few interfaces to worry about, the end user can relocate the terminal equipment and, more likely than not, the equipment plug will fit the new jack, and the equipment will continue to work properly with the ISDN network.

Well-designed user-network interfaces isolate the end user's terminal equipment from the network. Equipment on both sides of the interface continuously evolves and improves. Stable user-network interfaces allow incorporation of technology improvements into the ISDN network without affecting end-user terminal equipment. Conversely, new technology implemented in terminal equipment doesn't adversely affect the ISDN network.

Finally, a limited set of user-network interfaces promotes *end-to-end interoperability,* making it possible for the sending end-user's equipment to work properly with the receiving end-user's equipment. By limiting ISDN service capabilities to a small number of standard types, widespread implementation of all the capabilities is more likely. A set of standardized services must be complete in scope and limited in number.

To successfully transfer information, the equipment on either end of a connection must have interoperable service capabilities. Even pre-ISDN, when a telephone user dials a distant person, the user expects terminal equipment on either end to be arranged for *ciruit-switched speech.* But sometimes, the distant end returns only tones or beeps to the user originating the call. In such a case, the distant end-user equipment may not be a telephone, but a modem or fax machine arranged for a certain *circuit-switched data* capability. And you can achieve successful information transfer only when the terminal equipment at either end is arranged for the same type of circuit-switched data capability.

Standardizing and limiting the number of service capabilities provided over an ISDN user-network interface helps simplify the task of successfully transferring information from one user to another.

Message-Oriented Signaling

Traditionally, telephone signaling changes a condition (*stimulus*) at one end of a circuit to achieve an effect (*response*) at some other point along the circuit. For example, a telephone user who lifts the handset from its cradle creates a physical connection from one side of the phone to the other. This connection creates a path from the network battery through the phone and back to network ground, causing current to flow. This current flow activates a relay in the network, which connects the telephone user to a dial-tone source. This scenario is typical of the many *stimulus–response signaling* techniques used in telephony signaling.

Message-oriented signaling consists of *messages* sent from user to network and back again. Each entity, the user and the network, is expected to conform to scripts of behavior known as *procedures*. The messages are not prose-like text that tell us, for example, to "provide dial tone." Rather, ISDN messages are (for economic and performance reasons) more cryptic than English prose (more like "one if by land, two if by sea") and are specified in the ISDN protocol standards.

Under ISDN, each service requires its own set of messages and procedures. But because all the messages and procedures can operate over the same access line, message-oriented signaling offers a way to provide a *variety* of different services on the *same* access line. Moreover, you can add a wide range of new services by introducing new messages and procedures to support the services. It's like expanding the vocabulary for describing services. To understand and speak this vocabulary, both the network and the terminal equipment need to be able to handle the new messages and procedures. To do this, manufacturers typically provide software updates.

Customer Control

With ISDN, the end user can specify to the network what services he or she wants. Using message-oriented signaling, the user selects a service while the call is being established. The user no longer needs to *subscribe* to a service in advance. Extending this technique, we could establish the terms and conditions of subscription, such as bill payment and call forwarding. Today, an end user establishes these subscription terms when arranging for telephone service.

As new services are added to ISDN, users will be able to select them, providing, of course, their ISDN telephone or ISDN terminal has the necessary capabilities to use these services. When a new service becomes available in the network, users will have to reprogram their equipment so they can properly signal the network to obtain the service. In some cases, terminal equipment (for example, an ISDN videotelephone) should support the new service with no more than a software programming update; in other cases, more extensive changes would be required. For example, even if a software update allows equipment to signal for a larger capacity information channel, the equipment itself may be unable to use this larger channel without additional changes.

Users will gain control because affordable ISDN will be deployed almost everywhere—just as today's telephone service is available almost everywhere at affordable rates. ISDN users may be able to remotely control equipment such as heating or air conditioning units at distant buildings, send full-color electronic greeting cards to friends, and jointly work on documents with distant coworkers. Imagine working on a writing project with a distant coworker and, at the same time, following a meeting in progress via a videobox on your workstation screen.

1.4   ISDN EVOLVES FROM EXISTING TELEPHONE SYSTEMS

Given the substantial investment in and benefit from existing telephone systems worldwide, it should not surprise you that ISDN is evolving from existing telephony. Although much of the existing investment can be reused (for example, the ubiquitous and expensive copper wire *subscriber loops* that connect each end user to the telephone network), many pieces of most networks will need to be replaced or augmented. Although more detail is presented in Chapter 4, in general, to make the switch to ISDN, telephone companies will have to convert telephone network switches from analog to digital, make digital switches ISDN-capable (via hardware and software upgrades), add *signaling system 7 (SS7)*, and create *64 Kbps clear channel capable trunks (64 CCC)*. The conversion will include adding packet-service capabilities and trunks.

This huge legacy of assets and possible future investments offers choices to telephone network providers. They must invest prudently in this new ISDN technology to adequately reward their investors and provide new ISDN services and technologies to meet the needs of their customers. Not surprisingly, some network provider companies see the opportunity more clearly and are willing to invest greater sums of capital than others.

Social and political agendas are also wrapped up in the evolution of ISDN from traditional telephony. Some potential end-user beneficiaries want ISDN services now. These supportive end users want to cajole or even force the existing telephone companies to provide a comprehensive ISDN sooner. Other end users are not aware of ISDN, don't see any benefit, and don't care what happens—as long as their telephone rates don't go higher. Politicians and regulators are trying to satisfy as many constituents as possible.

After reading this book, you understand that ISDN, as available today, presents new possibilities to you and your business. In most geographic areas, ISDN is being implemented now as the first movement on the digital information highway. In other locations, ISDN is not yet evident because network providers are not convinced that their end users want it. Still other network providers want to wait for the next generation of technology, or perhaps the generation of technology after that, before moving to future technologies.

We are in the process of deciding how much we are willing to invest and what amount of benefit we want to derive from ISDN information-service capabilities. Our decisions will determine our competitive advantage both nationally and internationally. We should each consider where we want ISDN and future telecommunications capabilities. We need to responsibly participate so that currently proposed and debated laws and regulations will provide the most desirable outcomes for our society.

1.5 SUMMARY

ISDN is a forward-looking telephone-network technology, suitable for both traditional voice capabilities and more sophisticated digital computer needs. The five attributes described in the sections above—particularly the digital nature of ISDN—combine to provide the capability of serving both voice and computer needs. Understanding why the digital nature of ISDN is so important requires a fundamental grasp of the differences between discrete digital values and continuous analog values (which can take on any value).

ISDN is a communication network that can provide a large number of services over a single serving architecture through one limited set of interfaces. This network architecture is, first and foremost, an exclusively digital architecture. To request services and establish connections, messages are sent to and through the ISDN network.

Yet despite the dramatically improved capabilities of the ISDN network over existing telephony networks, ISDN was conceived to evolve from existing networks. ISDN uses existing subscriber loops—the twisted-copper-wire pairs—from the end user to the telephone-network-switching central office. Network providers can modify existing digital switches to provide ISDN, although they must replace earlier vintage analog switches. Some parts of the existing network are reused for ISDN, other parts are modified, and still other pieces must be added. Network providers reclaim as much of the pre-ISDN network assets as possible to provide ISDN.

ISDN, a radically improved technology compared to *plain old telephone service (POTS),* is available now at rates affordable to most of us. In the next chapter, we explore why we need ISDN now.

2

Demand Pull for ISDN

This chapter explores the demand for ISDN. Writers in the trade press often ask: "Why do we need ISDN? Isn't this just a technology looking for a user base?" But at industry meetings across the country, a groundswell of end-users are beginning to argue the opposite: they need ISDN; it's a user base clamoring for a technology that can meet their needs. Although users who clearly recognize the benefits of ISDN may still be in the minority, users' emerging needs demand ISDN solutions.

Moving data is a requirement of our information-hungry postindustrial society. ISDN is the state-of-the-art communication technology that fulfills this requirement. If ISDN did not exist, a similar service or set of services would emerge to meet the need. As the information age continues to evolve, so does the way in which we rely on information. Advances in technology both promote and respond to our increasing reliance on information.

This chapter will briefly highlight the economic evolution that led up to the postindustrial era. It then turns to a discussion of the nature of technology itself before moving on to a detailed examination of the technology of tools. Finally, it looks at technology as it relates to our societal systems and institutions.

2.1 EVOLUTION TO THE POSTINDUSTRIAL AGE

Socioeconomic evolution has moved along a continuum from primary industries (agricultural or extractive) to secondary industries (industrial or manufacturing) to knowledge industries (information based). Knowledge industries form the foundation of the information age that has only recently emerged.

Commentators have different opinions on when the information age began. Many assert the computer propelled us into this postindustrial era. Others suggest that communications technologies—in particular the global reach of television—brought about the evolution to an information-based society.

At the *TRanscontinental ISDN Project* (*TRIP '92*), the *National ISDN (NISDN)* network was officially established. The first historic ISDN call interconnected computers, videos, and imaging systems, enabling them to communicate over the newly created National ISDN network. The moderator at TRIP '92, Dr. Robert Metcalfe, christened that moment as the birth of the information age. Everyone recognized that using ISDN to connect disparate computers and computer networks provided the missing link in the push toward using information to improve the ways we live, learn, and work.

Primary to Secondary Industries

For thousands of years, humans relied on nature to survive; economic well-being was hard won in the contest between humans and natural forces. Although methods for obtaining food and materials improved over time, people were essentially still at nature's mercy.

About 200 years ago, however, machines and manufacturing began to dominate the economic landscape. For the first time in history, the vast majority of workers worked in factories rather than on the land. Farm workers in the United States declined as a percentage of the total work force—from the vast majority to well below 10 percent.

The industrial revolution redefined the nature of work; it became a man–machine phenomenon. Even in farming, workers came to use machines such as tractors, combines, and automatic milking apparatus to increase agricultural productivity. Work was transformed from a struggle between man and nature to a contest between man and machine. Even though farm employment dropped dramatically, agricultural productivity grew rapidly.

Inventors and manufacturers put tremendous energy into developing new, beneficial ways to use machines. The factory worker was the symbol of the era. Even low-skilled workers began to view a good living wage as an inherent right, negotiated by unions from enlightened companies and protected by progressive government. Our political system encouraged that view and appears to do so today. But the economic realities are changing.

Knowledge Industries

About 20 years ago, we began to enter what has been called the post-industrial or information age. The focus shifted again—from manufacturing products to applying information to achieve results. New technologies emerged in response to the movement toward manipulating information. As the symbol of the industrial era was the machine and the factory worker, the symbol of the postindustrial era is the electronic computer and the computer programmer. Computer programming involves constructions of abstract logic that operate on data to deliver an analysis of a problem or opportunity. Computer programmers—and other information system architects — design computer-based information systems to help realize organizational and individual activities and goals.

Using these information systems, staff workers describe a problem or opportunity, suggest alternative courses of action, and recommend the most desirable alternatives to achieve organizational goals. Staff workers are a creation (product?) of the information age. For these workers, information is the medium of exchange.

Today's staff worker—really a knowledge worker—abstracts and analyzes information to achieve organizational purposes. In other words, the knowledge worker relies almost exclusively on information. As the value of low-skilled production work continues to decline, so too will the wages and living standard of people who can perform only low-skilled work. This growing economic stratification represents a challenge to society to maintain productivity in all sectors.

2.2 NATURE OF TECHNOLOGY IN THE INFORMATION AGE

The underpinning of the information age is technology. Broadly stated, technology is a set of organized facts or ideas that can accomplish some result. Thus, technology is not limited to *technical* facts. Although we instantly recognize electronic integrated circuits as technology, methodology is also an example of technology. Methodology includes division of labor or the concept of interchangeable parts. Methodology also includes assembly-line mass production. As these examples show, technology is not just a collection of technical details.

Production methodologies in the information age have evolved beyond the idea of mass production to include the technological concepts of *mass customization*, *just-in-time delivery*, and *zero-based defects*. The combination of these three concepts illustrates the productive power of our knowledge-based society.

The first of these three concepts, mass customization, is a highly efficient production capability (at the low costs of mass production), coupled with flexibility (normally only found in custom production). Computer-based manufacturing machines perform tasks inexpensively and flexibly. Knowledge is embedded in the design of these machines; manufacturing capability can be as nimble as the knowledge, which can be changed or updated.

The second of the three concepts, just-in-time delivery, means supplying inventory to the production process no sooner or later than it is required. This method avoids costs and achieves efficiencies needed for mass customization. Appropriate supply inventory satisfies customer demand and enhances revenue. Successful just-in-time delivery is possible only because the computer-based systems of the postindustrial process can manage information to achieve a just-in-time delivery result.

The third concept, zero-based defects, is achieving the desired production the first time, thereby avoiding subsequent rework or surplus inventory. Not only does the manufacturer avoid the cost of producing a product more than once, the consumer also avoids the cost of acquiring a product more than once. The precision of computer-based systems provides the platform for achieving zero-based-defect results.

One of the most pervasive examples of the combination of mass customization, just-in-time delivery, and zero-based defects in a mass-production context is telecommunications services—more specifically, your telephone service. You can dial whomever you want and talk whenever you want at mass-production costs. ISDN goes even further. In automated fashion at mass-production costs, an ISDN network provides various types of voice and data information (such as electronic mail, images, computer programs, and spreadsheets) in real or near-real time, with virtually no transmission errors.

2.3 TECHNOLOGY EMBEDDED IN TOOLS

One of the key characteristics that separates the postindustrial age from the industrial era is society's reliance on knowledge and abstract logic rather than experience and craftsmanship. In the industrial era, a machinist developed his skill and learned his craft through a long apprenticeship before he could call himself a journeyman or master machinist. In today's knowledge-based society, a machinist who operates a computer-controlled machine-making device needs to to keep this device in good repair and know how to reprogram it (or at least alter the program parameters) when necessary to change the product design. But the actual *skill* needed to precisely machine a part resides in the device itself—both in its structure and instructions. The skills and abilities of the craftspeople now lie within the *computer integrated manufacturing* (*CIM*) equipment.

The skill residing in these tools reflects knowledge embedded in their design. ISDN can connect equipment to knowledge sources and destinations, so the equipment can stay current with new information and provide information where it can be used productively.

Word Processing

Even the simple task of putting words to paper has changed. In the industrial age, the typewriter reigned supreme. The typist needed a measure of skill to properly operate the instrument. Today, the computer-based word processor is common. Many of the instructions for creating documents are actually embedded in the hardware and software of the word processor. The operator may have no real idea of how the system executes margins, unlike the manual-typewriter operator who had to create the margins, moving the mechanical stops and watching the carriage bang into them after striking the margin-release key.

Health Care

The tools and procedures of the health care industry have also changed. At one time, surgical skill was the pinnacle of medical expertise. Who wasn't amazed and impressed with the manual dexterity of surgeons who performed the first open-heart bypass operations? Now, with angioplasty, surgeons visually identify blockages and directly remove them from blood vessels. Surgeons insert optical fibers into patients for direct visual inspections, and use lasers for precision eye surgery.

Using these recent technologies, doctors help patients with less intrusive methods that place emphasis on the knowledgeable use of technology in tandem with manual dexterity and skill. Particularly in laser-based surgery and diagnostic methodology (applying imaging and radioactive-tracing techniques), the role of the doctor has changed significantly from that of a performing virtuoso to a knowledge worker. Certainly, manual techniques and skill are still crucial, but surgeons now have technological tools that help them focus their skill with greater certainty.

Telecommunications

In the telephone industry, newer equipment contains embedded knowledge. This embedded knowledge has streamlined installation, maintenance, and repair work (for example, locating telephone cable faults and repairing them).

In the last decade or two, technologically advanced devices have assisted in the process of isolating cable faults so crews can go directly to the damaged areas without having to search or repeatedly dig. One such device works ultrasonically. Crews insert gas under pressure into the cable; then they can locate the leaking area using ultrasonic detectors. Another device is electronically based. A technician inserts a known signal source on one end of the cable. At the fault-point in the cable, the signal changes discontinuously so the fault-locating device can calculate the location of the damaged area. Technicians today must have the skills to operate this kind of equipment. Hence, there is correspondingly less of a need for trench-digging skills. When a telephone company needs to dig trenches, technicians instead need to be able to operate technologically sophisticated devices to dig them.

Home Entertainment

Only about 90 years ago, if you wanted to hear music, you had to sing, play a musical instrument, or be within earshot of others who could. Today, at home, we can listen to a much wider variety of music but are further removed from the skills of music making. The phonograph at least gave the user some sense of involvement. After adjusting the rotation speed and arm balance (tracking weight), the listener could watch the progress of the playback as the arm traveled through the grooves and then returned to rest. But compact discs have eliminated even this minimal listener involvement. The disc is swallowed by the machine, hidden from view, and simply plays music. Today's music listener is less involved with music making and with the means of music reproduction than in the past, but he or she does *interact* more with the reproduced music. The listener can program the compact disc to play any selection in any order and never have to listen to songs or movements that he or she doesn't enjoy. The listener can even program only parts of a selection—skipping the recitatives in an opera—or mix selections from different works —mixing songs of the Beatles with songs from the members' solo careers. So, as the listener's involvement with music making and music reproduction becomes more remote, the listener's involvement with the music itself may increase.

Perhaps future home-entertainment devices will more closely resemble *virtual reality*. Commentators suggest we may be able to achieve interactive virtual reality. Computers may create virtual reality through programs that project realistic images and audio reproductions and simulate four-dimensional time-space that seems real to the person who enters and participates. Perhaps we won't have to wait as long for virtual reality as we did for the real version of the submarine prophesied in Jules Vernes' fiction.

2.4 TECHNOLOGY EMBEDDED IN SYSTEMS

Technology is also embedded in systems—legal, educational, and political. Systems are the hallmark of our postindustrial society. These systems are characterized by the interdependence of societal groups and organizations striving toward common goals. Each element of a system relies on information obtained from other elements within that system to achieve goals. Effectively moving information—using ISDN and other technologies—is as crucial to knowledge systems as moving blood is to your physical body.

Educational System

Public school systems contain myriad examples of embedded technology, organized knowledge to educate our children, that are mostly unchanged from our own school years. Each academic subject (for example, English, music, mathematics) relies on knowledge-based teaching methodologies and tools. Flash-cards are appropriate for some of the memorization required in studying foreign languages. Textbooks, films, and illustrations are tools that support other methods teachers use such as lectures, homework, group discussion, and testing. Teachers learn how to teach through formal academic programs, with only a brief dose of experiential learning at the end of their formal training. This reliance on formal training rather than apprenticeship experience is typical of our postindustrial society.

In educational systems we need to improve the technology of measurement to help us better understand and predict the connection between educational methods (and content) and success at certain types of jobs. We also need to have better learning models: How do different students learn and why are some motivated while others are not? In our information age, models are crucial to understanding systems of ideas and information.

Although a great deal of technology is embedded within our educational systems, we need a great deal more to be effective in preparing our students for modern society. And we need to affordably embed that technology in ways that reach all members of society. ISDN has vast potential for supporting educational improvement efforts as well as for expanding the reach of educational programs through its distance-learning capabilities.

Political System

Knowledge is also embedded in the political system. But we need to integrate knowledge within the system and extend it to the general public. We need greater access to facts on governmental policies—perhaps via an interactive electronic information source. How does the government go about creating jobs? At what cost are jobs created? How does it measure the effects of its policies? To what extent do alternative tax-and-spend policies affect the number of jobs? Or the quality of jobs?

On the local level, electronic town meetings would enable homebound town residents to monitor and make their voices heard in the political process.

Manufacturing System

Manufacturing systems still exist in our postindustrial society. However, the operational aspects of these systems have changed. There are three key attributes of manufacturing in an information-based society: flexible automated manufacturing, just-in-time delivery, and zero-based defects.

We must examine flexible automated manufacturing in the context of mass production. Mass-production techniques set up an unchanging assembly line to maximize efficiency, then use repetitive techniques to produce goods in such large quantities that unit prices remain quite low. Mass production provides goods that we can afford. Manufacturers have fine tuned mass production to create flexible automated manufacturing. This type of manufacturing involves robots and computer-integrated techniques. A robot can produce each part more cheaply and accurately than an assembly-line worker (further diminishing the economic value of the low-skilled worker); labor in environments where people can't readily go (such as inside steel furnaces or human bodies); and produce work to tolerances much finer than any human can perceive.

Flexible automated manufacturing allows for continuous alteration while *still retaining the economies of mass production*. If someone develops a more efficient way to attach a hose to a metal opening, the manufacturer can make that change (almost) immediately by reprogramming the CIM or the robot and by asking the part supplier to do the same. Manufacturers can produce customized products (small production runs) upon request at economies previously available only through mass-production methods.

Just-in-time delivery prevents the problem of surplus inventory in which warehouses overflow with parts or materials in storage. In addition to preventing carrying and storage charges, just-in-time delivery allows changes at the production facility to ripple into the supply chain so the organization as a whole can produce the best possible product as soon as it is defined. ISDN and other communication technologies are crucial to expanding the use of these capabilities.

Zero-based defects means that whatever the customer wants the customer gets; anything else is a defect. Providing more than the customer specifies (for example, unwanted options) is of no value to the customer and therefore represents excess cost without corresponding benefit. Providing less than the customer specifies is a defect, because the (manufacturing) goal is to produce only products that fully meet customer requirements.

Changes are constantly occurring in the production process, which is a hallmark of flexible automated assembly. And instead of doing repetitive tasks (requiring some limited skill), the technician can now supervise a robot or CIM to obtain zero-based defects. The postindustrial factory worker must be able to apply logic, compile and interpret statistics, and read and understand technical instructions to reprogram or repair automated devices.

This same change in emphasis is manifest in the support side of the industry as well. Previously, a good automobile mechanic could make an educated guess at a point setting or choke adjustment. In the microprocessor environment, however, the mechanic cannot "sense" a failure within an integrated electronic circuit and intuitively know what he or she must adjust or replace. Ideally, in today's environment, the mechanic should have access to a database through a *wide-area network* (*WAN*) such as ISDN to scan for the information needed to make the repairs.

Using an ISDN wide-area network, the mechanic could use a PC to connect to a manufacturer's data base. The mechanic would have to be able to write a technical description of the problem to search the database and have the skill to interpret the retrieved data to meet customer requirements.

In an auto sales environment, a salesperson could use a terminal or PC over an ISDN connection to access manufacturing schedules and capabilities to provide near real-time responses to manufacturing questions. And manufacturers could conceivably custom produce cars in a matter of days, applying ISDN to just-in-time delivery capabilities. One result of using ISDN would be lower inventory on dealer lots, which would reduce dealer overhead costs and ultimately result in lower prices, higher dealer profits, and greater customer satisfaction. The auto industry could extend this mass customization concept to other aspects of their support system, such as the financial establishment, insurance organizations, government licensing operations, and consumer-information sources, to meet customer requirements.

Banking

Banking institutions use *automatic teller machines* (*ATMs*) because they provide just-in-time delivery (24-hour-a-day service), zero-based defects (no transaction errors), and flexible automated manufacturing (customized transactions). Clearly, the tasks of banking personnel have changed. Bank tellers must now understand computer networking. Wide-area networks, such as ISDN, connect ATMs to a bank database; similar networks connect banking personnel to a database that provides information on how the ATMs are functioning.

Retail

Many retail institutions use *point-of-sale* (*POS*) devices that provide just-in-time delivery (no waiting) to the customer making a purchase. For example, at some gas stations, a self-service patron can completely perform a gas purchase without having to walk to a cashier or wait in line to pay. The patron simply inserts a card into a flexible automated machine, which alerts the financial institution (through a wide-area network) that the customer wishes pay. The automated pump then allows the customer to pump gas into the vehicle. This convenience allows retailers to avoid costs (employees doing low-skill tasks) and remove barriers to sale (people with transaction cards but without cash). In addition, gas station owners can better plan the timing of fuel deliveries for maximum benefit to cost.

2.5 SUMMARY

Society depends increasingly on information. The changes described in the preceding sections are already happening — even without ISDN. The deployment of ISDN, however, has supported these emerging needs and other advances of the same type. Even if ISDN were not poised for deployment, society at large would demand something like it. In fact, political-action groups like the *Electronic Frontier Foundation (EFF)* are already lobbying to make ISDN a part of the communications infrastructure to increase global competitiveness and quality of life. Many in government and industry champion the concept of a digital-highway infrastructure as well. ISDN appears to be part of their agenda.

ISDN technology is the most readily available communications technology for building such a digital infrastructure. Using the ISDN digital infrastructure, we can design and implement systems to transfer information so that it is available where and when it can be most productively employed.

But to understand how to make the most of this information transfer, we need to better understand the nature of information itself and how its value changes with time. We explore the nature of information in the next chapter.

3

What Is Information?

We tend to assume that we know what information is and everyone else knows what it is too. But our own intuitive understanding of information is, no doubt, somewhat nebulous, and it's probably quite different from someone else's.

Information is data—a fact or series of facts. It is unorganized raw material. ISDN and other technologies of the information age move this raw material from place to place to provide benefits such as increased productivity. When information is organized to provide context and understanding, we call it knowledge. It is the knowledge of how to acquire and use information effectively through technology that differentiates modern society from the industrial age. Wisdom is a deeper, more thorough assimilation of knowledge that promotes judgment and insight. The technology of the postindustrial age is not a substitute for wisdom; rather, technology such as ISDN is a beneficial tool for those with the wisdom to appropriately use it.

A clear understanding of what the term information means is necessary to apply *information technology (IT)* in useful ways. IT harnesses technology—computers; communications; and other information processing, storage, and conveyance systems—to achieve some purpose such as solving a business problem.

In this chapter, we discuss information attributes to clarify how information—and its value to the recipient—is affected when transported. Similarly, in industrial transport, you need to understand the nature of the cargo to transport it effectively. If you are trying to plan a transportation system to convey strawberries from the grower to the grocer, you need to understand the nature of the berry itself (for example, its shelf life, its susceptibility to bruising, the ripening process). Likewise, if you understand the attributes of information (discussed below), you will more readily understand the communications and computing aspects of IT implementations.

3.1 INFORMATION ATTRIBUTES

Each information attribute requires particular capabilities from the computers and communications systems used in IT systems. Often the capabilities required for one attribute are in direct conflict with capabilities required by some other information attribute. (Consider how, for example, the automotive attributes of speed and performance often conflict with the attributes of economy and safety.) The information attributes discussed below are not an industry-accepted standard list of information attributes but are culled from the author's personal observations over more than 20 years. These attributes should help you understand requirements for planning IT systems in general and ISDN information-movement requirements in particular.

Volume (How Much?)

Larger amounts of information require more IT resources than smaller amounts. Even in precomputer systems, the amount of bookshelf space never seems to be adequate to store all the information that most of us choose to keep. In addition to consuming more storage space, larger volumes of information also take longer to move from one location to another—all other things being equal. Many of the newer information forms, such as graphics and video, are even larger piles of information than traditional *text* messages. The number of bits required to characterize these graphical displays can be immense.

In digital systems, the volume or size of the information is measured in bits. However, volumes of information are usually quantified in groupings of bits. These units of groupings are *bytes* (8 bits), *kilobytes* (*KB* or 1000 bytes) or *megabytes* (*MB* or 1 million bytes). A short (one paragraph) e-mail note is typically a few KBs of information. Entering the 1980s, personal computers commonly had 64 KB of internal memory and 100 KB of disk memory. Now they commonly have 8 to 16 MB of internal memory and more than 500 MB of disk memory—hundreds of times more memory than a decade ago.

Similar evolutions of capacity have occurred in the telecommunications industry. In the late 1970s, a major increase in data transport rates—from 300 bits per second (bps) to 1200 bps—was headline news. Today, modems of 14,400 bps are now common. With ISDN, these speeds aren't just increased, they are greatly increased. Using a basic rate interface, ISDN terminal-adapter cards today routinely provide 64 kilobits per second (Kbps) and 128 Kbps transmission to and from computers to data sources. This is hundreds of times faster than in the 300 bps days and is a tenfold increase over today's fastest analog-modem transmission speeds. These much faster ISDN communication speeds, combined with increases in processing power and memory capacity, make IT systems powerful enough to address needs that could not be addressed just a decade ago.

Form (How Is It Presented?)

Information can be conveyed in a variety of forms. We have all seen information represented as printed text. This book is an example. Information can also be presented as images such as photographs, drawings, charts, figures, and diagrams. A rapid flow of successive images creates a *video* form of information. Information can also be contained in *audio* form, such as voice, music, or other sounds. Some forms of information—smell, touch, and physical sensations such as balance—are not captured by today's IT systems.

In many information technology systems, there is a change in form even though there is no change in content. Everyday examples include charting (graphing) a series of numbers to illustrate trends more clearly than might be done with tabular data, and converting spoken words into printed text. Sometimes this change in form adds great value for the end-user. Sometimes it simply adds undesirable overhead.

To effectively use information, we need to be able to store and transmit it in its variety of forms. Almost all IT systems today use digital representation to store and process information of any form, whether text, image, audio, or other. Hence, it is crucial that ISDN be digital from end to end.

Using the same native digital language, ISDN promotes efficiency and avoids errors; it becomes a more productive partner in IT systems.

Language (What Is the Syntax?)

Each of the various forms of information also has a *syntax*, or rules for presentation. For example, information expressed as text may be in English or French or Italian. Information from a computer may be in the ASCII format or coded using some other format. An informational image may be created with black and white dots (like a newspaper halftone photo) or with a different syntax that allows each dot to be described with color, intensity, and brightness. If the form is voice, there may be several encoding schemes from analog to digital.

Of course, the person who receives the information must understand the syntax used by the sender for the information to have value. In IT systems, this usually means both sender and receiver must use the same syntax. Sometimes, the two ends can negotiate to a common syntax. For example, current fax machines, operating over analog telephone circuits, use a G3 encoding syntax. Older machines, however, often used a G2 encoding syntax. Many modern machines start sending or receiving at G3 but can negotiate down to G2 to accommodate an older machine not capable of conversing in G3.

The ASCII and G3 syntaxes described above are end-to-end syntaxes, meaning the end-user equipment at one end of the ISDN connection transfers data to the end-user equipment at the other end. The ISDN itself is generally independent of this end-to-end syntax, since its job is to convey information from one end to the other without altering the information or its syntax.

A major exception to this rule is the voice-encoding algorithm (syntax) used in telephony in the United States for over 20 years. When you select speech service from an ISDN network, all the pieces in the network and in the digital telephone instruments use the standard coding algorithm so that the basic service will interoperate from end to end and through all the network(s) in between.

Accuracy (Is It Without Error?)

To the extent that information is without error, it is considered accurate. Thus, if your bank correctly determines that you have a balance of $502.43, and you receive a bank statement indicating the same, there is no error and the information is accurate. In IT systems, the communication piece must convey the information without error to be considered accurate.

ISDN fulfills the need for accuracy. It is inherently more accurate than pre-ISDN systems because it has more advanced digital transmission technology (such as fiber-optic systems) and more advanced methodology (such as sophisticated error reporting and recovery processes). Early users of ISDN report that once their ISDN circuits were installed and working properly, they could *almost* forget about errors. Actual error performance on ISDN systems is vastly improved—sometimes hundreds of times better than previous systems.

Data must be accurate if we are to rely on it. But accuracy of data is not the sole determinant of its reliability and usefulness. While ISDN and other information transport systems can keep data errors to a minimum, we often need context and other information to recognize the value of the information we receive.

Freshness (Is It Still Relevant?)

Continuing with the bank balance example, if you examine a bank statement from 4 months ago, you most likely will not rely on it, even though it may be entirely error free—and therefore accurate. The statement simply has no relevance any more. On the other hand, if you use the checking account only for vacation spending, and you know you haven't written any checks since the statement came out 4 months ago, it would be entirely reasonable for you to rely on the balance indicated.

The value of some information ages much more quickly than other information. For example, information about human nature has not changed fundamentally in hundreds, or even thousands, of years. One need only look to William Shakespeare's plays, Niccolo Machiavelli's insights and observations, or the Bible's description of the human condition. Information concerning modern IT technology, however, ages very quickly.

You must consider the freshness of information before you apply it. With ISDN, the freshness of information depends mostly on the source of that information. On one hand, an ISDN high-speed transport system will speed out-of-date information to its destination just as quickly as current information. So using ISDN is not sufficient to guarantee that information is fresh. On the other hand, some pre-ISDN transport technologies are so slow that, in some cases, by the time the information arrives at its destination, it has gone from fresh to stale during the time it took to transport.

Urgency (How Soon Do You Need To Use It?)

Some applications need information more quickly than others. This requirement is not so much related to freshness of information but to the application's requirement for information within a certain timeframe. For example, if you are driving a car while receiving navigational directions from a passenger, you might want guidance *before* you pass through an intersection. On the other hand, you might feel comfortable waiting 1, 2, or even 3 weeks to verify a bank balance statement. The range of urgency for different applications can easily range from a few seconds to several weeks—a range of a million to one! It's not hard to think of other examples that have even more stringent requirements (antimissile defense systems might need to be notified in a fraction of a second) and others that have much more relaxed requirements (new insights from the dead sea scrolls, buried for approximately 2000 years, would be welcomed by scholars today).

Not surprisingly, requirements for *real-time* (absolutely no delay) or *near-real-time* (almost no observable delay) information create the greatest stress in information systems. But, in many cases, even if the system cannot acquire real-time information, historical information is still of value. For example, although real-time information may allow a motorist to avoid a traffic backup, delayed, slightly older information is still useful for planning future commuting to avoid backups.

In some cases, a system needs information so urgently that any transport delays become a significant issue. ISDN systems can establish a connection in as little as a fraction of a second compared to a pre-ISDN system that might take 15 seconds. And after connection, the ISDN system can convey the information from 10 to 100 times faster (depending upon configurations) than a pre-ISDN system. What might take less than 10 seconds for an ISDN system might require many minutes for a pre-ISDN system. Imagine the difference that this can make for IT systems tracking automobile traffic status to provide real-time congestion guidance! For IT systems that track investment status on many different trading exchanges, time delays of tens of seconds can mean a significantly different financial returns from real-time investment strategies.

Content (What Is It?)

This is what most of us think about when we think about information is. The message is, in effect, the information contained in the message. We need to turn left at the intersection. The bank balance is $502.43.

Since all information content can be represented digitally, ISDN is well suited to convey it. Whether the meaning is conveyed by text, image, chart, or sound, the ISDN transport capability can readily transport it. Only when the information source is massive does the ISDN transport capability become overwhelmed. For example, high-definition video transport and sophisticated computer-aided design systems are usually beyond the capabilities of ISDN. Future broadband implementations of ISDN and similar technologies will address these higher-bandwidth needs.

3.2 REPRESENTING INFORMATION IN IT SYSTEMS

Information technology systems operate on information and convey it to the appropriate location at the right time for the benefit of the person who actually needs it. After the form of information has been altered for use in the IT system, the information content can be stored or transmitted. Today, virtually all IT systems characterize information using digital representations (syntaxes). This section details how this is actually done. If you understand how information is represented digitally, you will have a better understanding of why digital systems, particularly ISDN, provide such capable systems for information technology.

Information in an IT system that is represented digitally is represented using a series of binary values (bits). Referring back to Figures 1.5 and 1.6, you see how numbers and letters are represented using binary values. Each *alphanumeric character* (number or letter) is represented by a specific binary value.

But what about other forms of information? How about music or voice? Some other forms of information involve continuously varying quantities, which we can approximate only by digital representation (just as the stairs in Figures 1.3 and 1.4 approximate the ramp). We can also digitally represent images and video (moving images). There are a variety of methods to do this. Video systems use special coding algorithms that compress the required bit rate by sending only information that changes rather than information that does not change.

Text

Even with all of the graphics-based systems around today, much of the information we use is still text (that is, letters of the alphabet, numbers, and special symbols). We know that computers can store this type of information, since we have all seen or used word processors or spreadsheets. The characters are mapped to the series of bits in a straightforward manner—computing machines simply consult a table to determine which *alphanumeric* character to associate with each bit pattern. And charts in almost any handbook on computers or communications show which characters correspond to which pattern (usually seven or eight) of bits. In Chapter 1, Figure 1.6 shows a few examples of ASCII values corresponding to each alphanumeric character. A different coding scheme such as *extended binary-coded decimal interchange code (EBCDIC)* will use different associations between bit patterns and characters. Once the computers identify the coding scheme, the sending computer can then translate each letter into encoded bit patterns, and the retreiving computer can decode the letters. In communications systems, after a letter is encoded, bit patterns are transmitted as a series of digital pulses and received at the distant end. At the receiving end, the pulses are assembled into groups of seven or eight and decoded using the same chart. The particular character is thus conveyed to the distant end by means of digital pulses. Figure 3.1 illustrates this process (omitting technical details, such as transmitted bit order and framing bits, for simplicity).

Continuous Information Sources

Speech and image forms of information are fundamentally different from text forms—they vary continuously rather than discretely. On one hand, in text, if a letter is an A, it certainly is not a B. It cannot "almost" be a B. It either is an A or it isn't. It is said to be *discrete*: it either is or it isn't. There is no sense of "almost." On the other hand, consider a clock time of 3 P.M. Although 3 P.M. is clearly different from 4 P.M., time is continuous from one hour to the next. There is a sense of "almost" 3 P.M. (one minute before or perhaps one

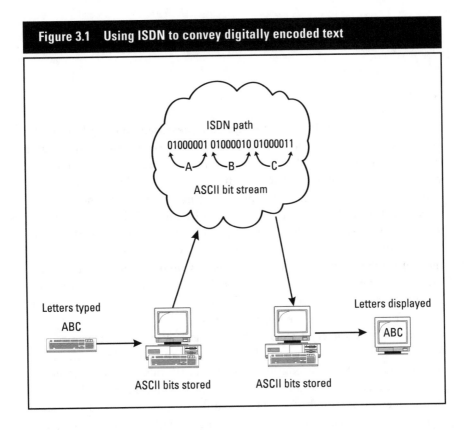

Figure 3.1   Using ISDN to convey digitally encoded text

second before). Since we know that digital systems have only discrete values, the question becomes "Can we digitally represent continuously varying types of information, and if so, can we represent them well enough?"

The difference between a continuous range of values and a quantized characterization is like the relationship between the ramp and the staircase illustrated in Figures 1.1 and 1.2. To try to visualize further, think about the way some building entrances have ramps adjacent to steps for wheelchair access. If you walk up the ramp, you will notice there are stairsteps corresponding approximately to heights on the ramp. To accommodate the average person using the stairs, each step is set at a rise of about 8 inches. But to make the stairs to look more like a ramp, we could insert many more stairs, making each step smaller, and setting steps at less than an 8-inch rise (see Figures 1.3 and 1.4). Imagine a staircase with a new step every one-tenth of an inch. From a distance of about 6 feet, it might look very much like a ramp. If steps were every 1/1000 inch, the staircase would look like a ramp even standing close to it.

Quantizing

Continuous forms of information can be represented digitally, but only in an approximate sense. Because the original piece of information has a naturally continuous quality, it is impossible to capture every point on the continuum as an accurate, finite amount. Instead, digital representations of continuous information are made by *quantizing* (assigning distinct numbers to bands of continuous values) over the entire range of the original source. The more quantizing levels you have, the better is the approximation—just as more steps better approximate the ramp. We can add discrete levels to the point where the user can no longer distinguish between levels. For example, compact disc recordings use 16 bits of binary data. Although manufacturers could design a system using 32 or even 48 bits, listeners wouldn't be able to hear the improvements.

Another common example of quantizing is how we quantize values from an analog wristwatch (the one with the big hand and the little hand). During the day, the watch hands continuously move. We quantize these values by saying, for example, it is almost 3 o'clock or it is quarter to 4. Quantizing time values on a digital watch is less subjective: each hour of the day is represented with a digital number. Minutes of the hour are represented in the same way—with a digital number. Since a digital watch only shows the hour and the minute, however, the digital watch is correct only at the beginning of the minute. Most of the time the digital watch is incorrect. It is appropriate to note that this entire band of time (1 minute) is characterized by only one discrete number representing the minute. The minute hand of an analog watch continuously moves; an observant person could possibly perceive this movement and have the "correct" time all the time. But even if you can't perceive the minute-hand movement, the watch itself truly does proclaim the right time.

Note that the digital watch displays a *quantizing error,* which at any instant ranges from zero to almost 1 minute. Many people find this error perfectly acceptable. Others want more precision. We can reduce quantizing error by selecting a digital watch that displays the hour, minute, and second, as some do. However, using the above observations and logic, we can still deduce that at any given instant even this watch displays a quantizing error ranging from zero to almost 1 second. This fineness of detail can be continued indefinitely—some watches display hundredths of a second! To sum up, we can, in fact, digitally represent continuously changing information. And we can bring the accuracy of that representation as close to the original as we desire—at the "expense" of using more bits and more processing power to generate that accuracy.

As an interesting digression, some of what we experience in life seems continuous but is in fact discrete. The chair you are sitting on is composed of solid matter. Even a hard, wooden chair is composed of a large number of molecules and atoms, which could be enumerated with appropriate technological aids. But to us it seems like a continuous piece of wood. We can cut it, touch it, sit on it—or even burn it, but it seems like a continuous piece of matter. It is actually composed of discrete pieces that approximate a continuum so well that we can't perceive the difference, and until recent times, we didn't even know that such objects consisted of discrete pieces.

Speech and Music

We are all familiar with one product that uses digital representation of continuous information—the digitally encoded compact disc. Many consumers prefer to obtain recorded music in this digital format because they know it offers superior reproduction from earlier analog technologies such as vinyl records or magnetic recording tape.

The technology was developed and deployed by the telephone companies over 30 years ago to more economically provide telephone circuits. In telephone systems, speech is sampled 8000 times each second. This sample rate accurately reproduces speech signals (which have a frequency range of slightly less than 4 Khz) for intelligibility in a telephone system. The rule is that the sample rate has to be twice the highest frequency of the sound to be reproduced.

Each sample of your speech on a telephone circuit is represented digitally by an 8-bit value. An 8-bit representation means that there are as many as 256 uniquely different values that represent the range of volume from the loudest to the softest. The volume of your speech is represented by this 8-bit value. The sampling algorithm determines the actual amplitude and assigns (from the 256 allowed possibilities) the one that is closest to the actual sample level. (For an analogy, see Figure 1.3, using a staircase of 256 steps to approximate various heights on a ramp.) The difference between the actual value and the assigned value is the quantizing error. On a telephone call, this quantizing error can actually be heard as a sort of "air noise." It sounds something like tape hiss, and it's noticeable only if you listen for it.

Using more digits to represent the value in each sample allows more than 256 possible values. You can obtain virtually any level of accuracy by using more digits. Compact-disc technology uses 16 digital bits for every sample, resulting in a quantizing error so low that none of us can hear the error, even though we know the error is there. (Compact discs have a signal-to-noise factor of more than 90 decibels.) The manufacturers could use 32 or 48 bits per sample to provide even better performance, but it would be pointless because we couldn't hear the improvement. In addition to using more bits per sample than a telephone system, the compact-disc system samples the sound source much more often than 8000 times per second. To provide accurate reproduction over the entire range of human hearing (up to 20 Khz), the compact-disc sample rate is slightly over 40 Khz.

Images

One of the earliest forms of digital representation of images is the half-tone photograph commonly seen in newspapers. It is simply a series of dots on a page. At each point in the picture, a black dot is either present (*a logical yes*) or absent (revealing the white of the paper, *a logical no*). Given enough points, the photograph can be of high quality. If you doubt this, look at a page printed from a laser printer, which approximates text characters and drawings using this method. Even the older machines at 300 dots per square inch look pretty smooth; the newer machines at 600 dots per inch render a better image (but you might not immediately notice the improvement for many images).

More sophisticated techniques produce almost-lifelike images. In computers, information about every pixel (picture element, or point of an image) is represented digitally. Every image attribute that the user cares about can have a digital value. Color monitors for *personal computers* (PCs) have attributes for color (hue), saturation (deepness of color), and intensity (brightness) for each pixel on the screen. The computer manufacturer can make images as lifelike as desired, using more and more digital bits to represent as many attributes as the user wants to see. For example, it is theoretically possible to represent the position of objects with additional attributes to develop truly three-dimensional images. Imagine designing a house floorplan layout with a PC design program that stores object-position information (including your own furniture). Wouldn't it be great to be able to wander through your newly created house and see how everything looks? From the family room reclining chair, can you see the dirty dishes in the kitchen? Find out before you build it.

There are many ways of digitally representing images. In fact, although we all like the flexibility that comes with variety and choice, there are so many alternatives of representing images that interoperability may be jeopardized. One of the success stories for image interoperability is the standard for *facsimile (fax)* transmission. Because fax has been standardized, the odds are quite high that sending and receiving users will select the same methods of facsimile digital representation.

Video Information

A series of images, presented with sufficient frequency, provide a sense of movement or animation. Images on television are refreshed 60 times per second, which appears as continuous motion. At very slow rates, movement appears to be jerky; at intermediate rates images are reasonably smooth but can be blurry when the subjects in the video move quickly. Higher bandwidths allow more images to be sent during a given period of time, which improves the quality of the video. Compression algorithms are constantly being improved, which means digital representation of video information requires fewer transmitted bits. Because of this improvement, ISDN can now transmit much higher quality video than even a few years ago, although the B-channel bandwidth hasn't increased.

Implementations currently available for basic rate ISDN are suitable for conferencing but do not begin to approach the video quality of commercial TV. Some of these ISDN systems transmit relatively sharp images at a very low rate, resulting in clear images but jerky motion. Other systems transmit images more frequently, but each image is of lower quality. This makes for smoother motion but more blurry images. Still other systems use multiple B channels to increase transport bandwidth to provide higher quality video.

Much higher bandwidth transport is being planned for broadband implementations of ISDN. Current plans for this future technology are to create bandwidth and coding algorithms that would support extremely high-quality video service — even for screens as large as a living room wall. In fact, some people speculate that commercial theaters may eventually use this technology to exhibit first-run feature films.

3.3 ILLUSTRATIVE EXAMPLES FOR PARTICULAR APPLICATIONS

Every application requires a set of information attribute values for success. In the next sections, we present examples to illustrate how information attribute values are determined in the context of applications. However, the sketches don't necessarily describe the applications sufficiently to be able in all cases to substantiate the precise values that appear in the charts. So if you feel inclined to challenge the values, you probably have a slightly different application in mind or your criteria for success are different from those assumed in the examples.

Group Calendar (Electronic)

A typical scenario is a group of about eight people in a work group who need to schedule meetings throughout the year. All group members need access to the schedules for everyone in the group. Since everyone works regularly with computers on a common *local area network (LAN)*, the group decides to use that platform to provide information for group calendaring. (Note: The group could use a wall chart, but due to travel, many are often out of the office.) Group members who are away from the office can access the LAN remotely via ISDN to find out the schedules. Some of the attribute quantities are arbitrary or negotiable. For example, although urgency is listed as 1 minute, 2 minutes might be acceptable and 10 seconds might be even better. The value of this application is that the group can schedule meetings for all its members or for a subset of its members, even though many group members may be traveling at any given time. But if the application doesn't work properly, group members may miss out on potential meeting times, which could reduce efficiency.

Urgency	Within 1 minute after using it
Freshness	Each person's calendar updated less than 1 week ago; date of update posted
Accuracy	Group members' schedules exactly as they entered them (i.e., without change or "error"); note that for this application to succeed, group members must not post meetings to wrong day or fail to post meetings
Format	Square boxes (for days); text (names); other formats OK
Language	Preferably, a standard computer language for graphics; ASCII for text
Volume	1 year (number of bits in .TIF file to convey info)
Content	For each individual in the group: date, name, purpose (e.g., name and location of scheduled meeting), phone number, calendar date of last schedule update

Shared (Electronic) Whiteboard

A typical scenario today is a work group that often uses a whiteboard during its meetings. Upon discovering a problem, opportunity, or an emergency, everyone in the work group gathers around a whiteboard. A moderator lists the key ideas on the board while group members jointly discuss aspects of the issue. After some discussion, the group members usually agree that they have adequately defined the problem, and at that point, they make a list of the tasks that they have to perform to address the problem. The group then disperses, each member carrying away a task for individual work. Later, the group reassembles and examines the results of individual assignments to develop a solution. The group reaches a joint decision.

Often, not every member of the group is physically in the same office location. But absent members could participate if they could work electronically with the other members of the group using a simulated whiteboard. A system that allows a shared computer screen (whiteboard) and audio conferencing would suffice, since the group members regularly work together and don't need to rely on visual cues to work well

Urgency	All group members to view changes made by any one group member within 2 seconds; voices synchronized with screen changes
Freshness	Everything produced on the whiteboard up to "now"; previous screens (whiteboards); current voices
Accuracy	Must clearly read words, see pictures, hear voices
Format	Replica of whiteboard: "handwritten" lines, text, and drawings in various colors on a white background; audio for voices
Language	Preferably a standard computer language for graphics; English language for voices
Volume	One entire board on a computer screen; voices of group members
Content	Free form; whatever can be made by a "marker" on a whiteboard and by a person speaking

together. ISDN is an excellent technology choice to connect remote members with the group.

Electronic Mail

A typical scenario is an end-user who wants to send a message to a colleague. Perhaps it is a simple text note, but often it is a compound document, containing other forms of communication such as drawings or images in addition to text. It's even possible that an end user may want to send a greeting card, containing a photo, a note, and a reproduction of a signature.

Issues other than information attributes (for example, connectivity, addressing, and the evolution of information attributes after passing through mail-switching gateways) are not considered in the table that follows—it simply attempts to characterize the information attributes where other factors are already resolved.

Urgency	Messages within 1 minute after requesting them
Freshness	Message should be available for the recipient to view 5 minutes after sending
Accuracy	Message and attachments unaltered in any way
Format	Text, drawings, pictures, and undefined binary files
Language	Various standard formats: ASCII for text; binary files for word processors, executable programs, G3 faxes, and so on
Volume	Essentially unbounded: often just a few Kilobits per second, usually less than 10 MB
Content	Text, drawings, photos (still picture images), and binary files: message to contain name and address of sender, receiving party's name and address; time sent; time received; and the message content

Availability (Paging)

A typical scenario is a group member who works remotely from the rest of the group yet must be accessible to the group. Sometimes group members may only need to ask the person for information; other times, the person may need to alter his or her schedule because of some change. The remote group member needs assurance that he or she can be reached when

Urgency	Knowledge of request within 2 minutes after it is made
Freshness	Requesting information must be current (within 2 minutes)
Accuracy	Every emergency request alerts remote group members; contact information is without error
Format	Alerting mechanism
Language	Text, ringing bell, beeping sound, and so on
Volume	Variable, but often fairly brief
Content	Who to contact; reason for request, relevant details

necessary — especially in emergency situations—and that he or she will get accurate, fresh information concerning what to do or who to contact.

Reading Resource Documents

A typical scenario is a worker who needs to read and understand some new methodology or assimilate news. This person may be writing a white paper and need information to do it. Or the person may be simply reading a newspaper, a journal, or a book while on an airline flight.

Urgency	Access documents within 3 minutes
Freshness	Information that is still relevant to particular need; often, messages within last few days (but some stay "fresh" for months); newspapers usually within the last week; books within the last few years, if technical
Accuracy	Ascertain words (letters), drawings, and so on as they appear on the page (readable print required — can't be too small, blurry, and so on.)
Format	Ink on paper: printed text bound in a hard cover
Language	English text; black-and-white line drawings; color photographs
Volume	350 pages (for example)
Content	Mystery novel; textbook; journal (for example)

Phone Voice Mail (Announcement for Callers)

A typical scenario is a worker with voice mail who leaves a message for anyone who calls. The worker intends to provide a message that will satisfy the needs of the person calling. The attribute requirements in the table below represent the needs of the person calling (and listening to the announcement on voice mail).

Urgency	Hear announcement within three rings
Freshness	Announcement less than 24 hours old
Accuracy	Clearly audible message; caller needs to understand the words and telephone numbers if provided
Format	Audio (voice)
Language	English language
Volume	About 30 seconds
Content	Name of person being called (to ensure callers reach correct person); when the person will return; when the person might return the call; where to reach person in emergency (if calling person has a high urgency requirement)

Phone Voice Mail (Message for Person Called)

A typical scenario is a worker with voice mail who receives a message left for him or her. Callers must provide details sufficient to satisfy the needs of the person being called. The attribute requirements in the table below represent the needs of the worker being called (and listening to the messages left by the people on voice mail).

Urgency	Determined by calling person (e.g., "please call by 3 P.M. today")
Freshness	Sufficient content to determine purpose (e.g., "I need the info for a 3 P.M. meeting; after that don't bother to obtain the info")
Accuracy	Clear messages so that words can be understood correctly
Format	Audio (voice)
Language	English
Volume	Less than 5 minutes
Content	Time of message; who called; why they called; degree of urgency; sufficient details to determine freshness; callback number

3.4 SUMMARY

We can characterize information by its attributes, only one of which is content or meaning. We must also consider other information attributes like volume, form, syntax, accuracy, freshness, and urgency. Each end-user application has particular requirements related to these attributes. Some applications stress urgency; others stress accuracy; still others emphasize a combination of two or more attributes. The end user obtains and uses a suitable IT system by carefully considering the information attributes in the context of his or her application requirements.

The forms of information include speech and music, text, images, video, and various combinations of these (i.e., multimedia information). All of these information forms can be represented digitally. That's why digital computers are so crucial to our society today. And we need ISDN and other similar digital communications capabilities to connect digital computers and other digital devices to provide IT capabilities. With the much-increased bandwidth provided by ISDN, we now have many more opportunities for applying distributed information solutions to our needs.

The illustrative examples showed varying information-attribute requirements. Upon examining them, we see that ISDN is particularly well suited to meeting these requirements, particularly compared to pre-ISDN possibilities. The very rapid call setup time of ISDN can satisfy higher urgency requirements than pre-ISDN systems. The digital nature of ISDN can provide a higher degree of accuracy, both because of error-control techniques common in digital systems (such as *cyclical redundancy checks* or *CRCs*) and because of improved infrastructure transport (especially true in fiber-optic systems that are many orders of magnitude more accurate). The higher speeds and corresponding throughput of ISDN allow a great deal more volume to be moved than with pre-ISDN systems with the same urgency requirements. The universal nature of digital representation of information allows a wide variety of format and language representations.

In other words, compared to other existing alternatives, ISDN technology can be more useful to us in applying information. In the next chapter, we explore how telecommunications networks are evolving to become ISDN-capable.

4

Supply Push

his chapter argues that the costs associated with providing ISDN will, in the long run, decline from being much higher to being lower than the costs of providing traditional communication services. The decline will occur as costs in switching and transmission equipment decline; in addition, the costs of operating and maintaining the ISDN network can be reduced. Lower cost potential—the push for ISDN—adds to the pull forces of demand to position ISDN to meet the needs of the information age.

Curiously, skeptics constantly harp on the "fact" that users have not demanded ISDN—vendors are pushing ISDN technology upon them. Possibly so. However, reflect back to the introduction of other technologies. How many potential automobile drivers in 1870 insisted that someone invent the automobile so they could commute to work each day? How many users asked for the invention of the electric motor? The steamboat? The airplane? The transistor, the TV, or the laser? Rather, each of these technologies was first invented or discovered; then, applications were found. It is difficult to think of even one technology that potential users demanded in advance. Regardless of whether users demand a technology, the vendor is at risk. Potential users make no guarantees prior to purchase.

4.1   TELEPHONE NETWORK ARCHITECTURE

Traditional telephone networks are perceived, designed, and operated as two major segments — *switching* and *transmission*. Although the very first telephone calls were connected directly, without switching, the need for switching soon became apparent. Developments in transmission technology, however, were largely independent of developments in switching technology, and vice versa. But in the ISDN era, these two formerly separate technologies are converging to yield more value. The promise of future technologies is that the distinctions between switching and transmission will disappear altogether.

In the past, a switched telephone call meant a circuit-switched voice telephone call. The talking path was established for the duration of the conversation, then cleared for use by other subscribers. Later, permanently reserved facilities, or *leased lines*, provided connections for as long as the user paid the leasing fee. More recently, packet-switched services were created to provide a more highly shared connection—with corresponding shared costs.

Our survey of the telephone network architecture begins with its mainstay—traditional circuit-switched voice service. Figure 4.1 shows the simplest of telephone connections—an *intraoffice call*. A caller at Main Street

Figure 4.1   An intraoffice telephone call: physical (top) and schematic (bottom) representations

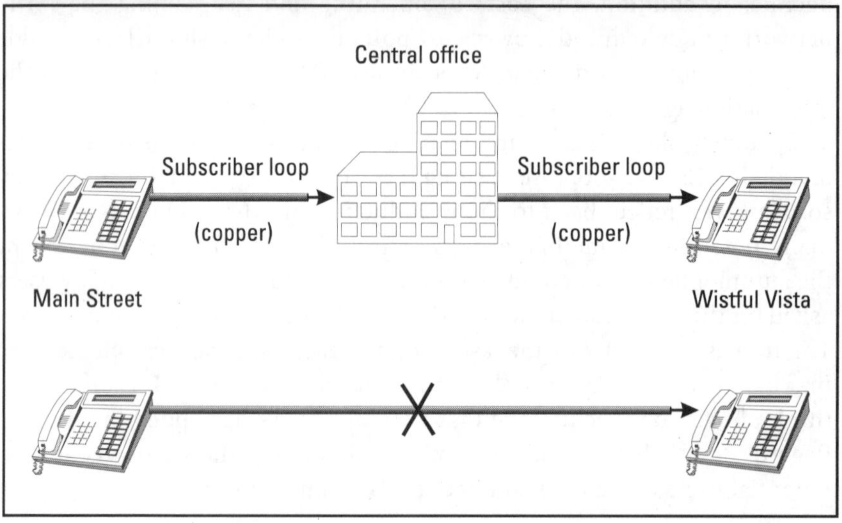

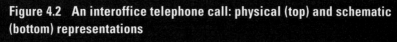

Figure 4.2   An interoffice telephone call: physical (top) and schematic (bottom) representations

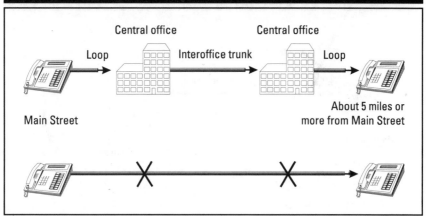

is connected to a caller in the same neighborhood at Wistful Vista. Each end user is connected to a *central office* via a *local loop,* which is a pair of copper wires, often simply called a *pair.* Typically, these loops are less than 2 miles long, although they can be much longer under some circumstances. Unless on party-line service, each end user is the sole user of a local loop. The central office houses the switching equipment that routes the call to the correct destination. The buildings that contain these switches vary greatly in size. Often the size of a house, they are sometimes as large as an office building or a high school, and sometimes no larger than a storage shed. Figure 4.2 illustrates a slightly more complex call, an *interoffice call.* In this case, the two telephone end users are separated by somewhat more geography (typically, more than about 5 miles in a suburban neighborhood). Architectural pieces similar to those of intraoffice calls support this connection. There is a central office and a trunk circuit connecting the end users (called an *interoffice trunk*). This interoffice trunk is typically about 8 miles long in a suburban location, but it is not unusual to find interoffice trunks well over 20 miles long. The transmission technology of interoffice trunks developed differently from the technology of loops because of the longer distances and shared usage and costs of the facility.

A telephone call to someone on the other side of a large town, as shown in Figure 4.3, is likely to pass through a *tandem switch.* This is a switch that acts as a hub—all of the subtending switches connect to it—that allows all

Figure 4.3   Routing a telephone call through a tandem switch: physical (top) and schematic (bottom) representations

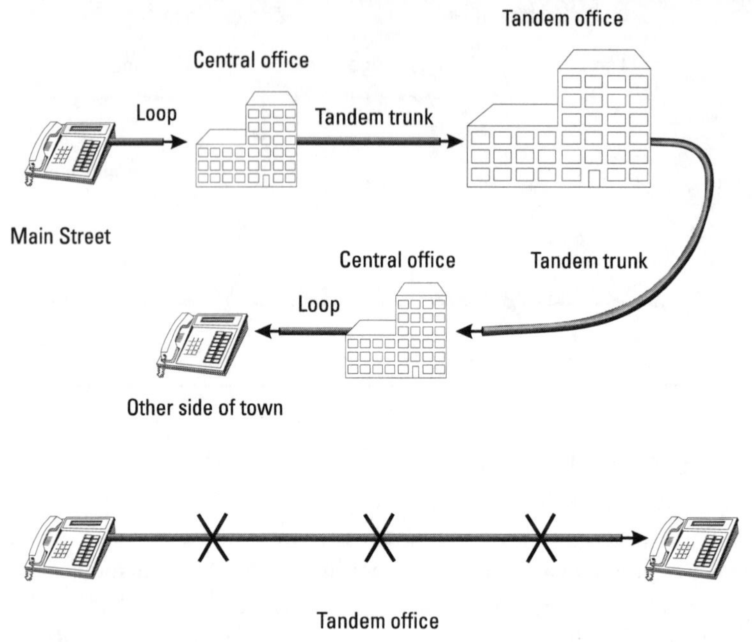

offices to be connected through that tandem switch. Without a tandem switch, offices would have to be connected directly (via *direct trunks*). While some pairs of offices might be in a community of interest that supports *direct trunking,* other pairs of offices might have no significant traffic. Routing through a tandem switch results in fewer overall trunks. Transmission requirements for tandem trunks have traditionally been much more demanding than requirements for interoffice trunks because tandem trunks are an extra link in the overall connection. Thus, a connection including a tandem trunk is comparable in quality to a direct connection. Similarly, requirements for the tandem switch are stringent because the switch affects so many calls.

Figure 4.4 illustrates long-distance calling within the United States. Since 1984, the United States (for telephony purposes) has been divided into 161 parcels known as *local access and transport areas (LATAs)*. You must connect to an *interLATA carrier* (as required by the U.S. government) to complete a telephone

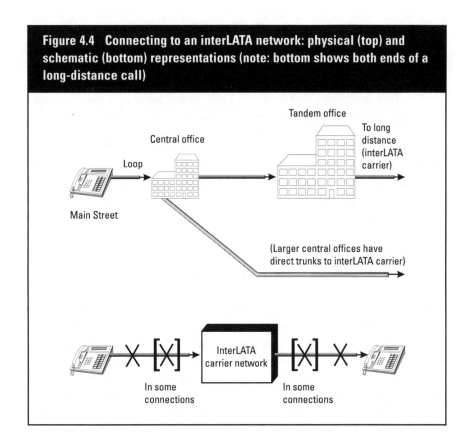

Figure 4.4   Connecting to an interLATA network: physical (top) and schematic (bottom) representations (note: bottom shows both ends of a long-distance call)

call to someone in a different LATA. Connections to the interLATA carrier can go directly through local central offices, but often these calls are routed through a tandem office. In each interLATA network, switching and transmission facilities operate in much the same way as the facilities in the local telephone network.

Ultimately, every telephone call is connected to a destination through a concatenation of facility links and switching connections. Each link must be designed so that every concatenation of links provides a good-quality speech connection.

Different pieces of this telephonic architecture have developed separately—particularly transmission and switching equipment. In the past, engineers and technicians who worked on switching systems rarely, if ever, were involved with transmission equipment, and vice versa. This tradition of total separation lingers even today, although recent efforts have been directed toward a more holistic approach.

The switching and transmission disciplines are fundamentally different. Switching systems establish circuits and provide services. Switching systems deal with physical elements that move to provide electrical contact (or assignments to particular time slots); statistical availability considerations; services (for example, call waiting and call forwarding); and a wide variety of support functions for buildings and power supplies. Transmission systems transport electrical signals from one point to another. These systems involve sophisticated electrical-transmission line analysis of signal strength and frequency, impedance issues, signal-enhancement concerns, modulation techniques, and a wide variety of support functions such as placing poles and splicing cables.

4.2 TRANSMISSION EVOLUTION

At its inception, telephony was an entirely analog system, consisting of electrical transmissions over metallic wires. Later, electronics were introduced into transmission systems to extend their range and to obtain more than one talk path connection over each pair of wires (or other metallic facility, such as coaxial cable). Using modulation techniques similar to those used in AM broadcast radio transmissions but contained within the transmission wires, transmission-system capacity was greatly increased and costs accordingly reduced. These analog carrier systems were deployed in the interior of the network, in trunks between telephone switching offices.

Beginning in the early 1960s, digital systems were introduced and gradually began to displace the analog carrier systems. By the early 1990s, almost all of the interior transmission systems were digital. Today, many of these digital systems are light pulses transmitted over fiber-optic strands rather than electrical pulses transmitted over copper wires. Increasingly, digital systems and fiber systems are making their way into the subscriber loop plant (and directly to the telephone user from the network). Logically extending this trend, someday all transmission systems will be digital and transmitted over fibers as optical signals.

This section provides a glimpse of the transmission technology details so you can get a sense of how the telephone network has evolved. While this overview is sufficient to give you an understanding of the basic concepts and trends that are consistent with the development of ISDN, the presentation is by no means complete, thorough, or rigorous. Perhaps the best single reference containing the most comprehensive discussion of the telephonic evolution is the well-known *Engineering and Operations in the Bell System*, which was updated in 1983.

Early Days

Telephony began with analog transmission. Figure 4.5 illustrates just how simple the basic idea is. We're all familiar with the idea of a battery and wires. When a circuit is closed, current flows. We also know that when there is resistance in a circuit, the resulting current flow is inversely proportional to the amount of resistance. The genius of early telephone design was the concept of variable resistance created by carbon granules: when you apply pressure to carbon granules, the resistance changes. As you put carbon granules under increasing pressure, the electrical resistance in the circuit decreases. When a person speaks, he or she produces sound waves, which are variations in air pressure. When a person speaks into the telephone transmitter, the varying air pressure strikes carbon granules inside the transmitter. In turn, the changes in air pressure cause increases and decreases in the electrical current flowing in the circuit. In fact, the electrical-current changes precisely "follow" the sound-wave changes.

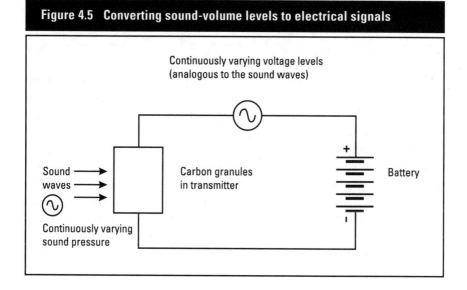

Figure 4.5   Converting sound-volume levels to electrical signals

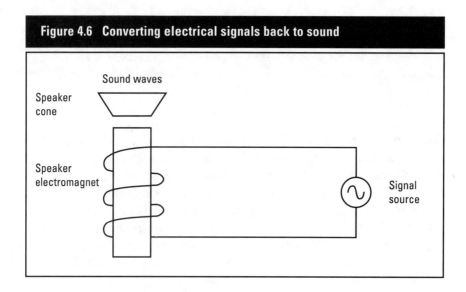

Figure 4.6   Converting electrical signals back to sound

Because the electrical current is analogous (in the dictionary definition sense of the word) to the voice sound waves, we characterize the transmission method as analog.

Once the speaker sets off this varying electrical current (the *signal source*), the current travels to the distant location and re-creates a facsimile of the original sound waves as shown in Figure 4.6. In a process that is conceptually inverse to the way the signal source is created at the transmitter, varying electrical current, traveling through an electromagnet, creates a varying magnetic field. A speaker cone, attached to a permanent magnet, is alternately attracted to and repelled from the electromagnet. This resulting movement of the speaker cone forces air to move in ways that sound very much like the original sound source. The person at the receiving end "hears" the person at the transmitting end speaking well enough to recognize and understand his or her voice.

Although fundamentally simple, analog transmission techniques became extremely sophisticated over time. Concepts such as *load coils* and *negative impedance* are but two examples of sophisticated analog-transmission systems elements that developed. Reading the notes and correspondence of telephone-transmission engineers written during the first half of this century makes convincing evidence that they were extraordinarily talented. It would be a mistake to think of these people and technologies as being in any way simple or primitive.

Over the years, transmission system elements have developed in distinctly different ways, depending on where they are located in the network. Transmission links between telephone switches, the *trunk* circuits, were the first beneficiaries of electronic transmission technology. Early electronic equipment used amplitude-modulation techniques similar to those used in AM broadcast radio. Over microwave or wire, a single transmission medium could carry many channels. Longer transmission paths were particularly good targets for this technology, since costs were almost directly proportional to distance. These long-haul systems quickly began using this technology almost exclusively. Short-haul transmission systems (the shorter transmission links between telephone switching centers) also used this technology, but to a lesser degree.

Introduction of Digital Systems

Starting in the early 1960s, T1 carrier systems were installed between central offices of local telephone networks, particularly in short-haul systems (that is, systems spanning a distance of less than about 50 miles). These carrier systems were the first digital systems to be deployed, hence the name *T1* (digiTal, 1st carrier system). In time, digital carrier systems became less expensive, and as a result, most new interoffice trunks (and tandem trunks) for local exchange networks were deployed on T1 systems. The widespread introduction of T1 systems into the local networks provided an economic base for future deployments of any network transmission equipment. Further, these massive deployments provided a technology base that made subsequent changes toward digital technology economically desirable. New additions to the network could take advantage of the benefits of these already-deployed digital carrier systems but suffered from the constraints and limitations of that technology.

These digital systems are radically different from the analog systems that preceded them. Rather than transmitting continuously varying electrical analog signals of original speech, digital systems periodically sample electrical signals, convert them into numbers, and transmit the (digital) numbers to the distant end.

Until recently, analog carrier systems continued to be the conduit for long-haul carrier systems, using coaxial cable and microwave systems.

Conversion to digital systems didn't seem attractive to the industry until the advent of fiber cable. But by the early 1990s, the norm for long-haul transmission became digital transmission over fiber-optic facilities.

As shown in Figure 4.1, the transmission link between the telephone subscriber (user) and the network is called the *subscriber loop*. Unlike trunk circuits, these loops are not shared; each loop is dedicated to one subscriber even if that telephone user is not currently using the telephone. Because each subscriber has the exclusive use of a loop, there are a huge number of them in a telephone network. In fact, a very large proportion of the network investment consists of these loops. Consequently, the cost of providing these loops must be kept as low as possible.

Until about the mid 1970s, telephone companies would provide a pair of copper wires from the local telephone central office to the subscriber location. Nothing else was generally needed to assure adequate transmission, except, occasionally, relatively simple load coils. (The use of load coils — very important to conventional analog telephony—is technically complex and not described in any detail in this book because it doesn't help explain ISDN.) Cable splicers were instructed to periodically insert load coils into the loops to improve transmission characteristics. Only in special circumstances were special analog design techniques, using specialized equipment (such as *E6 repeaters, dial long-line circuits,* and *loop extenders*), needed to ensure good voice transmission. This was good news for the accountants — no special design efforts meant no special costs; the only "design" expended on a loop was assigning physical resources, which were mainly cable pairs.

For very long loops, this simple approach to provisioning didn't work as well (too little line current, too much loss of voice power, and poor audio fidelity). During the rapid real estate boom of the 1970s, large quantities of long loops were often required. To address these problems and obtain more than one channel on each of these lengthy and expensive copper-wire pairs, telephone companies introduced the idea of subscriber carrier systems. The same technologies applied to the trunking networks were applied to the subscriber loop. Later, fiber-optic facilities were used for the sections of the loop (*feeder cable*) closest to the telephone switching office. Today, fiber is being deployed to crossconnect locations much closer to the end user. The last portion of the loop to the subscriber is via a pair of copper wires (or coaxial cable for higher bandwidth). The logical conclusion of this trend is to deploy of fiber all the way to the subscriber.

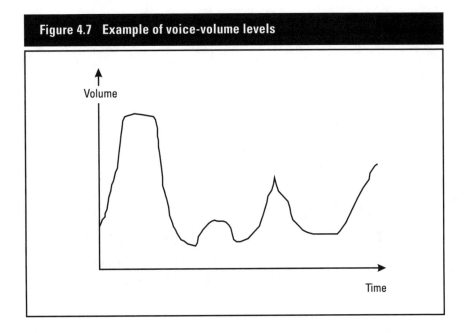

Figure 4.7   Example of voice-volume levels

Digital Encoding Details

Although it would be an exaggeration to claim that this section is highly technical, many readers may find it contains more detail than they want. These details are not prerequisites to understanding ISDN. Nevertheless, this section does provide a basic overview of how analog signals are converted to digital numbers (and back again).

Analog-to-digital conversions (*A/D conversions*) transform electrical analog signals to digital bitstreams. The continuously varying amplitude values of the analog signal (illustrated in Figure 4.7) are sampled so frequently (8000 times per second in a T1 carrier system) that it is difficult for a person to perceive the difference between a sequence of samples and the continuously varying source. (See Figure 4.8(a).) If this seems hard to believe, remember that visual action can be sampled as little as 24 times per second and still appear to be a "motion picture." So the sample rate of 8000 times per second renders voice signals quite well for telephony purposes. Each one of these samples is the value of the continuously varying analog (of a voice-volume level) signal.

Each value must be transformed into a digital number. (See Figure 4.8(b).) The most frequently used coding algorithm in the United States

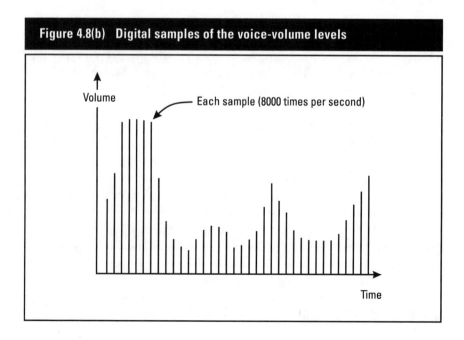

Figure 4.8(a)   Sampling voice-volume levels 8000 times per second

Figure 4.8(b)   Digital samples of the voice-volume levels

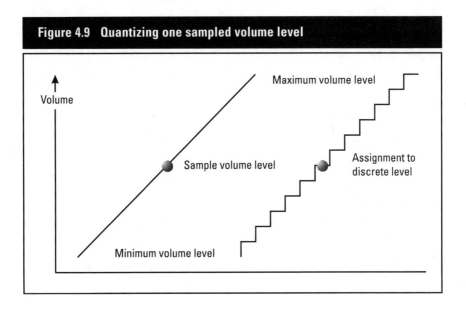

Figure 4.9   Quantizing one sampled volume level

is μ-*law encoding*. In a T1 system, a contiguous set of eight bits carries this digital number. After the value of the signal is obtained, the volume can then be mapped into one of 254 different numbers. (The 8 bits in the signal can actually represent 256 different numbers, but two are reserved for special purposes.) Notice how much Figure 4.9 resembles Figure 1.4. Any value along the continuum (the range of possible values from the lowest to the highest) can be mapped directly into one of the 254 discrete levels, just as any spot on our hypothetical ramp can be mapped into the height of the closest stair step. After this A/D conversion, the T1 carrier system conveys each 8-bit number, representing an analog sample, to the distant end. There, the inverse process (a D/A conversion) reconstructs each volume level (8000 times per second). The resulting signal is then processed (slightly) so that it can drive a speaker so the person on the receiving end can hear a voice.

In transmission systems, sending one channel after the other over one facility (such as a pair of wires) is known as *time-division multiplexing*. Each channel uses 8 bits, as shown in Figure 4.10(a). Shown in Figure 4.10(b) is the concept of *flags*, which are a special series of bits that indicate where to start decoding the line signal. Without a flag, the receiving demultiplexer wouldn't know where to start channel 1.

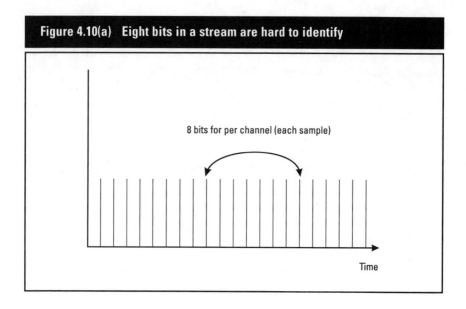

Figure 4.10(a)   Eight bits in a stream are hard to identify

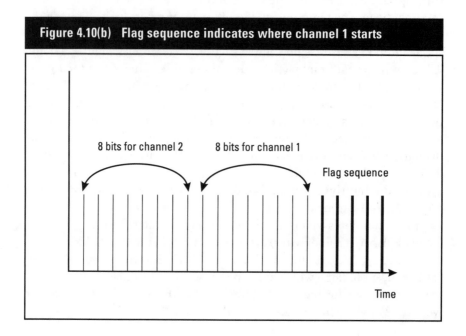

Figure 4.10(b)   Flag sequence indicates where channel 1 starts

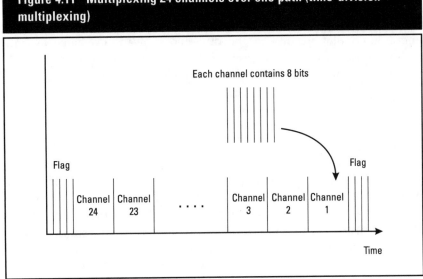

Figure 4.11   Multiplexing 24 channels over one path (time-division multiplexing)

The T1 digital carrier system time-division multiplexes 24 of these digitized voice paths onto one pair of wires for each direction of transmission. The eight-bit sample of channel 1 is followed by an 8-bit sample for channel 2, and so on, for a total of 24 channels. Additionally, as shown in Figure 4.11, a small number of bits are used at the beginning and end of the 24-channel sequence to *frame* the bit structure (to define where to start the process of decoding the samples for channel 1 and subsequent channels). Channels within the sequence of 24 are pinpointed by bit location within the frame. This cycle repeats continuously.

Fiber-Optic Systems

Typically, these T1 carrier systems used copper wires as the electrical transmission medium. However, you can convey information with optical digital pulses as well. If you have ever sent Morse-code signals by flashlight, you have done this. In fiber-optic systems, lasers replace flashlights, and fiber-optic strands convey and guide the laser light to the remote location. Constrained to obey the relevant laws of optics, light stays in the strand, which is sheathed with an opaque cover to prevent interference with adjacent strands.

Coding algorithms, line rates, and digital-format structures are the same for optical transmission as for electrical transmission. In fact, Figure 4.11 illustrates the synchronous digital hierarchy that makes up an entire family of transmission encoding and shows rates shared by both technologies. (Although the optical rates extend higher, which is consistent with their capacity for greater bandwidth over electrical systems.) Optical interface rates and formats are specified in the *optical carrier* (*OC*) levels (OC-1 to OC-48).

SONET Systems

Even though optical systems provide a much greater bandwidth than previous electrical systems, transmission architects wisely decided to build the optical rates-and-formats structure to mesh smoothly with existing electrical structures around the world. Because of the widespread deployment of T1 carrier systems, the basic building block of digital systems hierarchy is designed to be consistent with the T1 systems. In a T1 carrier system a line *digital-signal rate 1* (*DS1*) (1.544 Mbps) is used to convey 24 channels. Each of the 24 channels in the DS1 is referred to as a *DS0* and, as shown in Figures 4.10 and 4.11, consists of 8-bit samples, 8000 times per

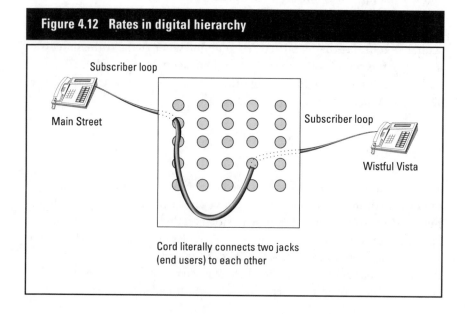

Figure 4.12   Rates in digital hierarchy

Subscriber loop

Main Street

Subscriber loop

Wistful Vista

Cord literally connects two jacks
(end users) to each other

second, to provide 64 Kbps of bandwidth. Just as a freight train is made up of many similar freight cars, higher signal-rate formats can be viewed as long strings of DS0 or DS1 digital streams. If you look at the systems for aggregating bandwidth shown in Figure 4.12, you see DS1s have been grouped together in a variety of ways to achieve higher overall rates. Current planning includes systems in the gigabit range, which contains thousands of DS1s. Traditionally, combinations of DS1s were not simple or elegant. To select one DS1 from a larger bundle, you had to demultiplex all of the DS1s, remove the desired DS1 from the bitstream, then remultiplex all of the other DS1s to send them to their destinations. Hence, *synchronous optical network systems (SONET)* was developed as an easier way to insert and extract the desired number of DS1s and DS0s from a larger digital bitstream. Today, national and international standards that define these rates and formats are largely complete. These standards have enabled SONET implementations to work with existing network infrastructure. (In fact, SONET works even better than some of the existing implementations in its ease of inserting and removing individual DS1s and DS0s from a very high bandwidth signal.)

It is unnecessary to count the number of DS1s or to insert or remove individual DS1s to meet the needs of newer services such as *high-definition TV (HDTV)*. Although a channel of 140 Mbps might contain a number of DS1s, what is really important is that the bandwidth is appropriate for conveying HDTV. SONET provides the way to apportion bandwidth in much larger chunks as well as in the traditional smaller chunks. The following table shows the relationships between the different synchronous digital-signal rates.

Rate	Payload (bandwidth available to user)
DS0	64 Kbps (8 bits per sample, sampled 8000 times per second); in pre-ISDN systems, signaling requirements "rob" some of the bits, leaving only 56 Kbps payload
DS1	1536 Kbps (24 DS0s in a frame)
DS3	43.008 Mbps (672 DS0s, 28 DS1s)
OC-1	51.480 Mbps (672 DS0s, 28 DS1s)
OC-3, 9, 12, 18, 24, 36, and 48 (integral numbers of OC-1 capacity)	

Wave-Division Multiplexing

Each optical bit stream in a fiber-optic system is generated by turning a light source on and off. The light source is a laser, which will, by nature, have a specific wavelength. You can operate additional channels over the same strand if the channels operate on different wavelengths. Researchers speculate that someday systems could be developed that allow hundreds or even thousands of different wavelength sources. To achieve this, very coherent laser light sources would be needed to prevent interference between channels. While it is not certain when or even whether such systems will eventually be deployed, if current research advances development, the capacity of fiber systems could multiply dramatically in future years, and drastically reduce the cost of digital transmission.

4.3   SWITCHING EVOLUTION

Switching systems were introduced into the telephone network for economy. They have evolved from manual systems, to automated electromechanical systems, and then to common-control electromechanical systems—arguably the earliest implementation of the modern computer. In the mid 1960s, stored program-control systems were introduced into electronic switching systems. Current switching systems use stored program-control technology with digital switching fabric. Future switching technologies will likely include higher bandwidths and additional features such as maintenance capabilities driven by expert systems. Researchers are even working on the concept of optical switches. In every case, technology has been advanced as a way to provide more or better telephone service at lower cost.

Early Days

Early telephony had no switching. Every telephone was directly connected to every other telephone. If you wanted to converse with other telephone users, you had to have separate telephone lines to connect you to each user. Each one of these lines had to go directly from your telephone to a specific other phone. Imagine: if you wanted to speak to 20 other people, you would have had to string 20 lines from your telephone to each of theirs. Running very short lines did not incur much of an economic penalty, but stringing lines across town would be expensive. Furthermore, to talk to a particular person, you would have to have a line installed in advance of the conversation. Instead of simply placing a call to talk with someone, you have to string up a line first! For telephony to ever move forward to the point where we could call virtually anyone in town, switching systems had to be invented and deployed in the telephone network. While this historical scenario of non-switched telephony seems quaint today, we, in fact, use an equivalent arrangement today when we use leased lines for data transmission.

The *cordboard* was the first switching system and was manually operated. (See Figure 4.12.) Each telephone was connected by a line to a centrally located switchboard. To switch a call, the switchboard operator would connect two lines together by plugging cords into the switchboard. Although we tend to romanticize the charm of these early systems, they had severe shortcomings. One of the less obvious disadvantages was that of operators favoring certain businesses—to their competitive advantage. If a telephone operator had ties with or interests in one particular business, she could recommend and offer to connect to that particular business. In fact, legend has it that just such a problem involving competing undertakers led to the development of the first automated switching system.

Major gains in productivity were achieved by automating the switching function—substituting capital for labor. If these automated systems had not been introduced, there would not be enough switchboard operators to switch all of the calls that are placed today, even if everyone were employed as a cordboard operator! Further, the labor costs would drive the costs of telephony so high that using a telephone would be a luxury most of us could not afford. In other words, we benefit from this cost-lowering automation in much the same way we benefit from mass production of products.

Early automatic switching systems were known as *step-by-step* systems. For every step in the dialing process, a piece of the switching machine would respond. After the first dialed digit, a piece of the switch would physically move and contact different electrical paths. The next digit would cause a subsequent switch change, and so on, until the dialed number was accepted by the switch and routed for call completion. A skilled technician could actually follow the progression of a call through the switching office as it was being dialed. Each piece of an electromechanical switching system contained its own control (or intelligence); it was a highly "distributed" system. The next phase of development was to implement control of the entire switch from one common-control area of the switch. Early common-control equipment, constructed of electromechanical relays, is considered by some to be the earliest form of computer. Although it consisted of relays rather than electronics, the logic behind this common-control equipment was similar to that of a modern digital computer. The instructions for this "computer" were "stored" in the way its relays were wired. Whenever a user desired different tasks, or wanted to perform existing tasks differently, the wiring needed to be changed!

Digital Control

After the development of the transistor, common-control portions of switching machines were reduced in size. The programming for these common-control machines could be stored as software instructions. Known as *stored program control* (*SPC*) switching machines, they became immensely popular because people could implement changes by inserting different software. The only real difference between the SPC telephone switch logic and a conventional digital electronic computer was that it had to be a great deal more fault tolerant, and it was optimized for telephony. The tremendous improvements in the computer industry were applied directly to SPC switches; likewise, improvements in SPC switches were applied within the computer industry. The transmission paths switched by these SPC machines, however, remained analog for a time. This made sense in an environment where most of the trunks and virtually all of the loops were analog. But as newly deployed trunks were increasingly digital, switching machine design was reconsidered and began to change, too.

Digital Switching Fabric

The push to use digital switching fabric in switching machines was driven by the need to avoid costly conversions from analog to digital systems and by the availability of low-cost digital building blocks from which to construct the digital switching fabric. Whether or not they were controlled by common-control technology, switches through the late 1960s required physical connections to route the analog signal from one path to another, as shown conceptually in Figure 4.13.

Switching machines in the telephone network perform a variety of functions to complete telephone calls. *Tandem* switches, deep in the heart of the

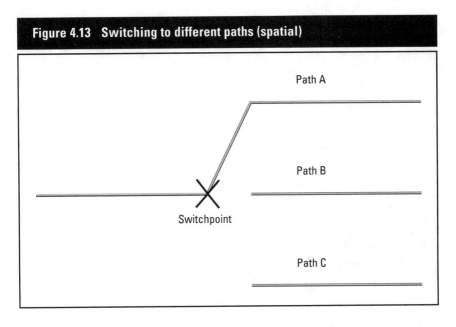

Figure 4.13 Switching to different paths (spatial)

Path A

Path B

Switchpoint

Path C

network, are designed to switch calls from one trunk circuit to another. In the past, a voice message represented digitally on an incoming trunk had to be converted to an analog signal to be switched to a machine with analog switching fabric. If the outgoing trunk was also digital, the voice signal had to be converted once again and coded into a digital representation of the voice signal. Relative to other network costs, this high cost added no value to the customer; it was purely and simply a change in *form* without a change in *content*.

Clearly, the unnecessary transaction costs of converting between analog and digital signals were targets for cost reduction. Since trunk circuits were becoming increasingly digital, digital switching fabric became necessary to avoid pointless signal conversions. As digital systems proliferated into the subscriber loop plant, the conversion problem was exacerbated, resulting in a push to provide digital switching fabric even for local switching machines. Fortunately, the push to avoid the costs of A/D conversions was accompanied by the availability of lower cost technology.

Just as the early switching machines could be considered the first computers, modern digital-telephone switching machines are quite similar to modern computing machines. Similar circuitry and programming techniques are used in their construction and component parts. In fact, components developed by the computer industry were used directly in the design of telephone switching equipment. The widespread deployment of

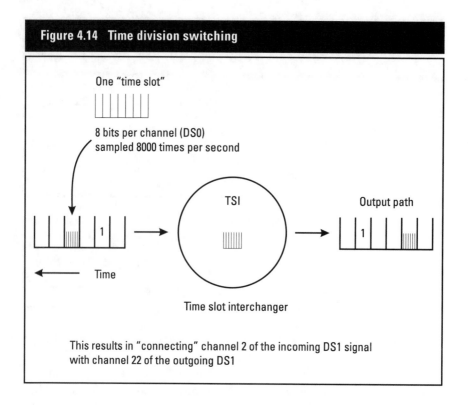

Figure 4.14   Time division switching

One "time slot"

8 bits per channel (DS0)
sampled 8000 times per second

TSI

Output path

1

1

Time

Time slot interchanger

This results in "connecting" channel 2 of the incoming DS1 signal
with channel 22 of the outgoing DS1

computer equipment made the availability and pricing attractive, particularly for *very large scale integrated (VLSI)* circuit technology. The telephone industry seized the opportunity of using these computer components and techniques to avoid costly A/D conversions.

These digital switching systems operate by moving signals in time, rather than in space. As shown conceptually in Figure 4.14, the *time slot interchanger* moves the input signal (the 8 bits of sampled volume level) from channel 2 of the input bitstream to channel 22 of the outgoing bitstream, which connects these two channels together. These techniques of digital switching are more similar to moving data blocks inside of a computer than they are to conventional telephone switching. The technologies of telephony and computers are merging into a single technology, allowing the economies of scale to lower costs for both industries.

As mentioned earlier, in the evolution of transmission systems, optical transmission systems are becoming popular and offer potentially very inexpensive transmission costs. If in the past we wanted to avoid conversions only of form (analog to digital), wouldn't we also want to avoid future conversions only of form (electrical to optical) by providing optical switches? Currently, researchers are laboring to do exactly that, although there are no indications that these kinds of switches will be available soon.

Operations, Administration, Management, and Provisioning for ISDN

Operations, administration, maintenance, and provisioning (OAM&P) are the four basic aspects of running a telephone network. ISDN offers the potential for a marked increase in productivity, providing management with more control and knowledge of network details and using less expensive component parts.

Reduced Design Requirements

Conventionally designed telephone circuits can be quite complex, particularly for data and special-purpose services, which are appropriately called *special services*. A wide variety of different equipment types are available, each of which requires insight and expertise to produce effective circuit designs. These designs meet a variety of end-user needs from data services to speech services with special signaling or quality requirements. Clerks and engineers assign specific equipment and facilities to provide each service; still more engineering and technician time is required to design and install each circuit. Additional time and effort goes into testing and accepting the final circuit for delivery.

Contrast the conventional scenario with an ISDN scenario. The user accesses the ISDN network from a digital terminal through the standard digital access loop. The user and the network exchange signaling messages describing the type of service desired, the kinds of terminal equipment in use, and other relevant details. Network intelligence in the switching machines or SS7 service-control points provides the connections and other capabilities requested by the end user. The network establishes ISDN services by selecting from the pool of interchangeable parts rather than selecting and assigning specific equipment.

Small Set of (Universal) Interchangeable Parts

The technology trends discussed above suggest that the ISDN network will move to a small set of interchangeable parts: digital transmission links, digital switching fabric, and digital stored-program control.

Historically, telephone networks have consisted of a large number of very specialized parts. Each part had a specific role to play and generally was not interchangeable with any other part. For example, some facilities were selected on the basis of geography or distance; switches were selected on the basis of the type of switching they did (local or tandem, voice or data, and so on). Signaling and the special equipment needed to achieve appropriate signaling were often the factors that complicated individual circuit designs.

In the ISDN network, signaling occurs by sending messages over a digital stream, more or less in the same way the data itself is transferred by one end user to another. The only real difference is that signaling contains messages from the user to the network (and within the network), whereas user-data transfer moves information from the sending user to the receiving user. Even with the increased use of fiber facilities, the actual use of a digital link (on either electrical or optical media) has more to do with the protocols and interfaces than with the details of the medium itself. The only perceivable differences in service have to do with cost (conversions from one medium to another) and performance (mostly error rates and transmission speeds). Consequently, the set of digital links can be thought of as an interchangeable pile: simply establish a pool of digital links and use them for whatever service is desired.

Interfaces between the user and the network are being standardized to a small number of possible types, based on existing and projected technology. ISDN is provided over existing copper facilities. The sets of digital format and protocol messaging details are few. Managing an inventory of a small number of interchangeable component parts, which can be assembled to provide virtually any user-requested service, has the potential of reducing operating costs and complexities while more completely meeting user needs.

Reusability

After the completion of a call, the interchangeable parts are released back into the pool of spares. Network intelligence constantly selects these spare parts to provide services, then releases them back into the pool as spares when they are no longer needed. Spared components almost certainly will be frequently reused.

In conventional special-services provisioning, in contrast, components can be reused only if a similar capability is requested at some future time by another end user. Even if this occurs, the odds of finding and reusing a component are not high because of the large set of very specialized equipment one would have to search. When components are reused in such situations, it is because costly computer-based management systems have been used.

Simplified Forecasting: Aggregate Demand

Without intervention, the demand for services could conceivably exhaust the supply of spare network components, and the user would be denied service. The prudent network manager tries to forecast, as accurately as possible, the ebb and flow of user demand for services and, on the basis of these predictions, arranges to periodically add to the pool of spare and available network components to balance (as much as possible) user demand and costs.

The reality of this balancing act is much more complex than this scenario implies. The network manager oversees quite a large variety of inventory, much of it specific to individual services. Consequently, the network manager has to peer through the crystal ball to estimate not only the aggregate demand for telephone services but the demand for virtually every type of service the user might need, including services that might not even exist at the time of a periodic planning effort. Even if aggregate estimates are correct, when users request services the network manager did not forecast, some stocked components will not be used and other missing components (not stocked) will be unavailable to provide required services. With ISDN, however, each network component helps provide almost every service. This general-purpose attribute frees the network manager from predicting future demands of specific services. Rather, the much simpler task of estimating the overall demand of all services suffices for adequate inventory.

Service Independent of Loop

One reason that users of pre-ISDN services have to negotiate with telephone representatives for service delivery is that there is no vast pool of universal components capable of providing many kinds of services. Making arrangements takes time and planning. With ISDN, such a resource pool of interchangeable parts could support subscribing to data and other special services *at the time a call is made*.

Under ISDN, if an end user is not currently using the subscriber loop at capacity, the user could obtain the new desired service simply by signaling for it over the access loop. Since network intelligence understands these messages and constructs the desired service from a small number of interchangeable parts, the network managers are better able to provide a sufficient parts pool because the cost of maintaining this much smaller number of parts is reasonable. Users can simply add services at will by requesting them directly of the network. When these services do not run simultaneously, new ISDN lines are not needed.

In other cases, more bandwidth may be required, and the user may request additional ISDN access. This would certainly be the case when the user needs several services simultaneously or when the user requests services requested that require a great deal of transmission capacity. But the fundamental reason for augmenting ISDN access is to add bandwidth, not to obtain a new service.

Inherent Capabilities: Performance

Conventional telephony implementations have provided a number of methods for assessing the performance of the network. In the message telephone network, trunks are tested periodically to determine how well they operate. But if such a test is performed only twice a year, a trunk circuit could be malfunctioning for as long as 6 months. When testing a particular circuit, it is common practice to insert testing capability into the circuit itself. This intrusive testing interrupts the customer's service with signal insertions, terminations, and measurements until the testing is complete.

Digital links used in ISDN can readily provide information to assess performance in mechanized ways that facilitate the task of maintenance and improve the quality of the result. The digital links enable monitoring of the bitstream for oddities such as patterns that should not appear when the circuit operates properly. (For example, in a DS1 bitstream, a *bipolar violation*, a failure of successive ones-bits to change polarity, is a positive indication of a malfunction.) *Cyclical redundancy checks (CRC)* of individual links in the communication path—which is an even more powerful assessment tool—indicates when there are errors in the transmission link. The receiver then requests retransmission of the data. Over time, a history of errors can be quite helpful in directing maintenance efforts and helping to assess the general performance level of the network or specific service links.

4.4 SUMMARY: LOWER LONG-TERM COSTS ENCOURAGE ISDN

We have seen how the network started as an entirely analog system. Digital links were introduced for economy. Once this happened, conversions from analog switches to digital transmission links were required. As more and more digital links were introduced, the number of conversions grew. Avoiding cost was one primary motivator for introducing digital switches. Another motivator was the revolution occurring in the computer industry. Digital components were declining in price at incredible rates. These digital components, such as VLSI, provided economical platforms for the design of digital switches.

When the telephone networks evolved to SPC switches, digital transport, and message-oriented signaling, they looked more like traditional computer networks than traditional telephone networks. The techniques for creating and managing this new network were virtually identical to the techniques used in the computer industry—and both industries benefited from sharing costs. ISDN technology has the potential to satisfy both voice and data end-user requirements.

Finally, we have seen that network management tasks may be greatly simplified in an ISDN environment. This is partly due to the small number of interchangeable parts used in ISDN, which can be used to construct a seemingly unlimited number of services. Simplification is also possible through the use of mechanization aides, which help keep track of components and their serviceability. Opportunities for network-management productivity gains appear to be substantial.

While short-run changeover costs to ISDN may seem overwhelming, in the long run, the costs of provisioning ISDN services may be lower than continuing to provide traditional telephone capabilities. This is good news for end users who want a wide variety of services. In the next chapter, we explore the scope of those services.

5

The ISDN
Network-Services Model

T he fundamental concept of ISDN is to provide a common access to a
wide variety of network services to support business and personal
applications. The logical question is "What are these services that are
integrated into one network?" This chapter addresses the scope of ISDN
services and explores some key services in detail.

From the early days of ISDN, developers thought that *open systems
interconnection (OSI)* services, such as file transfer and message handling, could be transported via ISDN. Accordingly, this chapter closes
with a consideration of ISDN as the lower three layers in the OSI seven-
layer model.

5.1 NETWORK BEARER SERVICES

A network *bearer service* transports end-user information from one location
to another. The adjective *bearer* is used to describe the function of bearing
end-user information. Ultimately, this is the payoff for the end user—it's the
primary benefit provided by the ISDN platform. We don't use the term
bearer service just to make life more complicated than it needs to be; it's

necessary to distinguish bearer services from supplementary services and teleservices and to distinguish these services from other functions.

When creating ISDN, developers selected a family of bearer services to span the entire scope of user requirements. Depending on what end users want to accomplish, ISDN satisfies a wide range of user needs. For example, a distributed office or work-at-home application may require transferring large computer files from one location to another. A very different application, like point-of-sale information transfer, requires quick transfer of a relatively small amount of information with a high degree of accuracy. Other possible end-user applications have still different requirements. Creating a family of services that spans the range of needs means that for every end-user application there is at least one bearer service with capabilities that satisfy the application requirements.

Although the range of needs is large, it is not necessary or even desirable to have a unique bearer service for every application requirement. A very large number of bearer services would be extremely confusing and complex for users to select from and for implementors to provide. Consequently, ISDN developers defined only enough bearer services to meet clearly understood end-user requirements. Each identified bearer service is sufficiently different from the others to provide some unique benefit to end users and therefore is self-justifying.

Many ISDN bearer services are replicas of existing services in the pre-ISDN telephone networks. After all, these existing services have already proven themselves to be useful and desirable. Nevertheless, developers add new bearer services to the list as applications needs arise, so the list will never be comprehensive.

Circuit-Switched Voice

Without ISDN technology, telephone conversations take place over circuit-switched voice channels. These connections are established at the beginning of the call, are used during the call, and are released back into a pool of available resources at the end of the call. During the call, there is a voice-path connection from one telephone user to the distant telephone user. On average, a voice call lasts for (that is, has a *holding time* of) about 3 minutes. The circuit connection is established only for the duration of the call; after the call is terminated, network resources such as trunks and switches are released. Subsequent calls reuse the same network resources.

It is theoretically possible to provide enough circuit capabilities, mainly switching capacity and message trunks, so that every person connected to the network could call someone else at the same time. As a practical matter, this isn't done because statistically only a small fraction of all people want to make calls at the same time. Network managers provision circuits by estimating the probability that circuits will not be available, causing a *blocked* call attempt. Circuits are provisioned so that the estimated blockage is quite low (typically 1 percent or less), yet still reasonably economical for users.

Many of the network switches and circuits involved in voice calls are digital now—a continuation of the evolutionary trend started in about 1960 that is heading toward the fully digital network of ISDN. Within the network, there are various switching machines and digital links. Figure 5.1 illustrates a user placing a long-distance call through the *local exchange carrier* (*LEC*), through an *interexchange carrier* (*IXC*), to the destination LEC. The talking-path

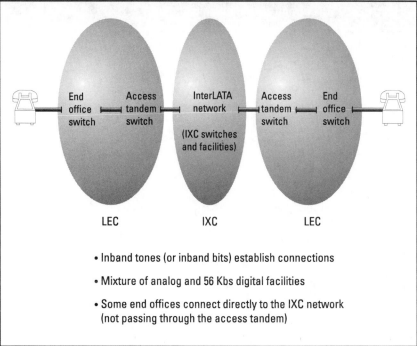

Figure 5.1   Pre-ISDN circuit-switched connections (circuit connection from one end to the other)

End office switch — Access tandem switch — InterLATA network (IXC switches and facilities) — Access tandem switch — End office switch

LEC   IXC   LEC

- Inband tones (or inband bits) establish connections

- Mixture of analog and 56 Kbs digital facilities

- Some end offices connect directly to the IXC network (not passing through the access tandem)

connection is often entirely digital (except for the analog loops from the network to the end user). Voice signals on this digital connection are encoded into digital bit patterns in today's pre-ISDN telephone network. The encoding scheme, called μ–*law encoding,* prescribes the way in which the voice signals are quantized and how bit patterns represent these quantized values. To signal the setup and clearing of the call, the system uses audible tones (known as *inband signaling*) over the same channel as the talking-path connection.

When using ISDN, the voice connection is established through one of the *B* (for *bearer*) channels. The digital connection for an ISDN voice call is 64 Kbps, but 56 Kbps for the voice bearer service, and some pre-ISDN technologies such as analog links are allowed. At each ISDN telephone, there is a conversion from voice (analog) signals to digital signals, using the μ-law encoding algorithm.

Like conventional telephony, the ISDN user forwards the telephone number to the network to establish a call. The end-user exchanges messages with the ISDN network via the *D* (D for *delta,* or change) channel, as shown in Figure 5.2. At the ISDN-end office, signaling information from the D channel

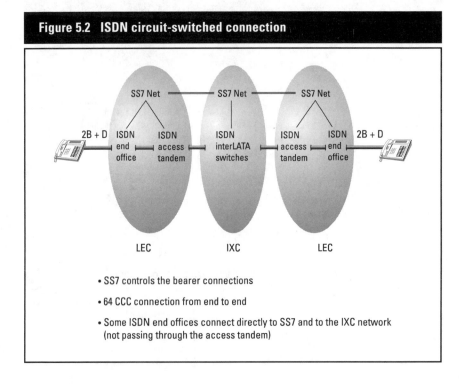

Figure 5.2   ISDN circuit-switched connection

- SS7 controls the bearer connections
- 64 CCC connection from end to end
- Some ISDN end offices connect directly to SS7 and to the IXC network (not passing through the access tandem)

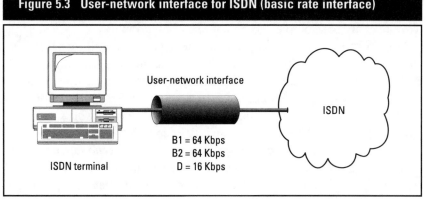

Figure 5.3   User-network interface for ISDN (basic rate interface)

User-network interface

ISDN

ISDN terminal

B1 = 64 Kbps
B2 = 64 Kbps
D = 16 Kbps

is inserted into SS7 messages. When the signaling information reaches the distant end-user's ISDN-end office, the SS7 releases relevant information into the D channel messages, which are then sent to the ISDN telephone.

Although ISDN circuit-mode voice service is very much like traditional telephone service, there are some significant differences that benefit the user. Since there are two B channels in a *basic rate interface* (*BRI*), you can put through two voice calls at the same time. (See Figure 5.3.) Even if both B channels are in use with telephone calls, the D channel can still receive messages for additional incoming calls. (The network doesn't necessarily perceive that the ISDN interface is busy.) There are various possibilities for managing these additional calls. The system can accept the new call, for example, by clearing an existing call to free up a B channel. Or, the system can send a "busy" message back to the network and not accept the new call. Still other possibilities are to invoke various *supplementary services* (such as call hold, call completion to busy subscriber, call waiting), which tend to be more powerful than their pre-ISDN counterparts.

The increased power of ISDN voice services is due mostly to the existence of two B channels (rather than one voice path) and the capability of messaging on the D channel (as opposed to the tones, ringing, and similar signaling methods of pre-ISDN telephony). The ISDN user sends and receives messages to the network and to the distant ISDN user. Sending and receiving messages supports adding beneficial functionality. For example, some ISDN telephones are capable of acting on received messages, illuminating buttons to show that a call is currently in progress on channel B2 or that a call is currently on hold on channel B1. These and other capabilities allow users to more easily use complex combinations of functionality.

Most of us, when placing a telephone call, just want to call and talk. ISDN speech-mode bearer service accommodates this need. Even though ISDN is defined as entirely digital, for this one bearer service, the standards definition permits an analog link in the voice path. This concession is to allow a graceful evolution from pre-ISDN telephony networks. Furthermore, it doesn't really degrade the quality of speech in an ISDN telephone call. Other capabilities used for speech service include *echo suppressors* (to prevent the conversation from sounding like it's taking place in a canyon) and other cost-effective techniques such as *time assignment speech interpolation (TASI)*, which allows other conversations to use your circuit-switched channel during quiet periods of your conversation.

There are several ISDN voice-bearer services. While they are all suitable for conveying speech, they each have a particular purpose. Most of us use *speech-mode* bearer service, described immediately above, to speak to others using ISDN. Another service, *3.1 kHz voiceband service*, is provided for modem users. For some time, there will be a lot of analog modem use, and it will be interworking with ISDN. Techniques that could impair the modem signal, such as analog links, echo suppressors or TASI, are not included in this service.

A third type of voice-bearer service is a higher fidelity speech-bearer service known as 7 kHz speech. Traditional telephony renders tones from about 100 Hz to about 3400 Hz, which is adequate to distinguish voices, but which certainly can't be mistaken for high-fidelity quality. Listening to 7 kHz improved-quality voice service is noticeably better than ordinary pre-ISDN voice quality, but it still falls short of true high-fidelity quality. Many people feel that this will be the preferred voice-bearer service for multimedia applications over ISDN. The encoding algorithm used for 7 kHz service is much more recent than the μ-law encoding algorithm described for the basic speech-bearer service; it offers superior results by more effectively using the information capacity of the same 64 Kbps bandwidth of the B bearer channel. For this service, the bearer channel cannot contain any analog links; it must be entirely digital from end to end.

To summarize, voice-mode ISDN bearer service is much like pre-ISDN telephone service. There are some added features and capabilities, however, and there is the capacity for better sound quality. Even though it might be somewhat "better," it is the same type of telephone service that we already know and use today. Many users won't notice much difference except in the speed with which calls are established and in the appearance of the calling number on their telephone.

Still, for some end users, such as those establishing help-desk support for their products, the additional *call management* features and capabilities provided by ISDN will make the critical difference in providing support using geographically dispersed personnel. And for end users who want *key telephone set* functionality, ISDN has much simpler wiring requirements and (no surprise here) lower costs than pre-ISDN systems. (Key telephone sets provide the user with call appearances for multiple directory numbers, allowing direct access and control so the user can select which line to use to make or answer a call).

Circuit-Switched Data

ISDN circuit-switched data service provides for transfer of end-user digital data streams at 64 Kbps. (See Figure 5.4.) To be useful for that purpose, the digital data presented on the calling side of the connection must be conveyed without any change to the other side of the connection. Conceptually, this circuit-switched connection is like a digital extension cord. If this extension cord were perfect, it would convey every bit from one end to the other, unchanged in any way. The ISDN connection is not the perfect digital transport, but for many classes of application it meets all requirements. It is limited to 64 Kbps per B channel and requires less than one

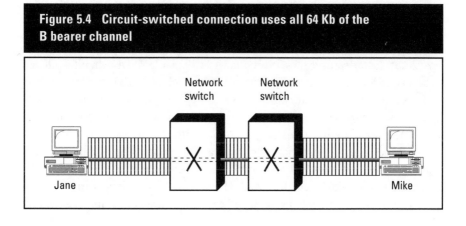

Figure 5.4   Circuit-switched connection uses all 64 Kb of the B bearer channel

second to establish a connection in the local calling area (somewhat longer
to establish a long-distance call). For a wide variety of applications, these
ISDN circuit-switched data performance characteristics are much more
than adequate, and in any event, much better than pre-ISDN digital services.

There are essentially two currently provided alternatives to ISDN circuit-
switched data in pre-ISDN telephone networks. The most common is the
modem, which operates over an analog voice circuit. The modem encodes
the digital data signals into tones, and these tones travel from one end to
the other. As a practical matter, without using data-compression techniques, this method limits most communications to about 14.4 Kbps over
a good connection, although some users claim higher figures. Consequently, using one ISDN B channel increases the speed of transmission by
a factor of about five. In addition to the obvious benefit of improved
transmission speed, another benefit provided by ISDN is vastly improved
circuit setup time and error performance. Call setup time is perhaps 10 to
15 times faster, and error performance is improved by a factor of 100 (in
some cases, by a factor as high as 100,000). Data-compression techniques
typically improve the effective throughput of data streams by a factor of
about two for both pre-ISDN analog services (to about 30 Kbps) and ISDN
services (to about 128 Kbs for each B channel).

Another existing type of pre-ISDN circuit-switched data service is switched-
56 or switched-64 digital service. It is provided by very expensive adjunct-
equipment additions to the analog network. Once connected, it can transport
data almost as fast as ISDN service, but its inband signaling does not allow
establishing connections as quickly as ISDN circuit-switched digital data
service allows. Probably even more important, the typical monthly service
charge for switched-56 digital service is often hundreds of dollars, whereas the
monthly ISDN service charge is tens of dollars. Even at such high pre-ISDN
prices, some users find that their particular needs justify obtaining these
services. But with ISDN, you will obtain much greater ubiquity, much lower
costs, and faster setup times. Now that it is available, ISDN circuit-switched
data service is much preferred over pre-ISDN switched digital services.

Some applications that cannot tolerate the long setup time of pre-ISDN
circuit-switched services are currently served with *dedicated facilities*
(facilities permanently dedicated to, not switched between, two or more
end-user locations). For example, transaction processing, such as credit-
card verifications, requires response times of less than 10 seconds for the
entire system. Pre-ISDN circuit-switched connections take longer than 10 seconds just to establish a call. Faster ISDN call-setup times allow for establishing

and clearing connections when data needs to be conveyed. Longer setup times result in what users perceive as sluggish performance and cause timeouts of LAN protocols because of 10- to 15-second time lapses. Improved call setup performance means that some users will be able to use ISDN circuit-switched data services instead of using pre-ISDN dedicated facilities.

Packet-Switched Data

Since ISDN was conceived shortly after X.25 packet service, it is not surprising that X.25 packet service was included as one of the bearer services in ISDN. This ISDN bearer service is almost identical to the X.25 packet service that many readers may already know. In fact, one of its virtues is that ISDN provides an improved, more reliable access to the packet networks. One key difference is that the ISDN packet service uses the same numbering plan as regular telephone service, the North American Numbering Plan (E.163 and E.164), rather than the X.121 numbering plan familiar to long-time X.25 packet users.

Existing packet-data networks, providing X.25 user-network interfaces, are generally available. For the benefit of those who are not familiar with packet services, they can be compared and contrasted with the circuit-switched service described previously. Like circuit-switched service, there is an end-to-end connection established to transfer information. Unlike circuit-switched service, the entire channel bandwidth (64 Kbps for a B channel) is not reserved for the use of a packet-switched call. Rather, the channel is subdivided so that many logical channels can be created over the one B channel. (See Figure 5.5.) Unlike circuit-mode services, packet-mode services are also available over the D channel at throughputs below 16 Kbps. It may seem odd that information would be divided into packets. Why not simply use the entire channel? The reason for packets is that packets more fully utilize telecommunications facilities. For certain types of information transfer, especially those that are bursty and interactive, little time is spent sending data; the circuit is idle most of the time. Packet services allow other users to send data during these long, idle time periods. Consequently, each user pays for only a fraction of the time, resulting in a more economical service for all users who share the facility.

Each packet of information is typically fairly small, consisting of about one kilobyte (1 KB) of information, which can convey slightly over 1000 characters of text. Each packet of information is then identified separately so that there is no confusion within the channel as to which packet of information belongs

Figure 5.5   Jane establishes three logical packet channels over one bearer channel

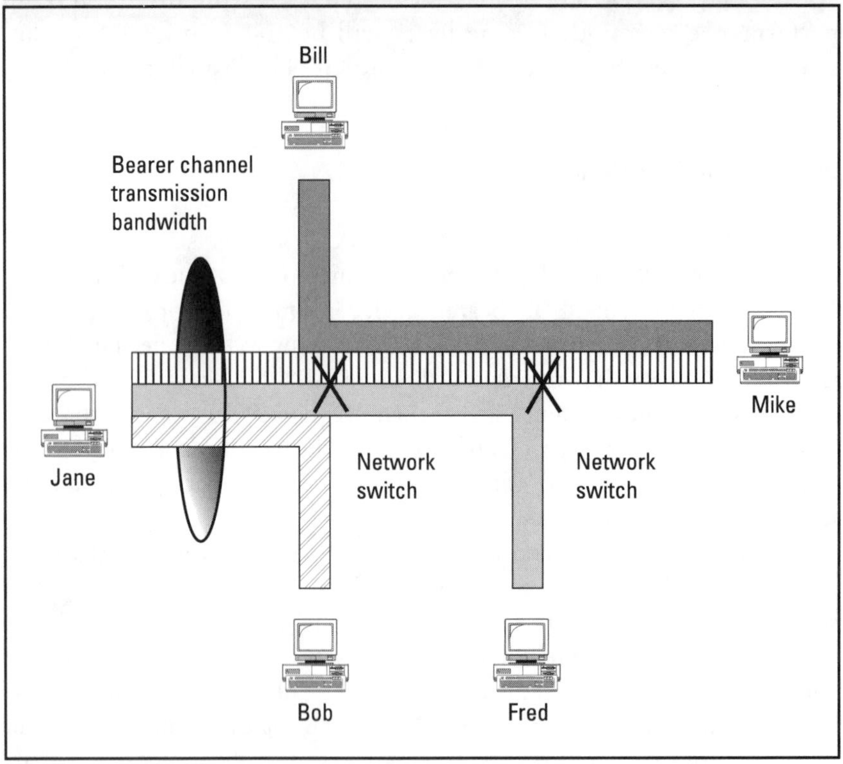

to which logical connection. For example, if you are sending one letter to your best friend and another to a business associate, you expect the text of one letter to be kept separate from the text of the other. Further, you want them assembled correctly so that the two letters are reconstructed properly upon receipt. These packets are identified and administered by *headers* and *trailers*. In addition to identifying the beginning and end of a particular packet, headers and trailers provide other information to keep packets within their logical channel and ensure that they are properly received at the other end. Often, each packet is in a single frame (the bits between two successive flags, as illustrated in Figures 5.6 and 5.7). While a more detailed exposition would reveal many differences between frames and packets, frames are sometimes used without containing packets to provide a simpler service.

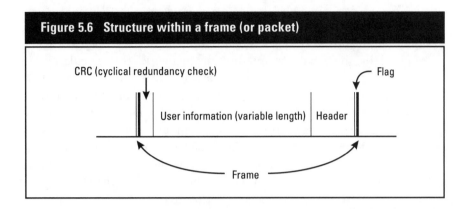

Figure 5.6   Structure within a frame (or packet)

Although we do not intend to go into detail about packet service here, it is important to note that there is a fair amount of network processing involved in providing this service. For example, there is a fairly comprehensive error detection and correction in packet-data service. In the trailer of each packet is a digital entity known as a *cyclical redundancy check* or

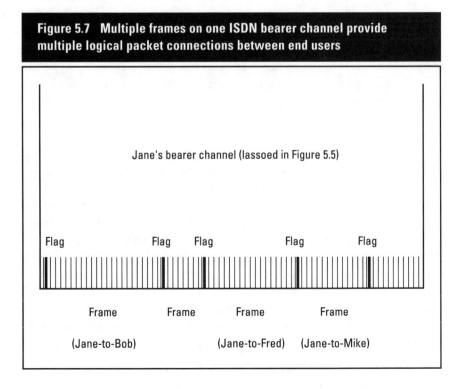

Figure 5.7   Multiple frames on one ISDN bearer channel provide multiple logical packet connections between end users

checksum. This value is obtained by performing a mathematical proc-ess on all of the bits in the packet before transmission. When the packet is received by the next node within the network, this calculation is performed again, and the value obtained is compared to the transmitted check-sum value. If the values match, the assumption is that there is no error in the received message. (Of course, mathematicians will quickly point out that there is actually an astronomically small probability of error even if the values match.) If the values don't match, the receiving node requests a resend of the packet (*retransmission request*) until the check-sum values do match. Only when there is a match does the receiving node transmit the packet to the next node in the network, and ultimately, to the far end user. Errors are pretty well scrubbed out in this process.

Another telecommunications network function has to do with network congestion control. Unlike circuit-switched service, where a caller may simply be blocked from making a phone call in heavy traffic, packet networks respond to heavy traffic with some delay in getting through. As traffic gets heavier, the delays get longer. It's possible to actually gridlock in such a system, but packet networks come with *congestion control* to avoid it. One congestion control measure is called *windowing*. When a packet is received at the far end, the far end sends an acknowledgment to the original sender that the packet was received without error.

But the original sender need not wait to receive acknowledgment before sending a second packet, or even a third packet. The number of packets that can be sent before receiving an acknowledgment is known as the *window size*. Should gridlock appear imminent, the network will slow down, acknowledgments will slow down, and new packets entering the network will be throttled. If necessary, networks can instruct users to reduce the window size during periods of very heavy traffic.

All of these extra administrative features (such as error detection and correction, congestion control, and others not described here) add value to the packet service but also extract a price in performance. It takes time to check for errors, request and obtain retransmission, and hold packets until the network congestion has cleared. For some types of applications, such additional functionality is not needed. The user can avoid the added expense and gain the benefits of speedier transmission. This gain is espe-cially valuable for applications where round-trip transmissions—seen by the user as response time—could be improved. Accordingly, new packet services have been proposed.

The *frame relay* bearer service was proposed to meet that need. This service consists of only the barest needed parts to delineate the frames (not even enough functionality is provided to warrant the name "packet") and route them to their destination. There are no capabilities for retransmission, sequencing, and so on. As the standards have progressed, different variations of this service have evolved (different types of frame relaying and frame switching). The marketplace of user demand will determine which variations are used and deployed the most.

Although packet services predate ISDN, there are obvious benefits to accessing packet services via ISDN. One of the main barriers to using packet service today is the cost and performance in accessing from the user's location to the packet network. With a special access loop, the quality is good but the cost is high. Using a normal access loop with a modem, the cost is lower but so is the quality. ISDN seems to provide the right combination of cost and quality to make using packet services desirable.

Permanent (Reserved) Channels

These are the ISDN equivalents of the dedicated facility (also known as a *private line* or *leased line*). In traditional private-line service, the user subscribes to a nonswitched channel (an information pipe) between two locations (a point-to-point circuit) or between multiple locations (a multipoint circuit). The user obtains this service for a fixed price each month, regardless of usage. Consequently, users with very high information-transfer requirements sometimes find this the most cost-effective service. The information pipe is always available to transmit data, so applications requiring little or no setup time may require these services whether or not the volume of data traffic is high.

Service providers originally constructed the private-line service by dedicating spare channels to connect user locations. Where necessary, wires are physically crossconnected within the network to provide this channel. From a user's perspective, the advantage is that the channel stays constant during the service life of the leased line. (Typically, users, on average, keep a leased-line service for about 3 years, then for a variety of reasons, such as changes in business needs, they will order a different service.) Since this nonvarying channel is always available to the user, the user can depend on fairly constant transmission parameters and does not need to be concerned with availability. During unusual conditions such as a snowstorm, or before a rock concert, when many users are bidding for network service, traffic jams may tie up switched services, meaning that most users will be blocked from placing a circuit-switched connection. But the private-line user is generally assured of service. The private-line facility is dedicated to that particular end user; there is no bidding for service as in a switched connection. Consequently, certain user-critical requirements are well served with private-line service.

Over the years, the methods for providing this dedicated service have changed. Rather than just physical cross-connects, digital cross-connects, using equipment designed expressly for this purpose, are now common. These special *digital cross-connect switches (DCSs)* are designed to economically route the information as though a physical cross-connect had been made, economically providing a connection for an indefinite period of time. The switched connection is made at the beginning of the service interval and then not altered until the end of the service interval, when it is "unswitched." Although, architecturally, these circuits are now actually "switched," the characteristics users see are unchanged. In particular, the channel is nonvarying in performance, because its parts are fixed. It is available during traffic jam situations, because only one user is connected to that portion of the switch.

Since many users have become accustomed to the availability and unique benefits of private lines, they have been adamant about continued availability of leased lines in the ISDN era. On the other hand, the basic proposition of ISDN is to provide one access to all network services. The apparent conflict suggests that adding a leased-line-like service to ISDN may be the way to go. Hence, the idea of *permanent (reserved) mode service* has come into being. Unfortunately, as of this writing there are no commercially available switches that economically integrate this bearer service with ISDN. This situation may well be remedied, perhaps by integrating DCSs into ISDN switches, so that a more complete offering of bearer services will be available to the user via ISDN.

Using ISDN Context for Defining Bearer Services

In a more rigorous exposition of ISDN, the architectural reference models described in this section would have been presented earlier and with much more precision. However, since one of the principle values of these reference configurations is to define bearer services (and other services described later in this chapter), the topic is introduced now.

The basic rate interface shown in Figure 5.8 contains *reference points* that show what parts are included in ISDN, and where they are. Some of

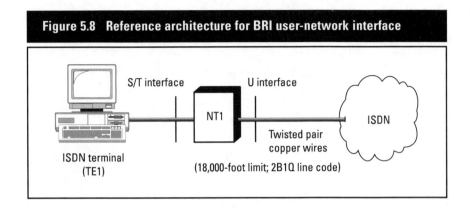

Figure 5.8   Reference architecture for BRI user-network interface

these reference points, such as the S, the T, and the U, have very specific definitions and therefore become *interfaces*. From the U interface at the residence or business of the end user to the ISDN network, a twisted pair of copper wires (the subscriber loop) carries the digital signals (two B channels and a D channel, as shown in Figure 5.3). The *network terminating unit (NT1)* provides various testing capabilities (like loopback) and also transforms the 2B + D signal into a different bitstream format. At the S/T interface, two pairs of wires (one for transmitting, one for receiving) are used.

This reference architecture is general in nature; not all of the interfaces must exist in actual implementations. For example, an ISDN terminal could be constructed in such a way that it contains the functionality of an NT1. In that case, the U interface would be physically realized, but the S/T interface would exist only conceptually somewhere inside the terminal.

A more complete reference architecture is shown in Figure 5.9. The simpler diagram in Figure 5.8 is often completely adequate for the use of

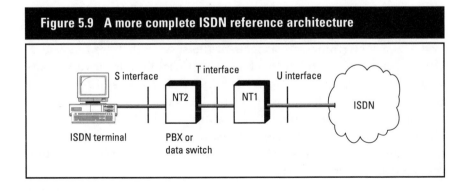

Figure 5.9   A more complete ISDN reference architecture

Figure 5.10   Where ISDN service attributes apply

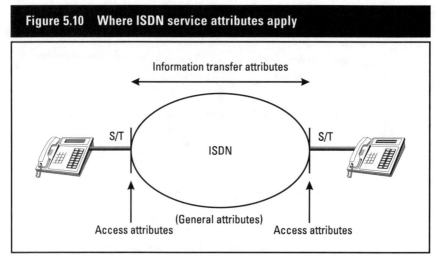

Fascicle III.7. Copyright CCITT Recommendation 1.210. Blue Book, 1988. Figure
B-1/1.210, "Relationship between the groups of attributes and fields of applicability."
Reprinted with permission from ITU.

an individual ISDN end user. Businesses often use local switches (PBXs).
In Figure 5.9, the PBX would be a particular instance of an additional
network terminating unit 2 (NT2). In this case, the T interface is different
from the S interface, since it terminates a primary-rate ISDN interface,
which has 23 B channels and one 64 Kbps D channel. The S interface in
Figure 5.9 has the same specifications as the S/T interface in Figure 5.8.

Definition by Service Attribute

Every ISDN bearer service is defined by its attributes. (See Figure 5.10.)
These attributes are of three general types: access, transfer, and general. Access attributes are aspects of the service that are relevant at
the user-network interface, such as which channels are involved and
what protocols are used. Transfer attributes are aspects of the service
that deal with what happens across the ISDN network, such as whether
the bearer service provides 64 Kbps, and whether the transport is
circuit-switched in a data stream or packet switched. General attributes
include just about anything else, such as quality of service, internetworking possibilities, and so on.

Attributes are not mysterious. They are simply a rigorous way to specify the details of the service so it is in context. The table below lists service attributes for circuit-mode, alternate speech-data bearer service. This is a service that allows you to make a voice call or a circuit-switched data call whenever you originate the call. Looking at the attribute list, you may notice that the information-transfer attributes include the mode of transport (circuit) and the bandwidth (64 Kbps). You can also see the capability for voice (μ-law encoding) or data (unrestricted, meaning data can be of any bit pattern combination). In addition, the *configuration* can be *point-to-point* or it can have multiple ISDN terminals (*multipoint*), which is particularly useful for situations where more than one type of equipment is required (to support different applications).

Notice that the access attributes define the circuit-mode bearer channel as the B channels, and set aside the D channel for signaling. The access

Attribute	Value
Information transfer	
Mode	Circuit
Rate	64 Kbps
Capability	Speech (μ-law in the United States) or unrestricted digital information
Structure	8 kHz integrity (octet alignment is preserved)
Communications establishment	Demand upon request
Symmetry	Bidirectional symmetric, unidirectional
Configuration	Point-to-point, multipoint
Access	
Channel	B for user information, D for signaling
Protocol	DSS1 (I Series for the D channel)
General (including supplementary services, quality of service, interworking possibilities, and operation and commercial aspects)	Further study required, based on 1.231

Fascicle III.x. Copyright CCITT Recommendation 1.231. Blue Book, 1988. Section 4.7, "Information transfer attributes, Access attributes, and General attributes." Reprinted with permission from ITU.

protocol for the signaling is *digital signaling system 1 (DSS1)*, the message-oriented ISDN-access protocol used by end users to obtain ISDN services. We will explore this further in the next chapter.

Finally, although this section has explored only the bearer-service attributes, there are attributes associated with other services. These attributes apply to specific reference points in the ISDN architecture. In the next section, we begin to look at *supplementary services*. They, too, are defined at the S or T reference points. Some of them have transfer attributes and general attributes. Some have attributes only at the S or T interface.

5.2 SUPPLEMENTARY SERVICES

Supplementary services differ from basic bearer services in a number of ways. First, a bearer service must exist before a supplementary service can exist. Each supplementary service is created or defined to add value to the underlying basic bearer service. Many of these supplementary services are very familiar to U.S. telephone users today: call hold, call waiting, and call forwarding are some examples. Other services, such as calling-line identification and call-completion to busy subscriber, are services that have come out of the ISDN era. But they are already part of existing telephone-network services, paralleling initial ISDN deployments.

There are about a dozen supplementary services that have matured to a point where relatively standardized descriptions exist. It seems likely that eventually there will be tens or even hundreds of these services available to the user analogous to the plethora of features offered by switching systems today. Each individual user takes advantage of only a small number of the available supplementary features because there are so many from which to choose. It is also difficult to use many of them simultaneously with conventional analog telephone sets. In the ISDN era, people will probably be using telephone sets that make selecting a larger number of supplementary services much easier. Anyone who has used a windows-oriented personal computer program can envision a group of ISDN supplementary service icons with explanatory dialog boxes that clarify the purpose of the service and convey the status of the service delivery.

Listed below are the supplementary services that are the most common and the most mature. This is somewhat of a judgment call; someone's favorite supplementary service is bound to be someone else's trivial additional service. Listing them all probably would not be possible—there is no central list, and new services are constantly being added. Just to make it even more challenging, the identifying names of standards occasionally change. Each ISDN service provider tends to use its own trademarked name for each of the supplementary services listed below, and there are many different trademarked names. Most service providers, however, can cross-reference the names below to their service offerings.

Call Hold

ISDN call hold is essentially the same service that you have today. If your ISDN telephone instrument (or terminal) has a *hold button,* you press it to place a call on hold. When you want to retrieve the call and speak to the person again, you press the appropriate button to return to the call.

This raises an interesting point. The supplementary services described for ISDN are mostly network-based. Although you must have end-user equipment to invoke these network-based services, the design and layout of ISDN terminal equipment is not even mentioned in the standard descriptions of supplementary services. For example, for the *call hold* supplementary service, one terminal vendor may implement the service using a latching call-hold button. Depressing the button places the call on hold; pressing it again releases the button and allows the user to retrieve the original call. Another vendor might use a screen, a mouse, and icons so the user can select the calls to place on hold and the calls to retrieve. Still another vendor might allow the user to choose which button on a set to use to put a call on hold; if the user decides that the one in the corner is better than the one in the middle, the user can change it.

Describing ISDN supplementary services is made more difficult because the use of common ISDN terminal equipment cannot be assumed. It would be much easier if we could describe supplementary services in terms of what you the end user must do to invoke the service (for example, press the hold button). Because there is no standard for this aspect of the service, descriptions have to be more general to accommodate the many possible implementations that the user might encounter. Accordingly, what you see here is a much less rigorous method of describing these services. Often, familiar telephone-equipment terms are used below where they make the explanation more understandable. But you cannot assume the availability of any particular type of ISDN equipment, so if you do not find a hold button on your equipment, you will find some equivalent to achieve the call-hold service.

On a closing note, be advised that ISDN terminal vendors may, and often do, implement supplementary services within the terminal equipment itself. From an end-user's perspective, the service may look and feel like the same thing even thought it may result in different network activity. Sometimes, the wider choice can allow you to find more precisely what you need in your home or business.

Call Forwarding

This is another ISDN service that replicates a pre-ISDN capability. Not only does this similarity provide continuity for users who have grown accustomed to this service, but it is a worthwhile and desired service for those who haven't had access to it.

In addition to pre-ISDN features, the ISDN *call forwarding* supplementary service has greater capability to keep the end user informed. For example, calls forwarded to you can contain the calling telephone number of the caller as well as the original number dialed. Having this additional information may help you decide whether you wish to answer the call. For example, you might not want to receive a call from your dentist when you are at a relaxing party.

Call Transfer

Again, this is an ISDN service that replicates the pre-ISDN service that many of us use today. Sometimes, the oldies are the goodies. The name of the service describes pretty well what it is. When you prefer not to receive a call that should be routed elsewhere, the *call transfer* supplementary service conveniently allows you reroute the incoming call to someone else's telephone.

User-to-User Signaling

User-to-user signaling (UUS) is a supplementary service that is new with ISDN. Because ISDN signaling involves messaging between the end-user equipment and the network, developers thought including the capability for sending short user-to-user messages was desirable. For the most part, this service was constructed to take advantage of extra space available in normally transmitted signaling messages. For example, when a call is established, a small amount of end-user information is inserted in the signaling message sent to the ISDN network. This end-user information is conveyed, unchanged, to the distant end user. Before the distant end user even answers the call, however, this information could be made available over the D channel. For example, it could contain the subject matter of the telephone call, very much like what you now see a subject line of an email message or a printed memorandum. This would allow you to decide which call is the more urgent.

Within the telephone industry, this service has been the subject of much debate and dissension. How would such a service be billed? Would nefarious end users keep pumping calls through the network to send very small amounts of information free, assuming that unanswered calls would not be billed? While it may seem unlikely that people would do this (a great number of calls would have to be placed to send the equivalent of a one-page letter), it has actually happened in some earlier packet networks. That offender was unofficially known as "Captain Crunch."

There are also subtle implementation variations to the *user-to-user supplementary service*. One variation allows sending user-to-user messages only during the times that a call is being established or cleared. Other variations allow this sending to occur during a call or even without having a call. The concern on the part of some network providers is that these messages are generally understood to be routed over the SS7 networks, because the signaling part of the messages is so routed. Effects on the SS7 networks are unknown, but the fear is that congestion on them could halt all telephone service.

So far, the network providers have moved cautiously towards user-to-user signaling. Probably the version that allows this signaling during call setup and clearing will be the first to become available, since network providers generally feel that such a service would generate no additional packets through the SS7 networks and the slightly longer packets would probably not adversely affect the network.

Calling Line ID Services

This is an ISDN-era service that some of today's telephone networks are also implementing. It seems to be more popular with lawyers and regulators than with the average telephone user wanting to know who is calling. Almost all of the media coverage of this service has to do with legal and regulatory considerations rather than technical details or opportunities for improving the way we live and work.

This service forwards the *calling-line identification* (*CLID*), which is the calling person's telephone number, to the person who is receiving the telephone call. In the United States, until recently, networks were not permitted to send the user name since that would involve a query to a database that has information contained in the telephone directory. Nevertheless, some end-user equipment does use the CLID as a search key to find information about the person calling. This information, when displayed to the end user, can be helpful to the user in dealing with the caller. One implementation uses the CLID search key to find and display a photograph of the calling person, which is helpful if you have met the caller before but haven't recently spoken with him or her. Another implementation might use the CLID as a search key to retrieve notes you made during your last telephone conversation with that person. Retrieving notes can "refresh" your memory and allow you to continue where you left off.

Like many of the ISDN supplementary services, variations on this service have been discussed. For example, if there was one particular person for whom you would be willing to interrupt your work, the calling-line ID service could be set up so that only a call from that particular person would ring your phone; other callers would be informed that your phone is "busy." The converse of that type of service would be that a particular person might be the last person with whom you wish to speak. The service could be arranged to exclude only calls from this individual. Within the industry, raging debates (actually good-natured discussions) have not resolved the issue of whether to name this "Mother-in-Law" Service or "Reject-a-Jerk" Service.

Call Completion to Busy Subscriber

Have you ever tried to call someone who is busy? Always busy? This is the service for you. After your call, the network at the called location will monitor the called person's ISDN interface for availability (nonbusy). When availability is detected, the network(s) initiates a call to you and the called person so that you can speak. This *call completion to busy subscriber* (*CCBS*) service adds value by helping a user complete a call that would otherwise not be completed.

In today's pre-ISDN networks, similar services exist. In most of these, however, the service is implemented in a fundamentally different way. Calls are initiated periodically (perhaps every 20 seconds) for a period of time (perhaps 30 minutes) until the distant end user answers your call. This is straightforward automation of continuing to try to reach a busy person. The ISDN version is much more elegant. When the distant end user finishes a call, the network at the distant end is aware of it (due to the messaging between the distant network and the distant end user). The distant network then initiates a call back to you (to make sure you are not on another call) and, if you are available, also alerts the distant end user. There is no need for a flood of network messages with this ISDN version of the service.

Message-Waiting Indicator Control and Notification

Wouldn't it be great if your phone could indicate to you that the ISDN network had a message for you? Because of the use of messaging to establish calls, when the network tries to complete a call to you, it already has a great deal of information about the call. It is not difficult to arrange for the network to store that information and signal your equipment (for example, light a message-waiting light) or even send text information to your equipment concerning the telephone number of the calling person, the time of day, and perhaps a small amount of calling-user information (adapted from the UUS capability described previously).

Supplementary Services

Everyone has his or her own idea of which supplementary services are the most important or interesting. Although listing a complete menu of these services defies the imagination, we have listed services below that have been discussed in standards bodies. These services may or may not survive the trials of the marketplace, but they do stimulate the imagination and pro-vide insight into the power and scope of ISDN supplementary services.

Advice of Charge at Call Set-up Time (AOC-S)
Advice of Charge During the Call (AOC-D)

Advice of Charge at End of Call (AOC-E)
Booked Add-On Conference (BAC)
Business Group
Completion of Calls on No Reply (CCNR)
Call Deflection (CD)
Call Forwarding: Busy (CFB); No Reply (CFNR); Unconditional (CFU)
Call Transfer: Explicit (CTE); Normal (CTN); Single Step (CTSS)
Calling-Line Identification: Presentation (CLIP); Restriction (CLIR)
Closed User Group (CUG)
Conferencing (CONF)
Connected Line Identification: Presentation (COLP); Restriction (COLR)
Credit-Card Calling (CRED)
Diversion-X
Emergency Service
Hot Line
ISDN Freephone Service (IFS)
Incall Modification (IM)
Line Hunting
Malicious-Call Identification (MCID)
Meet-Me Conference (MMC)
Multilevel Precedence and Preemption (MLPP)
Multilocation Business Group (MBG)
Multiple-Subscriber Number (MSN)
Outgoing Call Barring (OCB)
Present / Booked Conference (PBC)
Private-Numbering Plan (PNP)
Reverse Charging (REV)
Subaddressing (SUB)
Terminal Portability (TP)
Temporary Location for Outgoing Calls (TLOC)
Three-Party Service (3PTY)

5.3 TELESERVICES

In addition to bearer services and supplementary services, the ISDN standards describe many ISDN *teleservices*. These services are, in some sense, more complete because they are descriptions of the facilities, resources, and equipment users need to operate the service. For example, a *telefax service* would contain information about the facsimile machine, including the paper it uses. It would also contain information about the circuit-mode bearer service needed to convey the signals from your fax machine to the distant end user's fax machine. And, it would contain the coding plan to convert the scanned images into digital bit-streams. Anything else needed to provide the service, including marketing elements, would be included in the concept of teleservices. This sort of description is especially helpful in societies where one service provider supplies the entire service—from equipment to telephone connections.

In the United States, the competitive stance is that various suppliers will offer whatever they want. Functionality is not dictated to them any more than price or availability is dictated to them. This allows for a great deal more competition and innovation but can lead to confusion and failure to create useful capabilities from service and equipment offerings. In fact, *systems integrators* have emerged whose sole objective is to help steer end users through the maze of service and equipment possibilities. It seems unlikely that in the United States there will be any major push to agree to teleservices, as defined in international standards, even though that same functionality will be provided in a wide variety of ways.

As an end user, you should know that in some other countries, the telephone administrations do provide ISDN teleservices. Hence, acquiring them in those countries is somewhat different than acquiring them in the United States. However, even the European countries appear to be following the trend established in the United States over the previous decade.

5.4 COMPARISON OF ISDN TO OSI

A frequently asked question is: How does ISDN compare to the *open systems interconnection (OSI)* model? A related question is: How do the two work together? The very short and oversimplified answer to those questions is that they have many similarities and differences. Some of these issues can become quite esoteric, but the key aspect is that they are designed to work together.

OSI model applications are supported by the seven-layer stack. Any of a wide variety of network types can provide the functionality of the lower three layers. One candidate technology to provide the network services is ISDN. A specific example is OSI capability such as *file transfer and management (FTAM)* provided over an ISDN network connection.

There are many open issues and unresolved considerations concerning how OSI and ISDN work together. Ongoing standards work and market performance will shape how the two concepts are merged to do useful things for end users.

Background

Commercial voice telephony communications have been available for more than 100 years. Conversely, commercial data processing has been available for only about 40 years. The basic notion of telephone service has been fairly constant over those 100 years. Now, we have to dial more numbers, and in fact, we have to dial the number instead of asking for our connection ("Hello Central!"). But the basic idea is still that you pick up a phone, place a call, and speak to the person at the other end. In contrast, data processing has changed so much over its much shorter life that the distributed-information systems of today bear scant resemblance to the punched-card central-processing environment of the early 1950s.

In many ways, voice-communications and data-processing technologies and techniques have been quite disparate, due in large part to their uncommon heritage. However, in the information age, current and future needs are focusing on the common theme of information. The need for information is the same, regardless of the form it might take. Information needs to be stored, processed, and moved, regardless of whether it is represented in traditional voice form or traditional data form. Consequently, there are increasing signs of the convergence of data processing and telephony to create enabling information-technology platforms that meet user needs.

Differences: Telephony and Data

Except perhaps in the very early days, approaches to data-processing implementations have typically involved much preplanning and structuring to ensure that objectives are satisfied and pitfalls avoided. Remember, this environment often involved unattended machines, which had to be set up in advance to handle any deviation from the basic plan of operation (such as what to do when errors or strange events occurred). The term *systems analysis* was widely used to abstractly characterize existing and desired processes to ensure that relevant factors were anticipated and desired objectives were achieved. As it evolved, this systems analysis approach became more top-down and structured to meet the needs of larger scale data-processing implementations. Structured techniques were also developed to address the increasing complexity of the technologies used and to parcel work out to separate individuals and teams. Partly to facilitate the parceling of work efforts, OSI was conceived as a structured, layered model. Functions required for each piece were identified, as were the connections between adjacent pieces necessary to reassemble the pieces into a whole implementation. Along with this process was a parallel merger between data processing and data communications, resulting in *distributed processing*. This term not only describes the technology used, it also alludes to the geographical dispersion.

Development in the voice-communications world couldn't have been more different. From the very early days of telephony, there was an overarching vision of talking to someone who was at the distant end. It was very easy to envision, unlike the abstract idea of data structures in a data-processing context. That basic vision has remained largely unchanged for almost 100 years. Only recently has the world of data processing been considered to be part of voice telecommunications. Even so, early merger implementations were more on the order of voice messaging systems and voice-inquiry-response systems (for example, obtaining stock quotes and bank balances using a touchtone phone). Further, voice communications usage was rarely planned, and the user's objectives were almost always integrated into the communications themselves. In other words, a person who wished to call to make an appointment would typically equate the placing of a telephone call with the making of an appointment. To the user, the objective and the application was the process of making the call; typically, the user made no distinction between the application (making the appointment) and the process of achieving that application (making the call). Most people who check their "to-do list" will find "call dentist" rather than "negotiate date, time of day, procedures to be performed by dentist."

Neither of these approaches is wrong or bad. In fact, each approach seems to have been entirely appropriate for its historical period. In the data environment, the preplanned, structured approach allowed effective time investment and appropriate design of data terminals and processors. Each piece of the implementation was designed to perform the specific tasks identified. In the voice communications world, people could interact with the communications systems in more intuitive ways. Not only has the basic telephonic vision remained unchanged, but the idea of a telephone seems almost a natural extension of what we do when we intereact directly with others. People don't seem to have much trouble with the idea of holding a telephone to the side of their face, speaking into one end, and listening to the other. Sidetone (the hearing of your own voice in the receiver as well as that of the distant party) assures the user that the phone is operating properly and conveys a sense of how the other person is perceiving the conversation. Within limits, it conveys a sense of being there.

Convergence: Voice and Data Forms of Information

In recent years, the latest a newer trend has been to focus upon the use of information *content* to perform tasks. Such a focus does not emphasize the *form* of the data but rather its content and other attributes as described in Chapter 3. Consequently, the separation between voice and data no longer interests users, but the different forms have to be accommodated in different ways. Examples that illustrate this trend include the use of fax transmissions (and other imaging systems), video, and multimedia applications (for example, voice combined with images). It's no longer easy to determine which systems are in the voice domain and which are in the data domain. Even voice-mail messages are stored in digital form by computers.

Another result of focusing on information content is that users no longer find it profitable to isolate data processing to an area of geography; rather they must move it around to gain additional benefit. Often, information processing takes place in conjunction with moving information. For example, a sale transaction that sends information to the warehouse can also result in an order to resupply inventory. The worlds of voice and data communications and processing are merging into information systems technologies.

Data-Processing Connectivity Requires Open Systems

The origins of OSI seem to be consistent with the data-processing approach of preplanned, structured, and abstractly defined systems. The main objective is to provide an openness that allows assembly of pieces into a whole so the user can mix and match components at will, regardless of which vendors make which pieces. To help achieve this, the concept of layering was used, and the well-known seven-layer model was detailed. Even though this is an extremely broad effort, a lot of user applications fall outside the scope of OSI because of its innate structure and definition. For example, voice communications are not included, nor are multimedia applications (although, by the time you read this, OSI may include all these applications and more).

Voice Telephony Evolves to ISDN

ISDN is intended to provide data capabilities and is layered in the same sense that the OSI model is layered. ISDN includes as a bearer service the X.25 packet-data communications capabilities. This service is explicitly identified as being in the OSI construct (that is, it is identified as an *OSI subnetwork*). In these and other ways, ISDN seems very consistent with the OSI model.

However, ISDN provides both voice and data capabilities. The designers of the ISDN construct decided that out-of-band message-oriented signaling would suit their needs; OSI, on the other hand, did not developmentally accommodate the concept of out-of-band signaling. The development of ISDN has diverged from the development of OSI primarily because ISDN has evolved from telephony. It is based upon real networks with all of their heritage and history, including their limitations, their capabilities, and real internetworking problems and potentials.

Future Directions

Since ISDN and OSI have evolved from very different backgrounds, will these two constructs converge to become one concept and one implementation? Probably they will converge—ISDN was developed to be a layered implementation in much the same way that OSI is layered. Traditionally, however, this was not an objective for telephone network designers. Another positive indication that convergence is on the horizon is that users have demanded consistent implementations of information systems regardless of the form (voice or data) of these systems. This implies users are adopting a common approach to thinking about these systems rather than viewing them as two fundamentally different systems because of their differences in form.

There are also some rather practical reasons why convergence may well occur. Some of the problems and requirements uncovered in OSI development efforts have been helpful to developers of ISDN. The OSI ideas of conformance testing, certification, and recognition are being adopted within the ISDN community with very little change. (Why reinvent the wheel?) Some of the tools and techniques used in these OSI efforts, such as *protocol implementation conformance statements* (*PICS*) and *abstract test suites* (*ATSs*), are also gaining acceptance within the ISDN community. Similarly, the OSI community has concluded that the ISDN ideas of video, image transfer, and multimedia services are very worthwhile and should be incorporated into their developmental approach.

5.5 SUMMARY

End users obtain benefits from ISDN through the use of network services. Bearer services carry end-user information from one end of the network to the other. Packet-switched data bearer services, which existed prior to ISDN, are accessible through ISDN basic- and primary-rate interfaces. ISDN circuit-switched voice and data services are similar to those services end users enjoyed prior to ISDN, but circuit-switched data services are now, for the first time, available almost anywhere, cheaper, and better performing (particularly in reduced call set-up time and improved error performance).

Supplementary services provide additional value when using bearer services. From relatively simple services like call hold to more sophisticated services such as call completion and busy subscriber, additional services meet a wide array of end-user requirements.

In ISDN's early days, ISDN end users were more likely to use voice and voice-related services than data applications. While this is still true, an emerging trend favors using ISDN more for its data capabilities. Point-of-sale networks rely on packet-mode services and are helping consumers deal more easily with the necessities of life (such as buying groceries and gasoline). Circuit-switched data-mode services are often used to connect LANs and to provide remote access to LANs, which is often a requirement for people who telecommute. These progressive services and equipment are allowing many people to work and to live in ways that they only dreamed about a decade or two ago. ISDN may soon allow many of us to make the choice of where we live almost independently of where we choose to work.

In the next chapter, we explore how end users access services via message-oriented signaling.

6

ISDN Protocols

T his chapter answers the questions: "How do I signal for services?" and "What is message-oriented signaling?" We present illustrative examples and details to provide you with an understanding and appreciation of the answers to these two questions.

A rigorous review of protocols tends to be an overwhelming task for most readers. The discussion in this chapter is not intended to be rigorous, complete, or highly detailed. Rather, it is intended to familiarize the less-technical reader with some of the more salient technical aspects of protocols and signaling. If you decide that this material is just not for you, then you can skip it (or skim it) and still take advantage of ISDN technology. However, just as the automobile driver is better served by having a fundamental knowledge of how the automobile and its major components operate, so too will the ISDN user benefit from understanding some of the more technical aspects of how ISDN operates. Besides, this can get interesting.

If you find that you really enjoy this aspect of ISDN, this chapter will prepare you to read and understand the more detailed information listed in the Bibliography.

6.1 TELEPHONE SIGNALING

Bear in mind that you already know a great deal about telephone signaling. You have knowledge of and experience in the user-network interface because you use it every day. When you want to make a telephone call, you lift the receiver from its cradle (go off-hook). This signals the network that you want to make a phone call. The network obliges by preparing to receive the digits you will send to it. (It knows that you are going to be sending digits.) The network signals back to the telephone instrument and to you by sending a dial tone that you can hear. You know this means you can start dialing the number you want to reach. You dial by pressing the numbered buttons; hearing the tones assures you that the digits are being sent to the network. (You don't really still have a rotary dial set, do you? Same idea, different action and sounds.)

After you finish dialing, you hear a connecting noise and then ringing sounds, which assure you that the network has received the complete number and is trying to connect you with the person at the other end. (Incidentally, the "ringing" you hear is actually a recreation, not the actual ringing of a distant phone.) You also know from experience that if the audible ringing doesn't cease, no one is home. You also know about busy signals, credit card tones that signify it's time to enter the credit card information, and so on. You also know that when your telephone is ringing, someone is calling you.

The point of this exercise is to demonstrate that you already know a great deal about signaling in the telephone network. The ISDN versions of user-network signaling have functionalities very similar to the traditional telephone network with which you are already familiar. The key difference in ISDN signaling is that it is a message-oriented signaling protocol. Accordingly, we will encounter *messages* (for example, SETUP, ALERTing) and *procedures* to follow when messages are received (for example, begin to set up or establish the call, apply ringing) as we explore the ISDN user-network signaling *protocol*. Using messages for user-network signaling is different from the telephone signaling we all know how to use. Existing telephone systems use a series of *conditions* or *stimuli* in lieu of messages. For example, by pressing a series of buttons, you send tones (stimuli) to the network, which interprets the tones as a request to connect to the called person (*response*). In data networks and ISDN, the network accomplishes this process by sending a message, which is followed by some action (procedure) and often some returned message.

In the ISDN world, the messages are explicit and complex in structure. They consist of relatively lengthy bit patterns with precise rules as to what indications should be coded in what spot. ISDN signaling protocols consist primarily of defining those messages (bit patterns) and establishing their rules of use. Paradoxically, the complexity of ISDN messages actually makes for greater ease of use, because there is much greater precision. For example, with an analog telephone, a user might hear a stutter dial tone when a message is stored in the voice-mail system or when the user makes a three-way call. A user could be confused as to whether to respond with one action (get mail) or another action (add on a third party). Generally, however, the user knows from the context of the situation what to do. With the more complex messaging of ISDN, you have a much wider variety. Each message means only one thing and only very specific actions and reactions are permissible. This messaging is also potentially much more descriptive. For example, an incoming call in ISDN not only alerts the user but contains information like the calling-line identification, the type of bearer service suitable for terminating the call, and other information pertinent to completing the call. ISDN signaling is actually very practical.

As with more traditional telephony, most of us will never want or need to know the gory details of the various aspects of signaling. However, just as we have some intuitive idea about traditional telephone signaling, we should also have at least some insight into how ISDN signaling works. Of course, the user will actually interact with the ISDN telephone instrument, so what he or she does may be much more dependent upon the equipment at hand than any other single factor. Since instruments are designed by different manufacturers, it's likely there will be myriad ways to place calls, answer them, and so on. One terminal manufacturer might install buttons on the set for dialing a call. Other sets might have buttons for supplementary services, such as call hold. Yet another terminal might use a screen and keyboard and rely on icons and a mouse. Regardless of the manufacturer or style of design, you, the user, will want to make sure that you feel intuitively comfortable when using a particular ISDN instrument. Having a basic understanding of ISDN protocol will help you achieve this comfort level.

6.2   ACCESS PROTOCOLS: USER-NETWORK PROTOCOLS

User-network access protocols are the "rules of the road," defining how users interact with ISDN networks. Between the two entities of user equipment and network equipment is a *defined interface* (either S, T, or U). These are the same interfaces discussed in Chapter 5. (See Figures 5.9 and 5.10.) ISDN services are defined at and across these user-network interfaces. The access protocol is how these services are requested and obtained. Because the interface is a well-defined interface, all relevant details of operation at that particular reference point are explicitly defined so user equipment and network equipment are programmed to interact.

It is only at the interface that standards apply for the user-network protocols. On either side of the interface, user equipment and network equipment can be designed to perform as users want them to perform, as long as the appropriate messages and procedures occur at the interface.

Basic Call Control: ISDN Circuit Mode

Placing a telephone call starts with a *SETUP* message. If you want to call someone, you must command your ISDN telephone to send a SETUP message to the network. You may have purchased an ISDN phone that sends a SETUP message when you lift the receiver from the cradle and push the buttons to call the number. If so, you don't have to know much about the differences between ISDN and today's telephone operations, because your phone allows you to operate as you always have done. (Other users who select different types of equipment may have to learn new procedures to gain new levels of control.)

The conventions used to describe this type of signaling are the *calling* party (the user or user equipment that places the call) and the *called* party (the user or user equipment that receives the call). But this can be very confusing when reading a prose description, because as you try to follow the plot, it's pretty easy to misread or not notice the difference between "calling "and "called." So, we will use the terms calliNg and callEd, emphasizing the final two letters of each term and reinforcing this through a discussion of a person named Ng calliNg a person namEd Ed. (Although not exceedingly common, Ng is a not rare name, and besides, it rhymes with ring.)

Referring to Figure 6.1, we see that Ng is ready to call Ed. Ng follows the instructions provided by his supplier and commands his ISDN terminal to send a SETUP message to the ISDN network. The SETUP message contains a lot of information (the pieces of the message are called *information elements*), but the most crucial information element is Ed's telephone number. It also contains Ng's telephone number, the type of bearer service requested (Ng requests circuit-mode speech service), and other

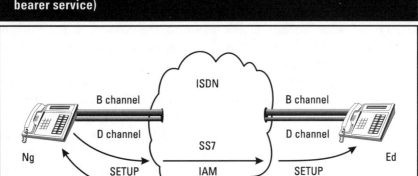

Figure 6.1   Ng Calls Ed (requests a circuit-mode speech bearer service)

call-information details that the network and the two end users ultimately will find useful. This should be familiar to you now—it's the list of bearer service attributes we saw in Chapter 5. The ISDN network conveys some of the information to Ed by sending a SETUP message to Ed's ISDN terminal.

To convey information through the network from Ng to Ed, the network packs the information it receives from Ng's SETUP message into an *SS7* message (specifically, the *initial address message (IAM)*) to be hauled across the network. After the IAM message arrives at Ed's side of the ISDN network, the relevant information is transmitted as another SETUP message to Ed. Ed's ISDN terminal (phone) knows about SETUP messages. It alerts Ed to the incoming call—by ringing, flashing a light, or some other method Ed selected when he bought the terminal.

Meanwhile, back at the originating end of the connection, a small fraction of a second has passed since Ng dialed the number sending a SETUP message. At this point, Ng's phone needs "reassurance" that everything is going well. To accomplish this, the ISDN network sends a CALL PROCeeding message to Ng. Without going into details, the receipt of the message means that everything is OK so far. In less successful scenarios, other messages would be sent to indicate errors. There are more messages and procedures for error conditions than for successful signaling.

There are end-to-end (transfer) aspects of this signaling effort (between calliNg and callEd numbers and the selected bearer service), and there are aspects of this signaling that are entirely local (between Ng and his side of the ISDN network or between Ed and his side of the ISDN network). Consult Figure 5.10 and the table on page 91 for an example of these aspects (bearer-service attributes).

There are two matters of local significance that occur with the SETUP message and the messages in response to the SETUP message that are important for establishing a call. The first is that the caller must *reserve* a B channel for the circuit-mode connection. Ng's SETUP message will include information about which B channel he wishes to use. The CALL PROCeeding message that comes back from the network concludes the negotiation; at that point, both the network and Ng will have agreed upon which B channel is *reserved* for the circuit-switch call. From then on, that B channel is not available for any other use until it is released at the end of the call. The other item of local significance that is important for establishing a call is that the caller must negotiate a *call reference value*. This is essentially a serial number that uniquely identifies a call so that the parties can make future reference to it. All messages in the access protocol will contain the call reference value. This is necessary because all messaging for all calls or all B channels occurs over one D channel, and with the call reference value, both the caller Ng and the ISDN network can keep track of which message to associate with which call. Ng selects the call reference value when he sends his SETUP message to the network. The negotiations are complete when he receives back the CALL PROCeeding message. Similarly, on the terminating end, the network then *allocates* a call reference value and inserts it into the SETUP message it sends to Ed. Once allocated, the call reference value cannot be used for any other call until the call is cleared.

In Figure 6.2, we see that Ed's phone has sent an *ALERTing* message back to the ISDN network. This simply informs the network that Ed's phone is ringing (or, in "ISDN speak," Ed is being alerted). The ISDN network takes the relevant information from Ed's ALERTing message, inserts it into an SS7 message (in this case, an *address complete message (ACM)*), then hauls it through the network back to Ng's side. The ISDN network then sends an ALERTing message back to Ng. At first glance, this may not seem necessary, but it simulates the ringing of the called phone on a pre-ISDN network. Figure 6.2 shows that in an ISDN environment, the network sends Ng an ALERTing message, rather than reproducing the "stimulus" of an audible ringing sound, to inform him that Ed's phone is ringing. If this is a voice

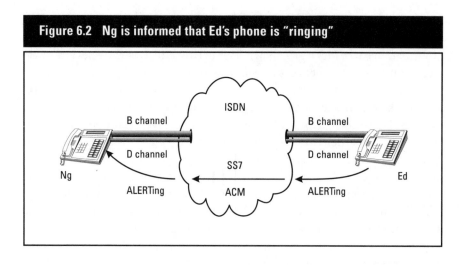

Figure 6.2   Ng is informed that Ed's phone is "ringing"

call (circuit-mode speech bearer service), Ng may have selected a network service that provides a ringing sound over the B channel, so that Ng actually can "hear" Ed's phone ringing, just as he did prior to ISDN. Or Ng may have chosen a phone that informs him in some other fashion (for example, flashing light, blowing horn, or a vibrating screen-based icon of Ed's phone). If interwork with pre-ISDN networks was necessary to get to Ed, other messages would have been involved.

Figure 6.3 contains good news for Ng. Ed decides he's going to answer his phone. When Ed accepts the call, his phone sends a CONNect message

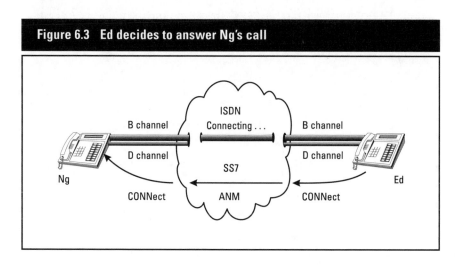

Figure 6.3   Ed decides to answer Ng's call

to the ISDN network. Again, the SS7 signaling network helps out by hauling the relevant information from Ed's side of the network to Ng's by inserting it into an *ANswer Message (ANM)*. The network inserts the relevant information into a CONNect message and sends it to Ng.

We are now getting to the heart of the matter—establishing the bearer channel so that the two end users, Ng and Ed, can obtain their ISDN bearer service. Up to this point, only the D channels have been involved. Ng is signaling to the network over his D channel, and Ed is signaling to the network over his D channel. The SS7 is relaying messages back and forth between the two. But when the B channels are connected to the network, there will be an actual end-to-end (Ng-to-Ed) bitstream connection over a B channel from Ng to the ISDN network, across the network, and then from the ISDN network to Ed over a B channel. Finally, the network connects the reserved B channels at each end to a 64 Kbps path through the network that connects the two ends.

We see in Figure 6.4 that Ng and Ed have established their circuit-switched connection. If this is a 64 Kbps unrestricted digital-information circuit-mode bearer service, a 64 Kbps bitstream path extends from Ng to Ed (in both directions simultaneously). The network ideally does absolutely nothing to that bitstream. Every bit that Ed generates gets to Ng unaltered in any way and vice versa. Of course, in real networks there is an absolute delay (the speed of light is still a constraint), and sometimes there are errors in the act of transmission. The potential for errors suggests that

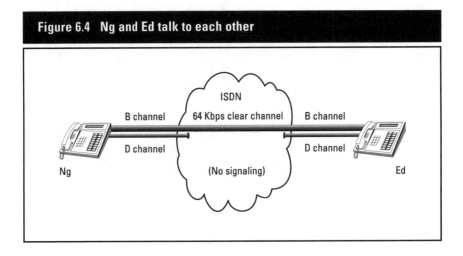

Figure 6.4   Ng and Ed talk to each other

Ng and Ed might want to use some sort of error-correcting protocol method between their two ISDN terminals.

If this is a speech circuit-mode bearer service, a speech path travels from Ng to Ed and, simultaneously, from Ed to Ng. Although the concept of ISDN supposes the path to be entirely digital from end to end (Ng to Ed), the standards allow analog links (for speech service) so that network providers can migrate from today's networks to fully digital ISDN without impairing the quality of service for ISDN users. In fact, it doesn't make much difference on a circuit-mode speech circuit whether there is an analog link in the connection. It still "talks up" properly, just as today's telephone circuits do.

Whatever the bearer service selected by Ng (with the initial SETUP message), information transfer occurs until Ng or Ed decides to end the call. While for voice calls this holding time is typically about 3 minutes, circuit-switched data calls typically last longer.

Figure 6.5 shows that Ng has decided to end the call, and therefore has sent a DISConnect message to the ISDN network. This message instructs the network to disconnect the reserved B channel from the network path at Ng's side of the network. We see in Figure 6.6 that the network responds to Ng with a RELease message, which instructs Ng's phone to release both the B-channel reservation and the call reference value. Ng's phone (or terminal) responds to the network with a RELease COMplete message, which also instructs the network to release the B-channel reservation and

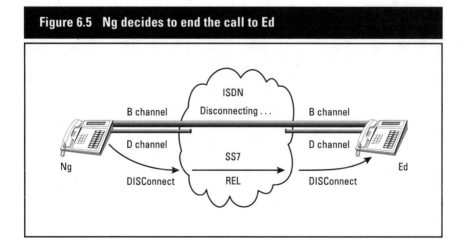

Figure 6.5   Ng decides to end the call to Ed

the call reference value. At this point, the B channel and call reference value are both idle; either Ng or the network can reuse them to establish another call connection.

Pertinent information in Ng's DISConnect message is hauled across the network by the SS7 network in the *release message*, and the ISDN network then sends a DISConnect message to Ed. Other information in the DISConnect message to Ed is entirely local in significance, such as the call reference value and the B-channel reservation information. When Ed's phone receives the DISConnect message, it responds with a RELease message back to the network, as shown in Figure 6.6. This causes the network to disconnect the B channel from the network path and release the B-channel reservation. The network sends a RELease COMplete message back to Ed's phone and then releases the call reference value.

At this point, the connection between the B channels and the network path has been severed. Call reference values and B-channel reservations at each end have been released. The network also tears down the various links in the network path and releases all of the links that were used to establish it. The call has been cleared, and all the piece parts can be reused (as they are *idle*) for the next call request.

The scenario above is a simplified view of what happens on a circuit-mode call; there are many other messages and possibilities that could occur. Most of these other messages and possibilities occur either because there is an error or problem in the network, or because of interworking considerations with networks other than ISDN. The signaling can become quite

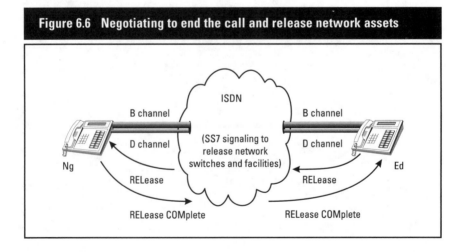

Figure 6.6 Negotiating to end the call and release network assets

complex, but the basic idea of sending messages and following procedures is illustrated by the example above.

Exceptions and Errors

This section provides a sample of the complexities that this book is, in fact, *not* covering in any significant detail. For those who want to pursue this further, many reference works that give this subject a more detailed treatment are available (see the Bibliography). For the rest of us, this section provides an overview of why there are timers, cause codes, and so many other kinds of messages in addition to the basic procedures of successful signaling described earlier.

Timers are used in protocol implementations in much the same way that kitchen timers are used when boiling an egg. That is, when the specified amount of time has expired, the controlling entity (either the kitchen cook or the protocol state-machine) needs to take action to ensure the desired results. As we have seen above, protocol messages flow back and forth between the network and the user. This cooperative effort means that after the network has sent a message, it must wait for the user to send a response. The network then reacts to that response by sending another message, and so on.

But what happens if there is no response? Unless some provision has been made, the network would simply wait (forever) for the response. Of course, the converse could also be true and the user could wait (forever) for a response. Neither condition is desirable or acceptable, so protocol designers add timers to the protocol specifications to deal with that problem. In the protocol procedures, when a user sends a message to the network (or vice versa), a timer starts counting. When the timer expires a certain action must occur. This action could be to resend the message or clear the call and start all over again.

This is not a particularly sophisticated concept, but you will find numerous timers, along with parameter ranges for their expiry, listed in the ISDN protocol standards. These protocol timers provoke debate over the interaction between timers, the implementation costs of providing them, and the need for any additional timers (where designers believe they have identified a potential problem that could be mitigated with the use of more than one timer).

Cause codes provide clues to the mysteries of where and why failures occur. For example, including the cause code in DISConnect, RELease, and RELease COMplete messages is helpful for determining what entity initiated the clearing of the call. Was it the originating user? The terminating user? Did an intermediate network cause the clearing due to operational difficulties? The cause code can provide clues. Values for cause codes are included in the ISDN standards.

The ISDN protocol provides many additional messages to deal with specific situations and provide a vehicle to carry needed information elements. Whenever designers identify a need to keep the network informed of end user conditions, or vice versa, they either piggyback onto an existing message to carry the information or a create new message. Over two dozen messages are used in the vocabulary of the user-access *digital signaling system 1 (DSS1)* messaging protocol.

Basic Call Control: Packet Mode

Packet mode comes in many varieties. A user can access the packet-mode service from the D channel or B channel. With the D channel, the packets contain a protocol discriminator so when the ISDN network receives D channel packets, they are not interpreted as signaling messages such as SETUP or DISConnect. Instead, the protocol discriminator identifies the packets as X.25 service packets. The signaling structure of messages and procedures is not described here but is in the ISDN standards and references listed in the Bibliography.

Packet-mode bearer service can also be accessed from the B channel. One way to do this is to permanently reserve a B channel for X.25 packet-mode bearer service. When you do this, the messages and procedures for establishing packet connections follow the standard and familiar X.25 process. Another service (on-demand B-channel packet-mode bearer service) allows the user to reserve a B channel at the time he or she wants to use packet service. With on-demand service, the SETUP message that goes to the network identifies both the B channel, and the packet protocol (X.25) to be used. This service does not require the user to reserve the B channel prior to requesting the service.

Supplementary Services

So far, we have seen how the user and network signal to each other to establish a basic call and clear the call when it is not longer wanted. In this section, we survey the signaling methods used to invoke the supplementary services of ISDN, such as *call hold, call forwarding,* and *call waiting.* There are three basic (and different) ways for a user to invoke these services from the network.

Functional, En-Bloc Signaling

Functional, en-bloc signaling is very much like the types of signaling for ISDN that we have already encountered. Messages, containing information elements, are used. For example, the user sends a message that contains an information element requesting call forwarding; another information element contains the telephone number for call forwarding. This method is called *en-bloc* because the entire message goes out at one time—in one block. Like the signaling described earlier, messages are sent and procedures are followed.

Feature Key Signaling

Feature keys were proposed to overcome one of the key limitations of functional, en-bloc signaling in providing supplementary services. When a new supplementary service is conceived, a long (usually a 4-year) period of standardization follows before the messages and information elements are approved. After that, equipment manufacturers must implement in accordance with standardized messages and their corresponding procedures, which can take still more years. Purchasing and installing equipment in a complex network comprised of hundreds or thousands of switching machines costing billions of dollars also takes a period of some years. At that rate, widespread availability takes 5 or even 10 years from the time a supplementary service is first conceived.

Feature key signaling provides a way to rapidly arrange to signal for new supplementary services. Feature keys are identified in a unique way—by number. When a user presses feature key #7 on his or her telephone, a signal is sent to the network informing it that key #7 was pressed. The network then associates that key number with a specific supplementary service. If the user and network agree that feature key #7 is to be used for call waiting, the user labels that key as call waiting. Keys can be reassigned to new services as they are created if the old services are no longer desired. Most users only want a few supplementary services; they can buy ISDN terminals with only a few feature keys to activate the features they prefer.

Keypad Signaling

Keypad signaling is very similar to the kind of signaling a user commonly performs today with existing custom-calling features. For example, in one particular telephone network, today's user presses the sequence *69 to automatically redial the number of the last person who called him or her. With ISDN keypad signaling, the signaling message also contains *69. The advantage of this method is that it does not require the addition of feature keys or messages programmed into the ISDN phone; another advantage is that it allows the user to continue using key sequences that are already familiar.

A disadvantage of keypad signaling is that feature keys are easier to use and remember and, therefore, are likely to result in higher use of and satisfaction with the supplementary services.

User-Machine Interface

It's easy to confuse these signaling types with different ways of operating a phone or an ISDN terminal. For any of these three signaling types, however, the terminal design could be the same. For example, the ISDN terminal functions could be performed on your personal computer. Perhaps you use a graphical user interface like Mac, Windows, or OS-2; you typically click on an icon. If this is the case, the computer itself could generate a special supplementary-service message, a feature key number, or a pattern of *69. Similarly, if you select an ISDN phone with buttons that denote call hold and call waiting, pressing these buttons could send a specific message, a feature key number, or even a pattern such as *69. Consequently, it is probably more important for most of us to understand how to use our ISDN terminal rather than how the particular signaling is implemented.

6.3   NETWORK PROTOCOLS

When the user requests a call through the ISDN network, the protocols within the network establish the connection. For ISDN, *Signaling System 7* (*SS7*) is the ANSI-defined protocol that achieves this connection.

Interworking From User-Network Protocols (DSS1)

The user who initiates a call uses protocols different from those used within the network. That is, user-network protocols (as described previously) are *different* from the SS7 protocol used within the network and between networks. Consequently, there is a need to interwork from one protocol to the other. For example, the SETUP message from the user to the network contains the telephone number of the person called. When the network switch receives the number, the switch removes it from the SETUP message and inserts into an SS7 message (the *initial address message,* or *IAM*). This message travels through the network(s) to the far end of the terminating network where the "called user" telephone number transfers from the SS7 message to yet another SETUP message, which is then sent to the person called. This procedure also occurs for the requested bearer service as well as for other information elements the caller sends across the network.

Signaling Within a Network

In addition to simply parroting information it receives from the user, the network also uses protocols to determine how to establish a call. For example, when the network receives the called telephone number, it must route the call. A series of trunk routes extend from each switching machine in the network to other switching machines. One trunk, connected to another trunk, connected to another trunk might make up the connection for a particular call. The network must "know" how to choose these trunks to provide for various ISDN bearer (and sometimes supplementary) services. For example, if the called user has invoked call forwarding, the network must perform additional signaling to reroute the connection to the forwarded location.

In the case of certain services, the network must signal for specific functionality. For example, when a user dials an 800 number, the network accepts the number but sends it via SS7 message to an information database. At the database location, the 800 number becomes a search tool for looking up a directory number (the more familiar area code and number), which is then used to complete the call. In the case of 800 numbers, the network directs billing to the terminating user. Similarly, credit-card verification and other services are provided using SS7 protocols.

Signaling Between Networks

In case you haven't made a long-distance phone call since 1984, you should know that the divestiture of the Bell System resulted in a new phenomenon—the separation of local from long-distance service providers. Entities called *local access telephone areas* (*LATAs*) were created for the *local exchange carriers (LECs)*; *interexchange carriers (ICs)* were created to provide the long-distance services needed to connect these LATAs. LECs, formerly within the Bell System, are only allowed to complete calls within a LATA. Consequently, a user placing a long-distance call often encounters three networks: the originating LEC, the IC, and the terminating LEC. However, an IC could provide the long-distance service directly from the originating user to the terminating user without using any LECs.

Because of the regulatory construct, it is likely that there will be many network-to-network connections on many ISDN calls. However, SS7 standards speak to the protocol rules within one particular network. Accordingly, bilateral agreements between each LEC and each IC can effectively connect two networks via SS7. Since each network presumably uses the same or similar SS7, the technical aspects of the interconnection should be possible to achieve (although tests to verify the interconnection between a particular LEC and IC take weeks). However, the business issues can be much more difficult. For example, if an IC does not choose to pass a particular information element over its SS7 network, the IC can't then provide supplementary services like *calling-line identification (CLID)* or user-to-user signaling to its users.

6.4   LAYERS OF PROTOCOL IN THE OSI SENSE

Historically, data systems have not been particularly *open*. Among other things, this has meant different systems were not compatible enough to be interconnected. Terminals from one system could not be used with another. Data from one system couldn't even be transported in a useful way for use in other information systems. Thus, data systems sharply contrast with telephone systems, which have generally interoperated everywhere around the globe.

Over a decade ago, a group of technologists in the standards arena decided to pose a general construct that would promote interoperability in the data world. That construct was the now-famous seven-layer *open-systems interconnection (OSI)* model. Figure 6.7 illustrates the structure of that model. ISDN, which followed OSI, was designed to be a network technology inhabiting the lower three layers of the OSI model, as shown in Figure 6.8.

This section presents a view of these three layers of ISDN protocol so you will have a basic appreciation of what they are and how they stack up to provide functionality. Note that the actual end-user applications (software) program is outside the scope of the OSI model. Also, the physical

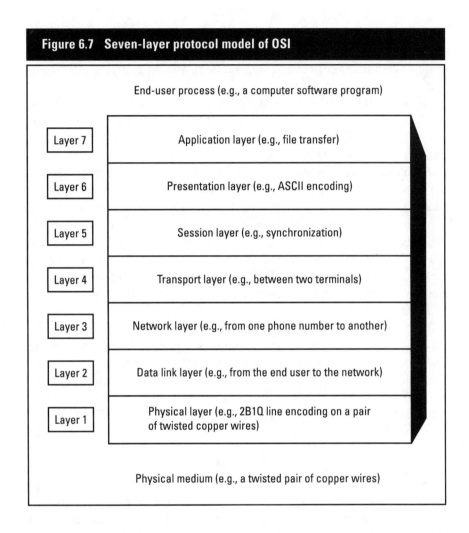

Figure 6.7 Seven-layer protocol model of OSI

End-user process (e.g., a computer software program)

Layer 7	Application layer (e.g., file transfer)
Layer 6	Presentation layer (e.g., ASCII encoding)
Layer 5	Session layer (e.g., synchronization)
Layer 4	Transport layer (e.g., between two terminals)
Layer 3	Network layer (e.g., from one phone number to another)
Layer 2	Data link layer (e.g., from the end user to the network)
Layer 1	Physical layer (e.g., 2B1Q line encoding on a pair of twisted copper wires)

Physical medium (e.g., a twisted pair of copper wires)

medium used to actually transport the bits from one end to the other is outside the scope of the OSI model.

Layers of ISDN Signaling

To be consistent with the idea of OSI, the ISDN has been defined in layers that are intended to be the same as the lower three layers of OSI. Consequently, an OSI end system (end-user equipment) that implements an OSI seven-layer stack might contain ISDN at the lower layers. This brings the power of ISDN to capabilities already defined in OSI (for example, *file transfer and management (FTAM), message handling service (MHS)*, directory services, and so on.).

Although this section deals with OSI and ISDN, we should note that services other than OSI also can use the ISDN network capabilities. For example, the well-known *Internet transmission control protocol (TCP/IP)* can use the ISDN network.

Each of the ISDN layers is designed to provide a useful service. So far, we have only looked at layer 3, the *network layer* of protocol. As we have already seen, layer 3 protocol establishes a connection for the transfer of user data from one user-network edge of the network to the other user-network edge of the network. The network connection is created when the user signals over the D channel to the network; this signaling creates a user bearer path between the two end users. The bearer path is carried over a separate channel known as the *bearer channel* (the B channel for circuit switched services).

Layers 1 and 2 are required to support layer 3. Layer 2 describes the digital connection between the end user's equipment and the serving network node (the user edge of the network). This protocol is used over the D channel for signaling. Layer 2 protocol establishes the link between the end user and the network for signaling. It is the responsibility of this protocol layer to ensure that data bits are reliably transmitted between the user and the network over this link (which is why it is also referred to as the *data-link level*). (It is via this reliable data link that layer 3 messages, such as SETUP, travel.) Layer 2 protocol in ISDN is a *link access protocol (LAPD)*, which operates on the D channel. Layer 2 protocol rules group signaling bits into frames, which serve as references for attaching meaning to the signaling bitstream (that is, identifying which bit in the stream is the beginning of the first character of signaling data).

Layer 1 protocols are required to support layer 2 protocols in creating a reliable link. Layer 1 protocols provide the details that describe how the signals (electrical or optical) are encoded onto the physical medium (copper wire or optical strands). These protocol(s) describe how the user data and signaling bits are transformed into line signals, then back again into user data bits. Each layer 1 protocol applies to and defines the B and D channels. For metallic (wire) ISDN service, there is a layer 1 protocol for basic rate (2 B + D) service, and another layer 1 protocol for primary rate (23 B + D) service.

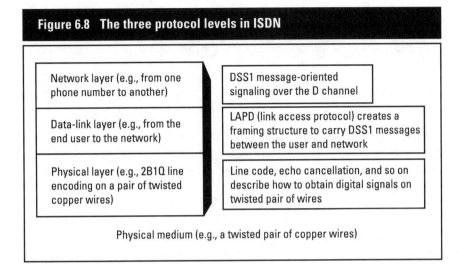

Figure 6.8   The three protocol levels in ISDN

Layer 2

Layer 2 protocol provides structuring of bits being sent between the user and the network. This structuring is generally called *framing*. In ISDN, in addition to providing a reliable link for data bits, layer 2 protocol rules also define logical channels. These logical-channel identifiers are identified by *digital logical channel identifiers (DLCIs)*. Two separate pieces of information identify each individual channel. First, the *service access point (SAP)* rigorously describes the services requested. The *terminal endpoint identifier (TEI)* identifies the individual terminal that accesses the ISDN services. The concatenation of these two pieces of information forms the DLCI. Typically, a two-byte header is used in the frame of the data-link layer.

The channels formed are used for signaling purposes, such as sending layer 3 messages to establish circuit-mode bearer channels. These channels are also used as individual channels for packet-bearer services. Only on the D channel are higher-level protocols used for user-network signaling. Although we will not explore the details of layer 2 messages and procedures, there are many fewer than at layer 3, consistent with the limited tasks of establishing a reliable link and creating individual channels.

In the late 1980s, it was proposed that the core aspects of these framing techniques form individual channels using the DLCI identifier on the B channel for circuit-mode data services. This would allow division of a (B-channel) connected data stream into many unique substreams (using the DLCI). For example, a host computer or server could receive a number of different channels from a variety of terminals all over a single circuit-switched connection. This represents the functionality of the *frame-relaying* bearer service.

Layer 1 Basic Rate Interface (BRI)

Layer 1 protocol provides the stream of bits between the user and the network and defines the B and D channels. On the D channel, this bitstream is structured into frames at layer 2 and carries the layer 3 messages described earlier in this chapter. On the B channels (and D for packet) this bitstream carries information from one user to the other. Layer 1 deals with the physical medium itself (wire, radio waves, satellites, fiber optics, and so on.). The bits travel along the physical medium, which is not actually part of the seven-layer model.

Developing this particular aspect of ISDN—the layer 1 for basic rate interface—was probably the most difficult task facing the designers of ISDN. To understand just how great a leap this was, you must understand that for traditional telephony, the bandwidth of transmission was from about 100 Hz to about 3400 Hz. It wasn't until the very late 1970s that modems were able to operate at speeds of 1200 bps. By the mid 1980s, modems of 2400 bps were about as fast as could be expected over the copper loops, although for short loops sometimes higher speeds of 9.6, and occasionally even 19.2 Kbps, were supported. The designers of ISDN determined in the late 1970s that they wanted much higher speeds over the same copper loops. They designated speeds of 160 Kbps, in each direction simultaneously, as the target. This target would provide 64 Kbps for each of the two B channels, 16 Kbps for the D channel, and 16 Kbps for *overhead functions*. However, existing technology was not capable of such high information-transfer speeds.

Although the technological barrier was huge, regulatory complexity made layer 1 agreements crucial to ISDN. In the international arena, the *International Telegraph and Telephone Consultative Committee (CCITT)* specifications detailed the S or T interface, which was between the user ISDN telephone (the TE1) and the network channel-terminating equipment (the NT1). (See Figure 5.8.) The interface on the other side of the NT1 and the telephone network was not defined. (The running joke was that the U interface stood for Undefined interface.)

The telephone administrations in Europe and the Bell System in the United States had planned to provide the NT1s as part of the ISDN telephone service. This meant that as line codes and transmission schemes developed and improved, newer pairs of NT1s and LTs (line terminations—the corresponding piece of equipment in the network that works with the NT1s) could be deployed without affecting end users with existing ISDN services. This plan seemed like a pretty effective isolation scheme to allow implementation of new technology breakthroughs into either the network or the terminal without one affecting the other. U.S. government regulators later decided that end users should own NT1s independently of subscribing to an ISDN service. This meant the industry had to create a new interface at the U reference point, which was on the network line side of the NT1.

Since interface specifications were nonexistent for this reference point, the standards committee (*T1D1* for basic rate access) worked to fill the void. The comittee could see that for this evolving technology, they would have to create standards so users could purchase an NT1 that would work with an LT deployed by a network service provider. Yet technologists in the early and mid 1980s were not sure how to make the system work. Further, if standards changed, users would own NT1s that could no longer function properly with the newer LTs. This curious interaction of regulation and technology has changed the way ISDN has emerged; in time, we will know whether users are ultimately happier providing their own NT1s than having network providers supply them as part of the ISDN service.

But back to the technology challenge—how could designers achieve these higher speeds? In the early 1980s, the technology of "ping pong" transmission was applied to create 56 Kbps access speeds. Using this technology, designers were able to achieve 56 Kbps speeds by transmitting in one direction at much higher speeds, sustaining a short idle period to allow the line to quiet, then producing another much higher speed burst in the reverse direction of transmission. This "ping pong" scheme allowed a net throughput of 56 Kbps in each direction "simultaneously." There was some thought that perhaps the same scheme could be used for ISDN, but clearly, these bursts of transmission would have to be at very high frequencies (that is, higher than 320 Kbps) to achieve the expected result.

Another idea proposed for ISDN was *echo cancellation*. In this plan, a small replica of the transmitted signal would be retained at the source and compared with signals received from the far end. Echoes from the transmitted signal would be recognizable by comparing the sample. Signals received from the far end would not compare to the replica of the transmitted signal, and so would be accepted as received signals. This system, which allowed simultaneous transmission in both directions, eventually was selected over the ping-pong method after much debate.

The debates for a standard turned even more heated when the proposed line signals were considered. A line code is how the data is encoded into signals that are transmitted over the copper loop. For example, in the 2B1Q line code, two binary data bits are encoded into one quaternary line signal (with the signal assuming any one of four values). A coding scheme like this requires transmission of only one line signal for every two data bits. Bandwidth requirements for the copper loop are thus only half of what they would be if every data bit was encoded into a different line signal. Further, the four values of the line signal can be selected so that the energy spectrum on the copper loop results in more acceptable performance. In the T1D1 meetings, participants proposed and debated other line codes over a year before 2B1Q was selected.

Since many of the proposed coding schemes were entirely new and theoretical, there was little or no practical knowledge to back up claims of performance benefits for any particular line coded. In fact, there was even a great deal of uncertainty about the amount of silicon real estate (that is, chip size and complexity that would be roughly proportional to the cost and complexity of the finished product). Debates raged as to which line code would allow use of the longest loops and therefore be able to serve the largest number of end users. At one meeting, a prominent professor or researcher would declare theoretical constraints that couldn't possibly be exceeded; at the next meeting, a scant 3 or 4 months later, a vendor would provide a working prototype that violated those theoretical constraints. A great deal of vendor prestige, development money, and time was at risk during these debates, and the debates often got quite heated.

From a local-exchange carrier perspective, the objective was to provide the functionality of BRI layer 1 at the lowest possible cost so that ISDN could be offered to the end user as cost effectively as possible. Achieving this objective essentially meant achieving two objectives: (1) requiring no special design when assigning copper facilities for ISDN access loops, and (2) attaining maximum range on real cable facilities. The first objective— simple facility assignment as opposed to designing individual ISDN services—has been a constant in the telephone companies for over 100 years. Designing individual ISDN services would add greatly to the end-user cost. The second objective also relates to the cost of providing ISDN. If the line code was sufficient for only relatively short lengths of copper wire, some sort of range extension would be required to serve many ISDN users. The most likely candidate for such an extension would be some form of subscriber-loop carrier electronics located between the user and the network serving switch—perhaps attached to a pole or located in a manhole. If a longer-range line code could be standardized, additional electronics would be needed much less frequently, and costs would be closer to pre-ISDN telephony.

In addition to transmission considerations (for example, echo cancellation, the 2B1Q line code, various electrical waveform details, and voltage levels), the ISDN layer 1 standards contain rules for maintenance capabilities. Although a BRI interface has 144 Kbps capacity for the two B and one D channels, another 16 Kbps is also used for maintenance and performance monitoring. Much of this capacity is used for a *checksum value*, which is used to determine whether the received information is in error. If the far end receives an error, it sets the *far end bit error* (*FEBE*) bit, which is transmitted back to the source. Consequently, both the near end and the far end possess the information that an error was sent. In the direction from the network to the user (from the LT to the NT1), bits also perform loopbacks (individual channels, all channels, and so on). The layer 1 standard contains bit values so that LT can send the appropriate commands to signal the NT1 to perform various tests, such as loopback on the B1 channel. The NT1 must interpret the particular bit value and provide the B1 loopback when requested. These kinds of capabilities provide remote testing and diagnosis, which minimizes the need to dispatch people with test equipment, and even allows regular, mechanized testing and logging of results to ensure that the access loop is working well.

Layer 1 Primary Rate Interface (PRI)

Unlike BRI, the set of protocol rules for primary rate access was not invented from scratch. Rather, the rules were based upon already existing and successful protocol rules used by DS1 transmission services dating from about 1960. In fact, layer 1 at PRI is unlike BRI in many ways: there are two copper loops, one for each direction of transmission, instead of one copper loop supporting transmission in both directions between the user NT1 and the network; periodic line repeaters instead of simple copper loops (although both PRI and BRI require electronics at the ends of the loop); 23 B channels instead of 2; AMI line code instead of 2B1Q; and different, although roughly equivalent, administrative and maintenance capabilities and coding. In short, ISDN layer 1 at PRI takes advantage of popular older technology and provides more capacity than BRI at greater cost.

Like BRI, there are overhead bits in the DS1 line signal to provide information for administration, testing, and fault isolation. There are, however, many fewer overhead bits available for use in the DS1 line signal than with BRI, which partially accounts for the difference in functionality and coding. For example, instead of sending a bit indication every time an error is received, the PRI protocol rules specify sending a bit indication if an error is received within the last second. However, similar functionality is provided to the user, namely line-quality performance and assurance.

Layers above 3

While we have focused mostly on layer 3 signaling messages within the signaling channel to establish connections and provide supplementary services, the real value of ISDN to users is in layers above 3 on the bearer channel; in these layers are applications that end users care about. (In the OSI model, the end user applications are above layer 7.)

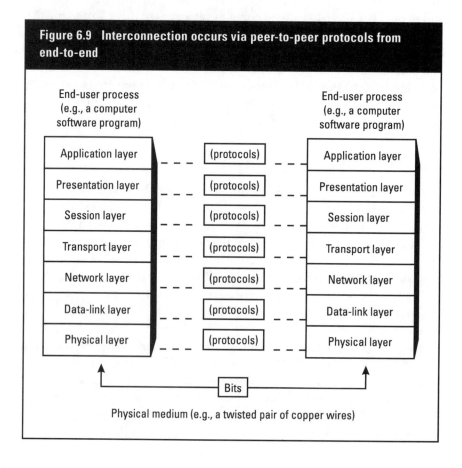

Figure 6.9   Interconnection occurs via peer-to-peer protocols from end-to-end

In the world of computer communications systems—in particular, within OSI—the layers above 3 are much more neatly structured. (Figure 6.7 illustrates the seven layers of OSI; Figure 6.9 shows how communication takes place between the peer entities.) Layer 4 (the *transport layer*) deals with transferring information between two terminals (called *end systems*). In addition to dealing with the user-network access issues of layer 3, it also deals with terminal issues such as buffering. Layer 5 (the *session layer*) deals with concepts of synchronization—or how to start and stop pieces of the application. Layer 6 (the *presentation layer*) deals with how to represent reality by coding (for example, the bit patterns for each character in the alphabet). Layer 7 (the *application layer*) deals with issues specific to the user application. For example, if the user application requires an inquiry-response element, you might use the layer 7 *remote operation service element (ROSE)*. Other layer 7 services include FTAM and MHS. Layer 7 even offers a service to coordinate all of the services needed by the application (*association control service element,* or (ACSE)).

When ISDN is used in the context of an OSI data-communications environment, it follows the strict rules introduced above. In such cases, ISDN is said to be a subnetwork of OSI and represents layers 1 through 3. But ISDN is often used in a context outside the OSI environment. In these cases, the layers above 3 are much more loosely defined—or not well-defined at all. Because telephony involves so much real-time human interaction, often there are no distinctions between the act of placing a telephone call and providing a user application.

End users who wish to accomplish applications using ISDN request ISDN services to do so. In Figure 6.10, for example, the end user might be using a software program that initiates a service request for a circuit-mode digital bearer service. The end-user equipment negotiates with the ISDN network for that service at each peer level (that is, layers 1, 2, and 3). The messages used in layer 3 require the digital link (established by layer 2), which in turn requires a bitstream (provided by the layer 1 protocols and the physical medium).

6.5 SUMMARY

The idea of message-oriented signaling is one of the five key attributes described in Chapter 1. This chapter focuses on the protocol used to accomplish

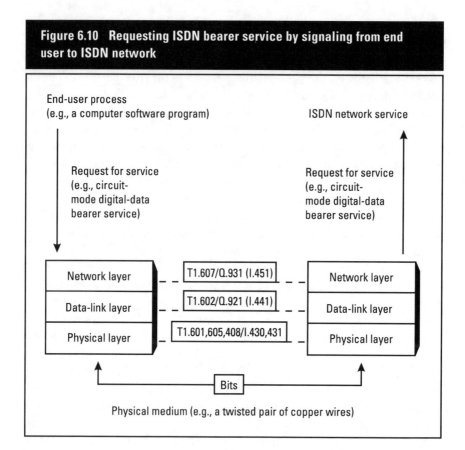

Figure 6.10   Requesting ISDN bearer service by signaling from end user to ISDN network

this method of signaling. Fundamentally, message-oriented signaling consists of informational messages sent back and forth between the end user's equipment and the ISDN network—a powerful capability indeed. This signaling system is the vehicle for ISDN networks to provide services to end users.

Data networks often use message-oriented signaling. It seems clear that data and telephone technologies and methodologies must merge to provide the communications systems we need and to facilitate the continuing development of information technology. Message-oriented techniques seem to be the best avenue to achieve this unity while providing the most useful and powerful capabilities.

In the next chapter, we explore the ways in which standards help establish well-defined protocols that can be used by equipment suppliers and network service providers.

7

The Standards Process

This chapter discusses how ISDN standards benefit users and make possible the implementation of ISDN. Various standards-development organizations, to varying degrees, meet the needs for standards. Each of these organizations has a particular scope of interest, and some of the organizational interests overlap. These organizations have made substantial progress in establishing standards (that is, in writing them and getting industry agreement to use them). Standards are fairly complete for the basic bearer services, many of the supplementary services, and the protocols. More is needed, however, in the areas of maintenance and management and for certain aspects of end-user equipment, much more is needed. The sections that follow describe the process of creating ISDN standards.

7.1 STANDARDIZING ISDN

As discussed earlier, standards are absolutely essential for users to realize the major benefits of ISDN. Standards set limits on the number of interfaces and services. Can you imagine a toaster that could be powered with 47 different types of plugs and sockets? The odds of ever successfully figuring out how to toast bread would not be very great.

In addition to establishing a limited number of user-network interfaces, standards address just about every other aspect of ISDN. The only way different ISDN network providers can ever hope to provide a similar set of services is to have standards-based descriptions of these ISDN services. Then, the end user who wants to use ISDN services across a concatenation of networks can expect applications to work properly and provide value.

Limited Set of Interfaces

One of the desirable aspects of ISDN is its limited set of interfaces. This simplification still allows access to an "information utility" array of services. The closest we come to this today is owning information-utility appliances such as television sets and radios. Both of these devices share the virtue of having a widely available set of limited standard interfaces.

The power interface for a TV set is standardized to be of only a few types: a two-prong 117 volt plug or a polarized two-prong or three-prong plug. Most modern wall sockets accept any of these plugs; older sockets won't and have to be replaced. The program signal feeds to the TV set via one of two standard interfaces: a 300 ohm balanced twin lead or a 75 ohm coaxial cable. If the antenna is of one type, the TV must be of the same type to receive the signal. Otherwise, you must use an adapter. There is only one U.S. standard for encoding the picture and sound. If the receiver can decode color and stereo, the user receives them; if not, the user still receives a program. The signal interface is simple, constant, and provides a very limited set of services (picture, sound, color, stereo).

In the ISDN world, 117 volt power will activate end-user equipment; thus, the same electrical-plug considerations as those described previously will be present. (We users may also want some sort of battery backup to continue service during commercial power failures.) The ISDN line signal (containing the user's data) is transported via standardized protocols and a standard physical plug. The interface protocols and plug are standardized for interoperability within North America, but standards in other countries may lead to some interoperability problems and limitations. (Interestingly, TV broadcast standards are also different in other countries, but we don't ordinarily receive direct broadcasts from them.) With ISDN, many users will make calls to users in other nations, making a globally consistent, standardized ISDN necessary.

ISDN Services

One of the first tasks in the standards-setting process is to agree on which services ISDN will provide. Next is the essential task of agreeing on how to describe each service. Chapter 5 showed that ISDN offers a relatively small set of bearer services that are appropriate for a large range of applications. All of these services have written standards.

Starting in the late 1980s, the standards-development community introduced the three-stage service description into the standards-development process. Stage 1 is a prose description of the service from the perspective of the end user. The descriptions are usually very straightforward, telling you what the service does and generally how it works. Stage 2 is an information-flow statement, describing the step-by-step procedures required to make the service work. For example, in call-forwarding service, the end user must send the network the telephone number to which the call should be forwarded. Understanding the information flow is essential to writing the specific protocols embodied in stage 3.

The protocol standards are the technical details of messages and procedures that allow different peer entities (for example, the user and the network) to negotiate services. Some claim that only protocol and architecture standards are needed to define services because implementors need to know only messages, procedures, and their applications. Skipping stages 1 and 2 has not been successful, however, because protocols alone are quite confusing to participants, especially those who have not been present from the beginning of the work.

When one user makes a call to another user, the user expects to complete the application. Today, when you send a fax message, you expect to use a circuit-switched connection and be compatible with the other (G3) fax machine. You dial the number and make the connection. The remote user terminates the circuit-switched connection. The user also has a machine that understands the G3 protocols. If there were 19 different types of circuit connections and 15 different fax-encoding protocols, the permutation of possibilities (15×19, or 304) would be so great that the likelihood of completing any call would be small. In a random world, the chances would be 1 out of 304 that you could get end-to-end service interoperability. Since we live in a chaotic rather than a random world, however, the odds are actually better that you could get some form of interoperability, but that situation would still be unacceptable.

In the ISDN world, the user must be fairly certain that the remote user can successfully terminate the connection, which means the remote network and end-user equipment must be hooked into the same or a compatible kind of service. (Also, as in the previous fax example, the user-to-user protocols, such as G3, must be compatible.)

The standards community is sensitive to the need to avoid creating too many new services, especially basic bearer services, unless there is a clear demand for a new type of service. Developing only needed services limits the number to a manageable range. Today's several different types of circuit-mode bearer services in ISDN address needs that have been clearly determined. Of course, there will always be disagreement about which services to standardize.

General Aspects of ISDN

Although ISDN standards are largely needed to define services and interfaces, there are other requirements that don't fit neatly into any particular category. Some standards efforts have defined ideas (for example, the basic ISDN idea of providing a multitude of services over a limited number of interfaces) and reference context (such as specific points within the end-user's equipment, points within the network, points of interconnection between networks, and the interface to the ISDN network). Only by using this common roadmap can we communicate about and use ISDN. For example, a service at a U interface has meaning only when you know what a U interface is, as described by its reference standard.

Other standards have general applicability. For example, some standards define vocabulary very precisely to avoid confusion. With a common understanding of context, including vocabulary, goals, and reference architecture, we can talk about ISDN services networks.

Networking Aspects of ISDN

Today, because so many different organizations and people are involved in networks, a single company, organization, or (even) country cannot simply decide how its network should work and issue specifications. Rather, the entire communications network community must have common standards. Standards, for example, provide specifications for the procurement of network equipment from a wide variety of suppliers. These standards also help to set priorities in the problem-solving arena, such as how to overcome congestion under adverse conditions.

One of the most well-known of the networking standards is *Signaling System 7 (SS7)*. As you saw in the call-setup example in Chapter 6, SS7 transfers information elements across the ISDN network(s) from one end user to the other. SS7, however, has utility beyond ISDN. (Often, networking standards cover a field broader than ISDN.) Many pre-ISDN networks use SS7 to provide advanced end-user services similar to the supplementary services in ISDN, along with other capabilities. *Advanced intelligent networks (AINs)* also use SS7 messaging to provide advanced services.

Clearly, ISDN needs SS7, yet it is not strictly an ISDN standard. Such broad applicability of certain existing standards makes it difficult to track whether all of the standards needed for ISDN are available and sufficiently complete. In addition, ISDN contemplates a new numbering plan, but many existing numbering standards are not necessarily considered to be ISDN standards, either.

Internetworking

Many standards deal with how ISDN interworks or internetworks with other services. Without these standards or some ad-hoc interworking units, an ISDN end user could not work with other end users who are not using ISDN.

Connecting one ISDN network to one or more other ISDN networks also requires standardization. In the United States, several different networks are likely to be involved in a given call. The interworking between the access signaling over the D channel (DSS1) to the network signaling (SS7) must be standardized to provide a common SS7 signaling set to interconnect ISDN networks.

Performance

Various aspects of ISDN performance are of interest to the end user and to the network provider. One example is error performance. For years, error performance has been estimated for data applications. Standards can define error performance, establish agreements for measuring it, and even establish acceptable error-performance levels. One example of error-performance standards might specify that a particular test pattern be transmitted for a period of time, such as 15 minutes. All detected errors would be reported as a total count of errors during this time period. Standards could also specify an agreed level of performance (errors counted) for end users to expect.

Another key performance aspect of ISDN is call setup time. One of the reasons end users want to use ISDN instead of other services is because data circuits can be established in less than 1 second. Again, standards could specify that a circuit-switched data call to be established and that elapsed time be measured.

Almost everyone in the communications-network community supports standardizing definitions of ISDN performance and techniques, particularly so they are measurable, can be assessed, and are clearly understood by all. While it seems reasonable to standardize a level of performance so that end users know what to expect, unfortunately, there are so many different organizations and networks involved in even a single ISDN call that disagreements over responsibility often impede agreement on such standards.

End-User Terminal Equipment

Many aspects of terminal equipment, such as rate adaption, may be standardized. Rate adaption is required to connect to a data source that operates at speeds lower than 64 Kbps. If, for example, you are an ISDN user operating at 64 Kbps and you connect with a user who accepts and transmits data at 48 Kbps, or even 56 kbps, you have a capacity difference. You have more bits at your disposal (over a given time period) than does the other end user. To sensibly convey information, the fewer bits (lower speed) are mapped into the higher number of bits (higher speed). This mapping informs the higher-speed location where to find the information among the larger number of bits sent from the lower-speed location. Two standardized and very popular ways of mapping are V.110 and V.120.

Other possibilities for standardizing terminal equipment include standardizing the man-machine interface. Such standardization exists in other contexts—for example, the brake pedal and steering wheel in our automobiles. Don't we want that same level of standardization in ISDN telephone terminals?

Operations, Administration, and Maintenance

Everyone wants to be able to manage the ISDN network (including end users), but very few are interested in writing the standards to make it happen. When

ISDN was young, the excitement came in defining the services, the architecture, and the protocols. Few people had much interest, however, in the "dog work" of support for the network. Nevertheless, ISDN developers created key maintenance capabilities at the same time they created protocols, services, and architectures.

Examples of these maintenance capabilities are quite mundane, yet greatly appreciated in times of need. If an end user experiences difficulty operating a particular ISDN service, someone must determine the cause. Within the standard BRI protocol definitions are capabilities for determining the fundamental health of the access line (that is, providing a very basic bit-error performance indication) and for isolating the source of a problem (for example, isolating the individual B channels and remotely looping a signal on them at various points in the circuit).

7.2 THE STANDARDS ORGANIZATIONS

It would probably be impossible to identify all the existing standards organizations. Even identifying all the organizations involved with ISDN and ISDN-related issues would be next to impossible. What follows is an overview of the major organizations that produce ISDN standards.

The American National Standards Institute

The *American National Standards Institute (ANSI)* recognizes and accredits standardization organizations and serves as the umbrella for the various *standards-development organizations (SDOs)*. While ANSI does not write standards, it accepts text from the SDOs for publication.

Committee T1

Committee T1 is an ANSI-accredited standards-development organization that produces the majority of ISDN standards appropriate for use in the United States. In 1984, the *Exchange Carrier Standards Association (ECSA)* established Committee T1, the first committee to develop standards for telecommunications. (Many people initially confuse the name of the T1 committee with the name of the telephone transmission system T1. There is no connection between the two names.) In 1993, ECSA broadened its membership to include all interested telecommunications industry members and became the *Alliance for Telecommunications Industry Solutions (ATIS)*. ATIS donates secretarial services to support Committee T1, but otherwise exercises no control over the committee or the standards it produces. To provide a complete set of telecommunications standards, the Committee T1 works internationally with the *International Telephone Union–Telecommunications (ITU-T)* sector, formerly known as the *International Telegraph and Telephone Consultative Committee (CCITT)*.

Committee T1 subsumes a variety of technical subcommittees (TSCs). Below is a list describing what the TSCs do with ISDN.

- *T1S1* is the primary TSC for ISDN. Previously, it was T1D1, and its entire domain was ISDN. Now, as T1S1, it deals with all signaling and services in telecommunications. Much of its work, however, still deals with ISDN.

- *T1E1* writes the layer-1 user-network interface specifications, including BRI, PRI, and even B-ISDN.

- *T1X1* writes the SONET specifications.

- *T1M1* addresses the maintenance aspects of ISDN.

- *T1A1* deals with the performance aspects of ISDN (formerly the responsibility of the now-defunct T1Q1).

- *T1P1* plans for the management of standards work for committee T1, including ISDN.

X3 Committee

This is an ANSI-accredited standards organization that, historically, has dealt with information-systems standards. There are a variety of subgroups within this organization (for example, X3S3, which deals with data-communications standards). The X3 committee works through ANSI to contribute to the work done by the ISO.

Until recently, this committee focused on data standards other than ISDN. By agreement, the Committee T1 was the domain of ISDN standards. For example, although the X3S3.5 subgroup wrote various packet standards, Committee T1 wrote standards for packet access via ISDN.

More recently, the ISO and X3 groups have undertaken efforts to produce standards for private ISDNs in addition to pure data circuits. Since historically many of the data networks using X3 and ISO standards have been private rather than public, the ISO and X3 groups see a role for themselves in addressing aspects of private ISDNs that other forums currently do not consider (for example, timing-synchronization issues in private networks).

Telephone Industry Association

The *Telephone Industry Association (TIA)* develops standards for equipment that is purchased by telephone end users, including telephones and PBXs. A subgroup (TR-41) deals with many ISDN issues. The TIA represents the *Electronic Industries Association (EIA)* for the telecommunications industry.

International Telephone Union—Telecommunications Sector

The ITU-T is actually part of the United Nations. Formerly the CCIT, it has for decades been *the* international standards body for telecommunications.

ITU-T membership is by country. The Department of State holds membership for the United States. Historically, telephone and telegraph administrations in most countries were part of the government (usually part of the postal administrations), which explains why government agencies hold membership. At least in theory, any differences between member countries can be resolved at the United Nations meetings.

The CCITT worked in 4-year study cycles; at the end of each cycle it produced a series of books that contained all of the standards agreed upon by the various members. During the 4-year cycle, the CCITT organized work by posing a series of questions to be answered during the cycle. CCITT first described ISDN in its 1980 orange books; in its 1984 red books, quite a few ISDN standards appeared, though not enough to support commercially available ISDN services. The 1988 blue books contain a much-expanded section on ISDN, and the 1992 white book recommendations contain still more.

The ITU-T has changed some working procedures, although the fundamental structure of the organization remains intact. Instead of producing a new series of standards every 4 years (the next would have been in 1996), the ITU-T now plans to produce standards whenever they are needed. Consequently, some revised and new standards will appear before 1996, while others will appear after 1996. For the next few years, you will find many of the CCITT recommendations still in force, while new ITU-T information and recommendations begin to emerge.

International Standards Organization

The ISO focuses on data-communications standards, whereas the ITU-T focuses on telephony. The ISO is well known if for no other reason than it produced the OSI model discussed in Chapters 5 and 6. The ISO constructed this seven-layer perception of protocol to facilitate interconnection between any two data systems (provided of course that they conform to the OSI model). Although few pure OSI products are available in the marketplace, many of the products and services that are available follow the basic layering concepts of OSI and, like OSI, often provide more openness than traditional systems.

Unlike the ITU-T membership, the ISO members are companies rather than countries. Because data-network and telephone-network communications technologies are converging, it is sometimes difficult to know where the role of the ITU-T ends and ISO begins. To promote universal communications, the ITU-T adopted the ISO concept of OSI into their standards by renumbering OSI standards into the X series of recommendations. ITU-T has adopted many other ideas that originated in ISO—message-handling systems, *protocol-implementation conformance pro formas (PICs)*, and *abstract test suites (ATSs)*, to name a few.

The ISO has claimed ownership of the private ISDN network standards and has also worked issues of ISDN into the context of OSI (addressing ISDN as a subnetwork of OSI). When ISDN conforms to the rules of OSI subnetworks, we can consider it a legitimate subnetwork of OSI (that is, it obeys the rules of the lower layers). However, the scope of ISDN extends well beyond the scope of OSI. Consequently, various organizations produce ISDN standards, each one with its own perspective on ISDN concepts. These different groups may potentially create problems by developing conflicting standards, thus confusing users. Many standards participants are struggling to minimize such occurrences.

The Society of International Electronics and Electrical Engineers

The *Society of International Electronics and Electrical Engineers (IEEE)* produces standards both in the communications industry and for computer languages. ISDN end users may be most familiar with the IEEE standards for *local area networks (LANs),* which connect workstations (various types of computers and PCs) throughout a single building or campus. LAN standards are written by the IEEE in the 800 series of standards. The Ethernet-like standard of *carrier-sense multiple access with collision detection (CSMA/CD)* is defined in IEEE's Section 802.3.

Participants ostensibly represent their own interests at these meetings on the basis of their IEEE membership. In reality, most participants attend at the behest of their sponsoring organization (usually their employer), and are there to represent their employer. This makes it difficult to determine whether a participant is speaking as an individual member of the IEEE, for his or her employer (as would be expected at Committee T1), or for their country (as would be expected at ITU-T).

Internet Engineering Task Force

The activities of the *Internet Engineering Task Force (IETF)* are often *on-line,* centering around the computer network known as the *Internet.* Originally conceived by and for the defense industry and later extended to the education community, this network of networks has grown to include virtually anyone who wishes to be on it. The IETF also produces the operational standards and relevant protocols for the network. It operates differently from the more traditional and formal organizations mentioned previously. Membership is based neither on country nor employer. To join the Internet, you simply need to connect and participate. It isn't necessary to travel to IETF meetings, but if you want to be influential, you should. The meetings are held throughout the year at various locations around the world.

The designation for standards in the IETF is the *Request for Comment (RFC).* You can access these RFCs by logging onto the Internet. (More detail is presented in Appexdix C.) To provide remote access to a LAN and connect LANs using ISDN, the IETF has proposed various protocols. The *point-to-point (PPP)* protocol is the most favored within the ISDN bridge-and-router community.

IETF work in progress—such as PPP protocol extensions for ISDN use—is available on the Internet. You can read draft documents by querying an archive host and downloading the document. You can participate in discussions of ongoing work by signing on to the appropriate mail list. Often, comments on a draft automatically go out to everyone on the mailing list as an e-mail message. This system saves travel time and expense, and results in more rapid development of standards than in the traditional standards-development forums.

7.3 THE STANDARDS PROCESS

The standards-development process is truly different from what most of us have experienced in other decision-making contexts. The standards community tries to obtain consensus to assure support for the voluntary standards they produce. Unless a consensus of the standards group solidly backs a standard, the individual organizations that comprise a standards body won't support the standard in their products or services. Hence, a simple vote is not sufficient to conduct business.

Within the telecommunications industry, implementors survey needs, compare needs to what is available to meet those needs, and then provide the best solutions they can provide. (See Figure 7.1.) In other words, the needs assessment and service offering are closely linked and very straightforward, providing the maximum benefit to the end user at the highest possible profit to the provider. Users specify what it is they need to achieve and look for minimum expenditure with maximum benefit. Often a small number of participants, recognizing a particular need or opportunity, produce substantive work on that need and forward it to the rest of the organization to review, modify, and ratify.

Volunteer Effort

The individuals who develop standards are volunteers. Organizations volunteer their employees, and sometimes, individuals volunteer themselves. Large organizations with a very large stake in the outcome of a particular standards-development effort typically volunteer more people for larger pieces of the work than organizations or individuals with only a passing interest.

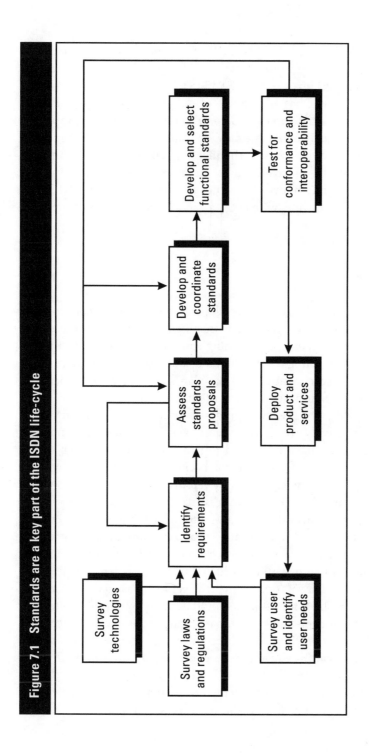

Figure 7.1 Standards are a key part of the ISDN life-cycle

Technical subcommittee T1S1 typically meets for a week at a time. Often more than 300 attendees from all over the world gather at each meeting. There are working groups within T1S1 (T1S1.1, .2, .3, and so on). Each of these working groups has a number of subgroups in it. A published schedule indicates what topics and *contributions,* or written proposals, are slated for particular meeting times. Volunteers bring word-processing and written resource materials to the meeting. Often, previous contributions are unavailable for reference at the hotel meeting sites. Instead, attendees devour many hours of meeting time laboriously reviewing one large document line by line, with every attendee penciling in changes on a paper copy of the document.

Contributions

The spark that starts the standards-development process is the contribution. Although details vary with each standards organization, a contribution is generally a written document proposing some idea or work effort to the standards body. At meetings of the standards body, participants discuss and may act upon these contributions. Standards-development participants frequently refer to their process as *contributions-driven.*

It may seem odd that the work process centers around written contributions, but it actually works reasonably well in the standards meeting environment. If you have ever tried to run a series of meetings with a large number of people from different backgrounds who may not have attended the previous meeting (3 or 4 months ago) and who may not attend the next meeting (3 or 4 months from now), you can appreciate the value of using contributions as a way to manage the process. Using a written document, participants may propose changes by suggesting specific wording. This process allows everyone to keep up with what is happening and also allows others who are unable to attend the meeting to review the work that was done. Further, everyone has an opportunity to have his or her say about how things should be done. By requiring a written contribution, the process forces each participant to clearly and succinctly make points. This contribution process ultimately saves time. Another advantage is that real-time reactions to contributions are captured in the meeting discussions.

When there is sufficient agreement, the participants begin a *baseline document.* Often a particular contribution serves as a baseline document.

This baseline document is used to record and include agreed-upon wording and eventually evolves into the standard itself.

Consensus

During the meetings, there is a very strict sense of due process, which centers around the ideas that everyone must have a chance to be heard, and consensus is the determining factor in making standards decisions. Unanimous support for or agreement on a particular standard is unusual. Somewhere between a voting majority and a unanimous endorsement lies consensus. Supporters of the consensus process explain that if an item under discussion is so contentious that consensus is in question, it is safe to assume that consensus doesn't exist. Consensus is very different than a simple majority vote or even a large majority vote. With voting, there are almost always some alienated participants, and alienated organizations or individuals will not adopt a standard if they remain alienated.

Standards groups have adopted a very practical method to overcome objections and the alienation of participating members. It is a formal method that involves *resolving comments* during the approval process. When there is a "no" vote on a particular proposed standard, the committee usually attempts to alter wording in the draft to address the specific issue raised by the objecting member. This comment-resolution process, when successful, often satisfies the objecting member without alienating other members.

Benefits of the Volunteer and Contribution Method

Although the volunteer-contribution system for standards development may seem strange to people who do not work in the standards arena, many positive benefits result. Probably the most important of these is industry acceptance. Since industry is not legally required to adopt these standards, it is to everyone's advantage to make the standards as acceptable to as much of industry as possible. As we all know, to obtain willing support from people affected by a decision, you must make sure they have a role in the decision-making process. This involvement is largely achieved through the contribution process described above.

Another benefit is the contribution process provides a relatively formalized method of including everyone's ideas and perspectives in the standards-development process and also gives everyone a chance to see what happens to their ideas and perspectives. A participant can ensure that his or her contribution is not swept under the rug. The participant may not get the verdict he or she wants but is guaranteed a public airing. In fact, most of the people at standards meetings are interested in hearing new ideas and perspectives. Generally, there is a high level of receptivity that greets each new proposal.

Still another benefit of this contribution system, at least in Committee T1, is that the volunteer effort is an open one. Any individual or organization that wishes to attend the T1 meetings may do so. Furthermore, like many volunteer activities, joining the organization is a very low-cost proposition, allowing any interested person to participate. The Committee T1 makes a genuine effort to ensure that potential participants are not disenfranchised because of location, size, or financial capability.

Problems with the Volunteer and Contribution Style

Most of us who don't regularly participate in a standards environment are used to a managed, goal-focused method of operation. We want to increase our company's revenue by bringing a new product to market. We want to improve our effectiveness by implementing a new inventory-management system. Or we want to provide better health care, education, and so on, by carrying out certain activities. So it comes as somewhat of a surprise that an area as important as ISDN standards is left to a group of volunteers who pursue the topics that interest them.

In the realm of ISDN standards, we do not yet have the full array of needed standards, and we definitely could have used some of them sooner than they actually materialized. In the context of a typical business organization, perhaps the results would have been different, with goals and timelines pushing standards development toward deadlines. Instead, because of the dispersed, volunteer-only nature of the effort and the diverse interests of the participants, only some of the needed standards are available.

The volunteer-contribution process runs the risk of slowing down or even destroying the process of standards decision-making and consensus. In fact, it could happen inadvertently without any intent to destroy the work. Participating organizations have all worked against the greater goal of creating standards—at least at times.

Even without hidden agendas, the process is long, tedious, and biased toward inaction and failure (to produce a standard). Allowing every individual to have his or her say is fair-minded, but it takes a lot of time. At a typical standards meeting, people travel from all over the world to discuss their contributions, and although the meeting may last for a week or two, there is a lot of work to accomplish in groups that are usually fairly large. Consequently, a large number of people spend a lot of time hearing the views of everyone.

Another problem with this system of standards making is that the participant who has a very small stake in the end result can exercise the same clout as a participant with an extremely large stake. For example, one participant may have invested *billions* of dollars in equipment to be consistent with emerging ISDN standards, only to find that a participant who has invested nothing is voting to change the standards so that they are inconsistent with previous work. This, some would say, undeserved parity can have a chilling effect on big industry participation but, even more significantly, it can curtail the adoption of final standards by the larger industry players. One safe way for these large industry players to avoid any technical conflict with standards is to hold off on implementing projects on products based on these standards until after publication of the standards. This industry hesitation is one reason why standards often do not emerge in products until 4 years or more after they have been published. If a large industry player tries to implement standards as they begin to emerge, the products may be ultimately inconsistent with the final standards. It's a no-win situation for both implementors and users. Because technology is changing so fast, time is an absolutely critical factor. Standards delayed are truly standards denied. Who wants a standard for a rotary-dial telephone? Perhaps no one does, but we have one.

National versus International Standards

Standards apply to a particular domain. Informal standards in a work group apply to specific individuals. More formal agreements might apply to an entire organization. Within a country, national standards apply. Other standards apply to regions of the world, and still other standards apply globally. While it would be easier if there were only one standard or set of standards to consult for any given product or system, such simplicity is out of the question, as the previous listing of standards organizations demonstrates.

Every country has certain unique needs that require unique standards. For example, in the United States, the legal-regulatory establishment has made certain decisions about ISDN that differ from decisions made in the rest of the world. For this reason, technical subcommittees within Committee T1 creates standards for the "U" interface. No other country considers such standards necessary, so these standards are unique to the United States. (Other countries may adopt these standards. If that happens, the U.S. legal-regulatory process will extend its domain to other parts of the world.) Where specifications satisfy unique national requirements, creating national standards to speak to those requirements is desirable.

It is only confusing, however, when a nation creates a standard that is unnecessarily different from a standard that otherwise would be globally adopted. This can confound end users and implementors alike. It also makes for more expensive ISDN. However, it is unlikely that this problem will ever completely evaporate. Standards organizations can only hope to exert some influence to keep these "nationalistic" impulses in check.

Government Involvement

For a variety of reasons, the governments of the world get involved in the standards-development process. First, standards have far-reaching commercial implications, and any given standard may directly affect the ability of a country to compete globally. Second, policies internal to each country mandate certain standards that may not be required in other countries. Generally, governments perceive themselves as major stakeholders in the standards process and promulgate standards that protect their interests.

Only governments are members of the ITU-T (formerly the CCITT). (Although an organization can be a *recognized private operating authority* (*RPOA*), which does provide a degree of nongovernmental status.) When the governments of the world assemble at the ITU-T, they address many issues in addition to telephony and ISDN.

The Department of State leads the U.S. delegation to the ITU-T meetings and represents the U.S. position. Company representatives may participate with the U.S. delegation at the discretion of the State Department. The U.S. delegation's technical positions are generally those agreed upon by consensus at the T1 technical subcommittee meetings. The State Department convenes meetings with industry to reach agreement on the contributions for the ITU-T and harmonizes differences of view at those meetings. Occasionally, the State Department overrides industry consensus and agrees with one particular industry viewpoint or makes its own determination as to how to proceed.

7.4   KEY ISDN STANDARDS

Listed in the following sections are the more significant standards (and standards in progress) that illustrate just how far the ISDN standardization process has come and how much more needs to be done. Curiously, such a checklist is not incorporated in the ANSI standards themselves (although the ITU-T recommendations do have a well-structured list of ISDN standards). Rather, the users of standards must determine what pieces are available and what other pieces they may need.

ITU-T (and CCITT) Standards

The ITU-T offers the most complete collection of ISDN standards, probably because ISDN standards work began there. The ITU-T specifications include descriptions, concepts, and architectures of ISDN. ANSI standards do not; rather, they assume that the architectural models of the ITU-T apply. ISDN recommendations are designated as I series. The numbering sequence is structured as described below.

The I.100 series of recommendations (I.110, I.111, I.112, and so on) introduces the general concept of ISDN. This series also contains the I-series structure, terminology, and general methods. The I.200 series deals with ISDN services. The I.300 series deals with network aspects of ISDN, and the I.400 series deals with user-network interface aspects. The I.500 series of recommendations presents internetworking (from ISDN to other ISDNs and from ISDN to other types of networks). Maintenance principles appear in the I.600 series.

Within each hundreds number, the tens deal with similar issues. So the I.110s recommendations concern terminology, whereas the I.120s deal with descriptions of ISDN, and so on. When the CCITT published the red books, all of the I recommendations were contained in one volume. Over the next 4 years, so much more was developed that the blue books of I recommendations grew to three volumes. The 1992 set of standards added even more, and work during the current cycle (1993–1996) promises to generate still more, in an effort to answer the study questions for the next 4 years.

The totality of ISDN recommendations extends even further. Other series of recommendations provide key requirements for ISDN. *SS7*, also known as *common channel signaling number 7*, appears in the Q series of recommendations, as do the protocol details for the *digital subcriber signaling system number 1*. These are the protocols that make ISDN work. Also relevant are other standards such as the G series, which specifies the coding algorithm for voice to digital (for example, the μ-law encoding specification and the A-law encoding specification). Other relevant CCITT recommendations are the F series (ISDN teleservices) and the V and X series of recommendations, which define data communications for pre-ISDN capabilities and, in the case of X.31, explain how to incorporate a pre-ISDN packet service into ISDN.

Almost all of the services described in the previous chapter on services are described in the I series of recommendations. Only a few of these services are unique to the United States and therefore not in the CCITT series.

ANSI (T1) Standards

Established after the divestiture of the Bell System, Committee T1 (and its various subcommittees) has been very active in working on ISDN standards. In fact, some of the most significant work done by T1D1 (later T1S1) has been to contribute to the CCITT recommendations. After review at the U.S. CCITT meetings, the U.S. contributions concerning ISDN are often accepted into the CCITT recommendations. A great deal of what ultimately appears as global standards originates in Committee T1. Consequently, we cannot easily measure T1's effectiveness by looking only at the number and quality of T1 standards, since so much of the ITU-T recommendations are generated by Committee T1. Figure 7.2 illustrates how the ANSI standards are centered around CCITT concepts and definitions.

When a separate U.S. standard is required in addition to the global CCITT recommendation, the Committee T1 ballots the standard to determine consensus, then submits it to ANSI for publication. These ANSI publications are numbered sequentially. Unlike the ITU-T, ANSI and T1 do not work in

Figure 7.2   Scope and timing of ANSI ISDN standards

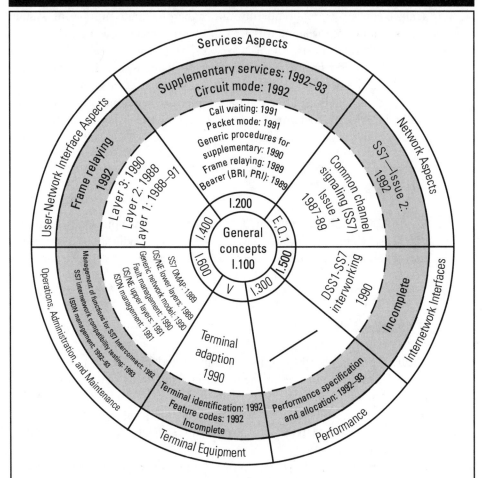

Note 1:   Figure is representative and does not include every standard.

Note 2:   Nonshaded areas indicate completed standards. Dates are ANSI-
approval dates.

Note 3:   Shaded areas indicate standards in progress with projected ANSI-
approval daates.

Note 4:   Application standards are not included.

a 4-year cycle and do not produce a complete series of standards at a specific point in time. Rather, they publish standards as they develop standards and achieve consensus. Consequently, rather than having a numbering system with a taxonomy, the standards are simply numbered sequentially.

ANSI standards deal with ISDN services, user-network protocols, network protocols (the SS7 protocols used in the United States, which differ from the global CCS7 specified in the CCITT recommendations), and internet-working protocols, such as rate adaption and terminal adaption. Generally, ideas seem to bounce from one side of the Atlantic to the other, ping-ponging back and forth as they develop.

ISO Standards

In addition to the well-known OSI standards, the ISO produces a number of other specifications that are relevant to ISDN. ISO specifications cover testing procedures and issues, maintenance methods, and private ISDNs, to name but a few.

IETF Standards

The IETF process uses the Internet to produce standards. The IETF RFC process is similar to what goes on in the traditional standards-development meetings, but anyone can participate by simply logging on to the Internet. Much of the existing body of RFCs concern systems programming, operating systems (especially UNIX), and networks (especially LANs and the inter-connection of LANs).

Within the past few years, the Internet community has been increasingly interested in working with telecommunications issues that will lead to *wide area networking (WAN)*, that is, connecting LANs together with public telecommunications networks. ISDN is one of the better choices of WAN technology to provide this capability.

Various RFCs address methods for using ISDN to provide remote access to LANs. RFC 1490 (replacing RFC 1294) describes one method using frame-relay procedures. RFC 1331–1334 describes *point-to-point protocol (PPP)*, which provides yet another method for using ISDN. Encapsulation techniques allow a smooth interworking of ISDN with TCP/IP, or with some of the other more popular existing protocols.

Generally, RFCs provide more pragmatic guidance for near-term implementation of ISDN applications than the standards emanating from other standards bodies, such as ISO or the ITU-T. Often, RFCs are based upon more fundamental standards produced by ANSI, ITU-T, or ISIO; sometimes they even tie in with popular commercial implementations — a practice atypical of the traditional *de jure* standards bodies.

7.5 SUMMARY

Standards organizations are stepping up to the role of producing ISDN standards and already have produced many of the needed standards. But with the proliferation of standards organizations comes the inevitable problem of competing standards. Users begin to ask: "Which standards should we use?" In the next chapter, we see that this question is only the first of many. Although standards are necessary to provide an interoperable ISDN, they are not in themselves sufficient to provide the full range of ISDN services, equipment, and interoperability that end users desire.

8

From Standards to Products

SDN *must* be interoperable. But contrary to our intuitive expectations, having standards does not guarantee that various ISDN services and products will interoperate. Sometimes standards do not provide as much guidance as you would expect, because they are the result of compromise, negotiation, and consensus building. The due process of achieving consensus is often emphasized over the content of the final standard. Hence, the content of a final standard may be subject to multiple interpretations. Finished standards products by themselves almost never provide a sufficient set of criteria for interoperability. Rather, standards documents are only the starting point for producing products and services that are interoperable in a multivendor environment.

In this chapter, we examine what happens *after* the standards are written to promote interoperability in a multivendor environment. Any vendor using poststandards documents and processes should be able to implement in an interoperable way with any other vendor who implements using the same documents and processes. Without these poststandards processes (however far from ideal they may be), we would not have achieved a relatively standard, interoperable ISDN.

We begin this chapter by exploring why standards alone are not completely sufficient. Next, we show how vendors introduce implementation agreements

Figure 8.1   Constraints promote interoperability

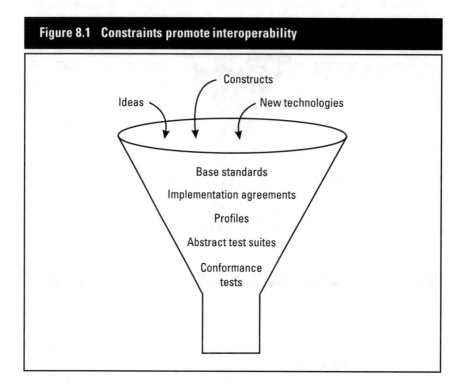

to satisfy the additional requirements for interoperability. Finally, we explore methods for assuring adherence to these implementation agreements and standards. Taken together, these constraints work to promote interoperability. Figure 8.1 shows successive constraints with each step in the process we explore in this chapter.

8.1   STANDARDS DOCUMENTS

It may seem odd that standards themselves are not sufficient for interoperability. But many standards for ISDN were written years before ISDN implementation. Often, the developers of these older standards did not focus on practical implementation considerations. When implementors later tried to build ISDN products and services from these standards, they found that the standards were imperfect documents.

Standards are the result of compromise: it is a difficult and delicate process to achieve consensus among the participants who develop the standards and to obtain approval from the sponsoring organizations. To reach agreement, standards-development committees sometimes settle on standards that aren't in the best interests of interoperability. There are three main areas in which standards fail to assure interoperability in implementation. First, most standards contain implementation *options*, which means that a vendor may (or may not) implement a particular capability or there may be two or more different procedures for doing the same thing. Second, many standards contain *parameters*, which are variables that have a range of values. Such paramenters, if too loosely specified, allow two different implementors to choose two different values (within the range specified in the standard) that don't interoperate. Finally, standards often contain vague or fuzzy text, which may be interpreted differently by vendors are otherwise not in communication. Standards texts that can be reasonably interpreted more than one way will prevent interoperability. These three interoperability deficiencies are "unfinished business" that must be resolved before implementors can produce interoperable products.

Options

Standards that contain options may describe more than one way of providing the same capability. Sometimes, developers build options into a standard to provide implementation flexibility. This can be a benefit and doesn't always create a barrier to interoperability. For example, an ISDN telephone has the option of using either functional or stimulus methods when signaling to the network. Clearly, a stimulus signaling method (for example, tones or voltages) is not compatible with message-oriented signaling. Assuming the network supports both methods, either method will work. The ISDN telephone at the remote end of the connection doesn't need to be using the same method to interoperate. This flexibility allows a lot of different types of equipment to interact, from the simple and inexpensive to the highly capable and highly priced. This type of option does not require implementation agreements to resolve interoperability barriers. Since some options in standards affect interoperability and some don't, it is necessary to review all of them to determine which ones present barriers to interoperability.

On the other hand, options are sometimes present in standards because implementors cannot reach consensus on two competing methods. Perhaps one implementor has already implemented a particular technique, whereas another implementor uses some other method. Even after protracted discussion, neither side can convince the other which particular technique is preferred. If the two parties cannot reach a consensus, there will be no standard. Ultimately, a standard that incorporates both techniques may seem preferable to no standard at all (at least the possibilities are narrowed to two). One solution is to allow both techniques to coexist within the standard as options.

When options create interoperability problems, we need to find remedies. Having everyone select only one option is one way to remedy the problem. (But if this were so easy, the standards developers would settle on one option when they write the standard. Sometimes this happens because implementors get so tired of conflict that they are willing to settle on any one option rather than having interoperability problems.) Another way implementors overcome interoperability is to provide an additional technique that tolerates two or more options. For example, if either end of a connection can negotiate which option to use, negotiating to a common option may provide interoperability. These remedies appear in *implementation agreements*, which implementors (and sometimes users) write. The *North American ISDN Users' Forum (NIUF)* produces many of these agreements. Within the NIUF, users and implementors are much closer to the actual deployment and use of ISDN and are anxious to obtain interoperability.

Insufficiently Specified Parameters

Parameter values are also important, and if insufficiently specified, can raise barriers to interoperability. Often, parameters are only loosely specified; frequently, only maximum values appear in a standard. Sometimes, the interoperability issues and parameter requirements are obvious, such as the need to agree on a precise bit pattern (within a wide range) to identify aspects of the service. In other cases, the need for certain specific parameters is more subtle and doesn't crop up until implementation. For example, if a parameter controlling the amount of data to be sent before receiving a positive confirmation is very large, manufacturers must develop terminal equipment that has a larger buffer to accommodate the larger amount of data. If an implementor makes assumptions leading to inadequate buffer space, certain equipment will not work well with other equipment under some conditions.

As an example of needing to precisely determine bit patterns describing services, users needed an implementation agreement to clarify the ANSI protocol standard for basic rate ISDN (T1.607). When a user places an ISDN call, the coding that identifies the desired bearer service is defined only as a range of values. The protocol standard (T1.607) calls for a SETUP message between the ISDN telephone and the ISDN network. Inside the SETUP message is information that identifies which bearer services the user is requesting. If the user wants the network to provide a packet-mode bearer service, a certain coding in the SETUP message is used to indicate the request. A different coding is used to request the circuit-mode digital bearer service and a still different coding to request the circuit-mode voice bearer service, and so on. The user must identify the bearer service because an ISDN terminal needs to be able to request a variety of different services from the ISDN over the same access channel.

Unfortunately, there is a bit of an interoperability loophole in T1.607. The specific coding values for each bearer service are not in the standard! Guidelines (parameter ranges) are there, but specific bit patterns are not associated with particular services. In this particular T1.607 standard, examples of values that you may select appear in the appendices of the standard to illustrate how an implementor could follow the guidelines. But material in any appendix or annex is only informational; it is not part of the standard itself. Although we could speculate as to why the standards body was unable to achieve consensus for these coding values, the reality is that, in the absence of standardized values, manufacturers can be in compliance with the standard, yet select code values completely different from other manufacturers for selecting ISDN bearer services. In fact, in early implementations, ISDN switch manufacturers didn't all use the same *codepoints*, or bit pattern values, for the same bearer services.

This practice of each manufacturer specifying unique codepoints to identify services simply wasn't practical for ISDN end users or service providers. Every ISDN service provider obtains network equipment from a variety of manufacturers. Consequently, a user accessing the network for service might be signaling to network equipment manufactured by any of the suppliers. That particular end user probably wouldn't even be aware of which suppliers provide the equipment—and wouldn't care to know. The truth is, most end users just want to plug in their ISDN phones and get the service they need.

In large businesses, ISDN telephones may be in a number of different user locations served by different network operators using equipment from many different manufacturers. That's why you can't have a solution that might work at one location, using a particular coding for bearer services, but not at another because of different manufacture. Pre-ISDN, end users are still able to move their phones around and use them just about anywhere. ISDN shouldn't constrain that flexibility.

Vague or Fuzzy Text

Finally, the third interoperability problem not completely resolved by standards documents is vague or fuzzy text. Why, you must be asking yourself, would a standards writing group write unclearly? Part of the answer is that standards text is written by a committee and approved by an even larger committee. Different people have very different ideas. Many of the standards people are of different cultures and languages, making it more likely that there will be differing understandings of the same words and phrases. Some foreign-born editors write text that is confusing (but in all fairness, other foreign-born editors write crystalline text that serves as a model). However, that doesn't completely tell the story.

Participants attending standards meetings want to protect the interests of their sponsoring organization. Suppose that a particular sponsoring organization has implemented or started development on particular equipment that conformed to an emerging standard as it existed earlier. Now, suppose development of that standard takes a sudden shift in an unexpected direction. It might be difficult for any participant to convince the others to return to the original path. But if participants write the text vaguely enough, it can be interpreted to include divergent implementations as well as those intended by the majority. A compromise is struck, but it may have odd results. It is quite common when reviewing the text of a standard in the presence of people who wrote it to receive an historical explanation of confusing text. Typically, stories go something like this: "Well, you had to be there to know why we did it that way. Mr. A from XYZ corporation wouldn't agree to anything that kept his implementation from being consistent with the standard, so we had to word it such that . . . [lots more story]." The story is usually lengthy, often involves many conflicting parties, and is seldom told exactly the same way twice. The problem, of course, is that these explanations about why the text is not clear and what it really means are not embedded in the standard document itself.

Another reason for confusing and vague text is incredibly banal. Work on these standards is performed under mostly undesirable conditions. Usually, the week-long session for writing national standards is held at a hotel, and the individual meetings are held in hotel ballrooms. These ballrooms often have elegant chandeliers remininiscent of the nineteenth century. Similarly, the manuscripts for the standards are produced in nineteenth-century conditions. Although each attendee should have a written copy of the baseline text, often there are insufficient copies. Each attendee manually notes changes to the text on his or her copy. Should there be subsequent revisions, the first revisions are crossed out and new ones added—each revision in successively smaller handwriting. Work may go late into the night, and the awkward nature of capturing the changes leads to sloppiness. Often, two or more comparisons the next day cannot resolve what changes were agreed upon. Photocopies of new text (from the editor) often cannot be produced and distributed until the following day (at best) and are typically handwritten and barely legible with all the crossouts. Incredibly, the only reference, word-processing, and secretarial support for these standards writers is what they can stuff into their suitcases—already bulging with all the necessities for a week-long meeting.

8.2   IMPLEMENTATION AGREEMENTS

Implementation agreements are written documents, created after the standards are written, that focus on details for promoting interoperability. These agreements specify which parts of a standard must be implemented by the vendor or service provider so that products can interoperate. They also clarify fuzzy standards text, select parameter values, and select options, if necessary, for interoperation of equipment.

The goal of the implementation agreement is to create a document that implementors can use without any other document or information to create products that interoperate with each other. That means that everything that needs to be covered by the document must be explicit and clear.

A major reason for having and relying on implementation agreements is because the various network providers and equipment manufacturers haven't been able to design, build, and deploy *all* of the many details of the complex ISDN standards in the first iteration. Even when manufacturers and providers intend to address all of the details eventually, they typically phase in only certain capabilities with each iteration. Consequently, if phase 1 is some subset of the total universe of details, interoperability will only be possible if all the stakeholders agree to use the same phase 1 subset (the same options). Network providers, network equipment manufacturers, customer equipment manufacturers, and all other stakeholders must agree to the same subset. Later, all players must adopt a common subset for phase 2, and so on. In this way, users can purchase ISDN terminals that work in meaningful ways with other ISDN elements as ISDN emerges. That's why we have *National ISDN–1 (NI–1)*, *NI–2*, *NI–3*, and so on.

These implementation agreement documents are keyed to one or more base standards, but there is no standard way of writing them. Some of them have been created by simply marking on existing standards. However, standards documents are copyrighted, and in the past, the owners of the copyrights did not allow publication of marked-up standards documents. Other agreements have been written from scratch and are re-created from a variety of standards to clearly state what the agreements contain. Because these documents differ in form from the base standards upon which they are based (that is, they do not track the standards word for word and chart for chart), detractors have claimed that they are not "the standards." Proving that the agreement is consistent with base standards can be a lengthy process, since the forms of standards and agreements differ significantly. The steps required to create an implementation agreement are:

- Select applicable base standards;
- Search for barriers to interoperability: sometimes uncovered through implementation experience and sometimes uncovered in vendor testing;
- Agree on how to overcome the barriers;
- Document results.

Protocol Implementation Conformance Statements

Some standards are so complex that they contain hundreds or even thousands of details pertaining to a particular protocol. Variance from even one of these details can prevent interoperability. Yet for a given product, only a small fraction of these protocol details may be implemented. To keep track of which details are implemented, you really need to have a way to keep score, much like a baseball scorekeeper uses a scorecard to keep track of game details.

The *protocol implementation conformance pro forma* has been developed so that implementors can proclaim (state) which details are in their implementations. The pro forma is essentially a blank questionnaire or form that asks which pieces of the standard are implemented. The *protocol implementation conformance statement (PICS)* is a completed pro forma—that is, a filled-out questionnaire. Using the PICS, you can determine what capabilities are implemented in a particular ISDN product. It's important to know what capabilities are implemented, because one implementation using a particular capability may not interoperate with another implementation using a different capability. For example, an ISDN fax device sending G4 encoded faxes over circuit-mode data connections will only provide value if another device can terminate the fax call over the same bearer service and encoding algorithm. Yet that other device may not be able to terminate a circuit-mode data ISDN call, or it might use only a G3 encoding algorithm. If so, the PICS would indicate that the device doesn't support those parts of the protocols.

A product may incorporate only a subset of capabilities because the vendor may want to produce a less expensive, less flexible product to perform a certain function only. For example, if a vendor offers a cheaper fax machine without speech capability, some users may be pleased to obtain the functionality they need without the added expense and functionality that they don't want. By relying on the PICS, purchasing agents can determine what capabilities—particularly those more subtle—are in the products and services they obtain.

Now more often, base standards come with a PICS pro forma as part of the standard. This pro forma provides a standardized way of capturing implementation conformances and suggests a future vehicle for creating implementation agreements. (For example, mark the PICS pro forma to indicate what compliance is required to be consistent with the implementation agreement.)

Profiles

Application profiles, as developed in the *NIUF,* are designed to capture back end-user requirement and collect the implementation agreements needed to satisfy that requirement. These profiles therefore capture protocol *stacks*—vertical concatenations of standards and associated agreements—that together satisfy the end-user needs.

These profiles bear some resemblence to the OSI profiles, but there is actually a great deal of difference between the two. One of the key differences is that the end-user environment is not considered at all in the OSI context, but it is central to the NIUF concept of an application profile. The components of a profile are:

- Description of end-user requirement:
  - Environment of application,
  - Benefits, and
  - Generally *real* considerations;
- Possible architectures;

- Process flow;
- Applicable standards:
  - Based on end-user application needs,
  - Refer to collection of implementation agreements, and
  - Refer to appropriate ATSs;
- Protocol stacks.

8.3 CONFORMANCE CRITERIA

A user intending to use ISDN capabilities to solve his or her business problems must depend upon a mosaic of suppliers: the software writer(s) for the application; the vendor(s) for the ISDN terminal and other equipment; the local exchange network provider; and the interexchange network provider. The user must also have a reasonable expectation that the remote user he or she calls will be compatible with the applications and platforms. Even with the best of implementation agreements, the user must verify, directly and indirectly, that each piece of the mosaic complies with implementation agreements that promote interoperability.

Conformance criteria consist of a series of tests that the product vendor must pass. Static criteria include conformance statements from the vendor that the appropriate parts of the appropriate standards and implementation agreements have in fact been implemented in the product(s) under consideration. Dynamic criteria include specifying an actual series of tests that the product must be able to pass. These test cases include a preamble, which sets up the product to be tested; the actual test itself; and the postamble, which returns the product to a condition from which any other preamble may be initiated for the next test case. A series of test cases are written so the product can be thoroughly tested. It's the abstract logic of the tests that constitutes the conformance criteria. These tests are developed with the idea that the product to be tested is a black box: the only concern is how it reacts to external stimuli over the defined interface (as defined by the standards and implementation agreement).

The logic for these tests is, by convention, written in a particular, formal descriptive language: *tree-tabular combined notation (TTCN)*.

This formal, descriptive language can be used as the basis for an actual computer program written in a particular computer-language program. In fact, cross-compilers are available that convert from TTCN directly to the C programming language.

The actual test campaign consists of the collection of tests to be performed. There are different philosophies for conformance criteria specification. For example, some test campaigns emphasize protection of the network, since badly behaved terminals can congest or defraud the network to the disadvantage of network providers and, ultimately, to the disadvantage of other users. Other test campaigns emphasize interoperability assurance: the user must be able to have some reasonable expectation that when the terminal is plugged into an ISDN network, the device will work. Both test objectives are reasonable, and both should be incorporated into the series of tests.

8.4 CONFORMANCE TESTING

The electrical and physical implementation of the tests are exercised against the product in the actual conformance test. (See Figure 8.2.) That is, real computers and simulators are used with the product. If the product responds appropriately, the product is said to be *conformant*.

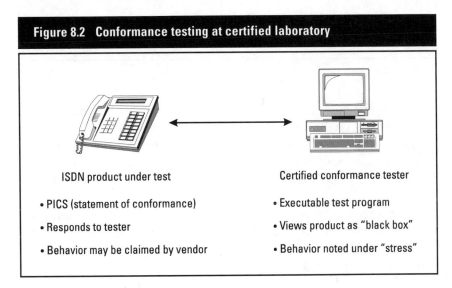

Figure 8.2 Conformance testing at certified laboratory

ISDN product under test

- PICS (statement of conformance)
- Responds to tester
- Behavior may be claimed by vendor

Certified conformance tester

- Executable test program
- Views product as "black box"
- Behavior noted under "stress"

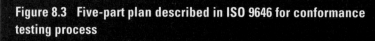

Figure 8.3   Five-part plan described in ISO 9646 for conformance testing process

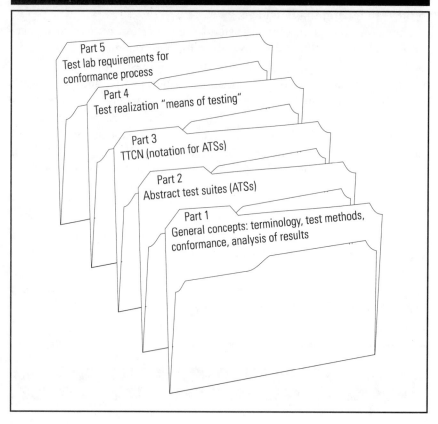

If the product does not respond appropriately, it is not conformant. Not surprisingly, the engineers who devised this plan (which is described in ISO 9646—see Figure 8.3) also allowed for judgments such as *inconclusive* and *inopportune*. Although these appear to be "waffle" statements, they are actually quite rigorously defined as conformance statements.

There are protocol analyzers and testers available in the marketplace for the those who intend to be deeply involved with protocol details. The rest of us will probably get more assurance from the process of certification, described in Section 8.5.

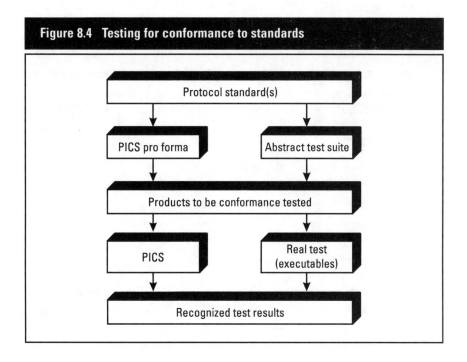

Figure 8.4   Testing for conformance to standards

8.5   CERTIFYING AND RECOGNIZING TEST RESULTS

Often overlooked, the process of certification and recognition is key to the whole idea of conformance. (See Figures 8.4–8.6.) After all, as a user, you want to know that the product has been properly tested and conforms to the relevant criteria. When you buy a toaster, you know that a UL label is reasonable assurance that the product is electrically safe (or at least not dangerously unsafe). In the case of ISDN, assurance is provided to end users, perhaps via a list of successfully tested products or by a product mark, that the vendor's product will work with the ISDN network. Within the United States, testing and certification for ISDN is specified and performed by the *Corporation for Open Systems (COS), Bell Communications Research (Bellcore)*, and the United States government.

COS also certifies testers for various testing laboratories. Although it surprises some users, equipment manufacturers are encouraged to test their own products at their factories and to certify the products themselves. Known as *first-party testing*, this inhouse testing often makes users wary. The first reaction in the user community may be that they are uneasy with having the "fox in the henhouse." In actuality, the process works to

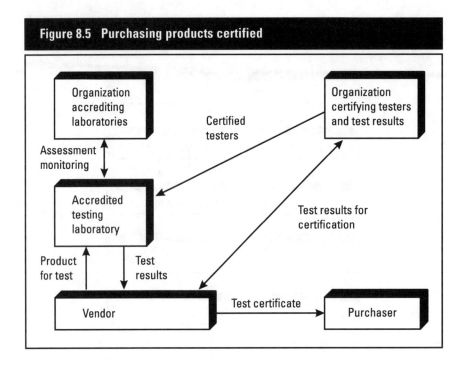

Figure 8.5 Purchasing products certified

everyone's advantage. Because it is easier and less expensive for the manufacturer to test inhouse, the manufacturer can offer more participation and lower prices than would be otherwise possible. Because certification is a process accredited by COS, there is outside control over the process.

Many people are working hard to provide certification that can be recognized everywhere so that tests don't have to be repeated in every country. Repeating the same tests unnecessarily is expensive; tests performed in a slightly different way in every country might be prohibitively expensive. Because testing agencies and certification authorities are beginning to multiply around the world, we must resolve the issue of standard certification to make ISDN a global phenomenon.

8.6   INTEROPERABILITY TESTING

Interoperability is what we all desire. Yet, as we have seen in this chapter, most formal techniques focus on conformance testing. In part, this is because

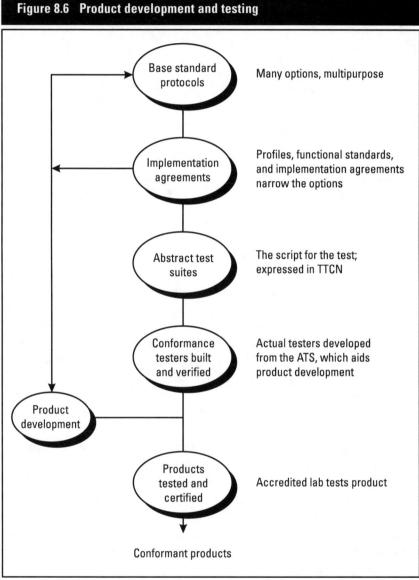

Figure 8.6   Product development and testing

Base standard protocols — Many options, multipurpose

Implementation agreements — Profiles, functional standards, and implementation agreements narrow the options

Abstract test suites — The script for the test; expressed in TTCN

Conformance testers built and verified — Actual testers developed from the ATS, which aids product development

Product development

Products tested and certified — Accredited lab tests product

Conformant products

formal methods for testing for interoperability lag behind the development of formal methods for conformance testing. Nevertheless, work is progressing on developing interoperability tests. Intuitively, it makes sense to directly test the capability desired, that is, interoperability itself. (See Figure 8.7.)

Figure 8.7   Interoperability tests between two vendors

ISDN product under test by vendor 1

- Vendor claims compliance to standard

- Responds to peer product; informal test campaigns

- Interoperability claimed by vendor in advertisements

ISDN product under test by vendor 2

- Vendor claims compliance to standard

- Responds to peer product; informal test campaigns

- Interoperability claimed by vendor in advertisements

Meanwhile, many vendors test for interoperability informally. That is, they arrange with other vendors to simply try to make the products work. Many times, they are successful. When vendors uncover problems, the problems shed light on how other vendors have interpreted the specifications. Sometimes a vendor will "fix" the problem by complying absolutely with specifications. At other times, a vendor will take a band-aid approach to expediently solve a problem.

Once two different vendors achieve interoperability, end users can be fairly confident that the products interoperate. But since there are no formal test campaigns, scripts, evaluations, and stressing (testing in unusual or unspecified conditions), it is still possible that some unexpected product behavior can materialize after vendors' interoperability tests.

Some vendors claim that their interoperability testing is preferable to conformance testing. They claim it is cheaper, faster, and more directly results in useful product fixes. In fact, these vendors resist the whole notion of conformance testing as being too cumbersome, bureaucratic, and expensive. Although they acknowledge that generally conformance testing will speed the process of interoperability testing (since some of the problems will be discovered earlier), these vendors are not likely to voluntarily subscribe to the idea of conformance testing anytime soon.

The reason many in industry are concerned only about interopability testing is that even if two vendor products interoperate today, these products will evolve over time and eventually their changed nature may jeopardize

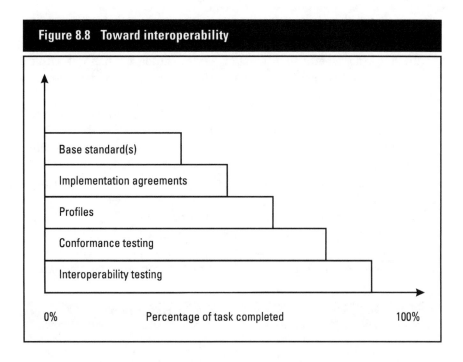

Figure 8.8 Toward interoperability

interoperability. Testing to conformant testers and scripts seems more likely to capture evolving products in ways that will promote interoperability over time (that is, make them backward- and forward-compatible with other products).

Still, not enough evidence has yet been compiled to establish which method provides the most assurance of interoperability with the best cost. The path to interoperability is depicted in Figure 8.8. In the near future, you will probably mostly encounter products that have been tested—informally—to be interoperable. Formal conformance and certification may be preferred only by very large user organizations and some network providers.

8.7 SUMMARY

This chapter has made the case that although standards are necessary to achieve interoperability, more needs to be done. First, standards documents need to be supplemented with implementation agreements to clarify the various standards for a particular product or service. We need to set up some sort of conformance criteria to establish what it means to be compliant with a standard or implementation agreement. We also need to be able to determine, through testing, whether a product or service is in fact consistent with the standard or implementation agreement. The path from standards to products is illustrated in the table below.

Providing interoperating, conformant ISDN equipment and services is neither simple nor straightforward. Organizations, most notably the NIUF, are writing implementation agreements to promote interoperability. Other organizations, such as COS, are involved in testing, certifying, and recognizing test results so that end users and others will be able to rely on conformance claims made by vendors.

Other organizations provide still more support for end users who want to purchase equipment that conforms to standards and implementation agreements. The *National Institute for Standards and Technology (NIST)* writes *federal information processing standards (FIPS)* to guide ISDN purchases

Milestone	Substance	Characteristics
Standard	Published agreements on technology and methodology	• Often written years before implementation • Typically general guidelines and options
Implementation agreements	Published statements that are unambiguous on technology and methodology	• Written closer to actual implementation • Typically more detailed guidelines and options • Stresses interoperability
Conformance criteria	Published abstract test sequences	• Written in formal description language • Contains test logic
Conformance testing	Performed actual testing or certification of products	• Performed with hardware and software • Typically results in certification of some kind

within the U.S. government. Similarly, Bellcore writes *technical references (TRs)* to help their clients in purchasing ISDN equipment to construct public ISDN networks that conform to standards and implementation agreements.

In the United States, public ISDN service providers have supported National ISDN, a standards-based ISDN, specified in the TRs written by Bellcore. The first phase, National ISDN 1 (NI-1), was introduced at the end of 1992. National ISDN 2 (NI-2) is scheduled to begin appearing at the end of 1994, with NI-3 to follow in the mid 1990s. Each phase adds capabilities.

9

The Users Speak Up

Society is changing, and within the telecommunications industry, change has been especially dramatic. No single organization can effectively plan for ISDN. Rather, many different organizations need to agree to a common ISDN vision and commit to achieving it. Equipment manufacturers must commit to producing standards-based equipment; telephone companies must commit to purchasing network equipment and deploying it to provide ISDN services; and end users must have the opportunity to purchase the communications services and terminal equipment they need and want. Historically, the Bell System has been the driving force behind telecommunications in the United States. Today, no specific organization or system can hope to single-handedly coordinate all aspects of telecommunications in our society.

We need a new paradigm to successfully plan the new communications infrastructure. In response to that need, the *North American ISDN Users' Forum (NIUF)*—the earliest and most successful of the ISDN users' organizations—began to examine telecommunications issues from the user's perspective. All of the stakeholders in the value chain of ISDN services and equipment have participated in NIUF meetings to make sure the purchasing end user will want the ISDN services and products they produce. The value of the NIUF and other users' groups lies in its ability to assess and publicize end-user needs so that, collectively, the various producer stakeholders can commit to providing an ISDN that meets those needs.

9.1   THE NORTH AMERICAN ISDN USERS' FORUM

It has been my pleasure and good fortune to have been involved with this organization from its beginning. Consequently, most of what follows comes from first-hand experience and observations. Other information comes from the NIUF documentation or other participants.

The Inception

In August 1987, a small meeting was held at the National Bureau of Standards (now the *National Institute for Standards and Technology (NIST)*) to discuss ISDN technology transfer. Participants expressed concern that end users did not understand the newly emerging ISDN enabling technology well enough to use it. At that time, ISDN was not widely deployed, and for the reasons (among others) discussed below, it seemed it would not be widely deployed any time soon.

First, the available ISDN was not standardized. Each manufacturer of network equipment provided a version of ISDN different from anyone else's. Before acquiring and using ISDN terminal equipment, end users had to find out the manufacturer and the vintage of the particular network switch serving them. One of the major concerns participants voiced at this first meeting was that different conformance testers were being developed for each of the manufacturers' telephone-network ISDN switching machines. While expedient in the short run, these differences would further delay the convergence of the various implementations into one standard. A common standards-based conformance tester would encourage the various manufacturers to adhere to a common standard, and the results of such a test would clearly show the areas in which particular implementations did not conform.

Another concern expressed at that early meeting was that end users were not having a large enough say in the development of ISDN. Although the industry assumed it had written standards and planned services to meet users' needs, there really was no forum for end users to interact with implementors. Providing such a forum would allow end users to state their needs, clarify issues for implementors, and question implementors directly about what was being planned for ISDN. In other words, the end users and implementors could work together to provide an ISDN that the end users wanted and could actually use.

This was such an unprecedented approach to technology development that it deserves further comment. Do you know of any other end-user group, open to anyone who cares to attend, that provides input to industry as it develops new technologies? Although unusual and unprecedented, this approach seemed likely to benefit both end users and producers: end users would get what they actually wanted and the producers of ISDN products and services would find a receptive market for their products and services.

Getting Started

The NIUF charter was signed in February 1988, at the OSI Implementors' Workshop, held at the NIST. Surprisingly, existing groups, especially user groups, were hostile to the idea of creating the NIUF. Although none of the existing groups had worked on ISDN issues to any great extent, they reacted strongly as though their domain—their turf—was being invaded. As we gained experience in the NIUF, we found that one of the general characteristics of user groups is a strong sense of purpose and ownership. Perhaps with more insight we might have expected other user groups to initially react to the formation of the NIUF as trespassing. In any event, this initial resistance did not turn out to be a lasting concern; people who were interested in ISDN simply came to the NIUF.

From that uncertain start, momentum picked up for the NIUF. The first meeting for end users, held in June 1988, was called the Users' Workshop of the NIUF. I particularly remember that meeting because at the beginning of it I presented an overview of ISDN. Having worked in U.S. ISDN standards bodies for over three years, I expected to be able to provide some new information to the assembled end users. But at the beginning of the presentation, when I asked how many in the audience were familiar with ISDN, I was flabbergasted to see almost everyone raise their hand! From that point on, end users and implementors have been trading visions and expectations to work toward an ISDN that users need and want.

The second meeting, held a month later, was for implementors. It was a bit rough around the edges, but industry participants were trying, for the first time, to reach the goal of a standards-based ISDN supported by all the major stakeholders.

It was the third meeting that convinced me that the NIUF would be successful. In September 1988, in St. Louis, a well-attended joint meeting of the Users' Workshop and the Implementors' Workshop was brimming with enthusiasm and ideas. It was at this meeting that the first harbinger of TRIP '92 emerged. The end users in the NIUF were establishing credibility with the people who mattered the most to them—the implementors who could provide and deliver the ISDN they wanted. And as work progressed, it became clear that the providers of ISDN really did want to provide what the end users wanted. From then on, although there were some ups and downs, the NIUF generally made progress.

Although perhaps procedurally imperfect, the NIUF is one of the most open and effective users' groups in achieving its goals.

ISDN Users' Workshop

The *ISDN Users' Workshop (IUW)* is made up of and chaired by persons who are (or want to be) end users of ISDN. Generally, they do not produce ISDN products or services as part of their responsibility in their company or organization. IUW meetings provide a forum for end users, not implementors, so users' needs are aired in their most pure, undistilled form. This separation between users and implementors is important because it gives users in the IUW the opportunity and freedom to set goals, targets, and direction for the NIUF.

The IUW is made up of various industry groups (such as manufacturing, process, service, financial services, government services, computer and communications, and small business). At each IUW meeting, attending end users submit their needs in the form of a written application statement describing what ISDN capabilities they need to achieve the results they want. The IUW has submitted over 100 different applications to the implementor side of the NIUF.

Success Factors

Users insisted upon running the NIUF and setting goals for industry. One of the goals they established early in 1991 was to have ISDN available to 80 percent of the population by the end of 1994. Not only that, they wanted the telephone industry to change some of its plans about how it would support ISDN. They insisted that ISDN be interoperable and standards based; easier to order than in earlier implementations; more accessible in terms of information to the end-user community; and more focused on ISDN capabilities in support of the more significant user-stated applications. They even conducted a popularity contest to determine which applications were the most desirable!

At first, it was difficult for the industry to deal with this proliferation of user requests. The industry had never heard anything like it before; responding to such requests was totally without precedent. Somewhere along the line, implementors reached a turning point, stopped questioning the validity of end-user requirements, and began to look for ways to meet the requirements. With guidance from users, implementors gradually began to work out ways of answering users' questions, providing deployment information, and—most important—providing the ISDN that end users wanted.

Obtaining Information from ISDN Implementors

As partners in the process of developing ISDN, NIUF end users wanted to know when and where the telephone industry intended to offer ISDN within the next few years. For a variety of reasons, the telephone industry had never offered such carefully guarded planning information to end users in the past. But end users correctly pointed out that to plan and budget for ISDN use, they really *did* need to know where it was going to be available.

Furthermore, end users voiced their frustration with the plethora of ISDN tariffs throughout the United States. Since there is now a wide array of telephone companies providing service in North America, end users were having to wade through numerous tariff filings and product names to develop an estimate of costs suitable for budgeting purposes. Users wanted ISDN to be tariffed over the entire nation as soon as possible, and in the meantime, wanted to know what ISDN offerings were tariffed in each area.

Also, as ISDN began to mature and National ISDN-1, -2, and -3 were developed, end users wanted to know exactly what was available in existing implementations, what was to be included in future implementations, and what were the implications of each offering for achieving the applications they had described to the implementors.

Integrating Industry Planning with NIUF

For end-user requirements to stimulate worthwhile products, industry has to listen and act. In a number of instances, this fortunate combination has occurred. After the first meeting in 1988, one company left the meeting with a very clear product plan in mind based upon what they had heard at the meeting. About three years later, that very company produced and began to successfully sell a product that allowed end users in different geographic locations to work as a team in answering large numbers of incoming calls (for example, at a catalog sales desk or a product-support help desk). This ISDN version of the classic *automatic call distributor (ACD)* allowed attendants to be geographically dispersed rather than situated at one location. It used the ISDN D-channel to signal the various pieces of the whole so that the functionality could be dispersed anywhere in the world. Other manufacturers followed suit with products and services culled from suggestions at the NIUF meetings.

Telephone companies and the major telephone-network equipment manufacturers had to cooperate and provide ISDN capabilities to make the ideas real. The planning teams for these combinations of organizations working on ISDN looked to the NIUF for requirements. The *Regional Bell Operating Company (RBOC)* and Bellcore ISDN planning teams were receptive to the NIUF as one of the better proxies for end-user sentiment and requirements. Network equipment vendors seemed to concur.

In late 1990, the *Corporation for Open Systems (COS)* suggested forming a group of telephone-industry executives to help move ISDN from the planning stages to reality. This group, also trying to meet end-user requirements coming out of NIUF, was the catalyst for industry agreement to provide deployment of a single standards-based ISDN. COS also determined early on that the NIUF was *the* significant ISDN user group. Later, the two groups—COS and NIUF—would combine efforts to put on TRIP '92.

Transcontinental ISDN Project 1992

In 1991, ISDN was still more of an intellectual construct than a reality. The purpose of *the Transcontinental ISDN Project 1992 (TRIP '92)* was to demonstrate the reality of ISDN and begin deployment of a nationwide network that people could begin to use. At one extreme, purists wanted to see absolute adherence to every detail of the NIUF agreements, with conformance tests completed for every piece of equipment used in TRIP '92 demonstrations. At the other extreme, end users and vendors wanted access to ISDN products and services as soon as possible. Early in 1991, when the 1992 TRIP date was set, it looked very reasonable. In late 1992, organizers encountered unexpected problems and delays, but many worked tirelessly to provide ISDN capabilities for TRIP '92. Dr. Robert Metcalfe, the moderator of TRIP '92 in Reston, Virginia, declared that providing National ISDN-1 was the beginning of the information age. Coming from the inventor of Ethernet, this was quite a declaration of the importance of ISDN-1.

The TRIP '92 demonstration required an unusual degree of cooperation among telephone providers and required that they file numerous tariffs for ISDN that they might otherwise not have filed so soon. Equipment vendors and service providers could no longer buy time with ISDN just around the corner. All of the end users who pushed for TRIP '92 truly influenced and hastened the deployment of a national standards-based ISDN.

During the TRIP week, about 170 end-user and implementator locations around the world (the vast majority in the United States) hosted open houses to demonstrate their ISDN applications to interested potential users. At the central Reston, Virginia, location, many vendors provided demonstrations of their ISDN products and services, and offered structured programs centered around particular topics, such as telecommuting and health care. At the end of the week, the beginning of a national ISDN network was in place.

ISDN Implementors' Workshop

The *ISDN Implementors' Workshop (IIW)* is made up of and chaired by persons who are producers of ISDN products or services. Although most of these implementors are also end users, they have a major stake in producing ISDN products and services. Most of the responsibility for achieving the goals and targets set by users in NIUF belongs to the implementors of ISDN.

The IIW consists of various industry members involved with providing ISDN. Many of the *local exchange carriers (LECs)* are involved, as are the *interexchange carriers (IECs)*. A wide variety of hardware and software suppliers in the computer, telecommunications, and information technology industries participate in different ways.

Many more people participate in the IIW than the IUW for a variety of reasons. Implementors are bigger stakeholders in ISDN technology; it is usually their main concern within their organization. While end users attend meetings to facilitate getting the ISDN they want to use in their organizations, their primary interest lies in supporting their organizational goals with whatever communications capabilities they can select from a wide variety of technologies. As ISDN has become available, they often use it to their benefit. But users have alternatives to ISDN, and they also have many other concerns about making their organizations successful. Because of the level of implementor commitment, the IIW understandably has become a larger organization.

The IIW is a complex organization, and it keeps changing. Some of its groups are constantly active, while others only intermittently produce results. Nevertheless, the various groups listed below have been quite successful in fulfilling their missions.

By the time you read this book, the IIW will probably be somewhat different from its characterization here. It still seems worthwhile, however, to describe the current structure, because it readily captures the IIW's work efforts.

Expert (Technical) Working Groups

Within the IIW, many groups work on a particular piece of the technology. Because the overall scope of the technology is so broad, no one knows enough to work on the entire technology. Consequently, groups were formed around various specializations. Some of them are described in the following sections.

Generally, each of these groups defines implementation agreements, as described in Chapter 8. In doing so, the groups have to agree to a set of applicable standards, determine whether there are any barriers to interoperability in those standards, and (for those barriers they do identify) agree on how to overcome the barriers.

Change within the organization is inevitable. Therefore, when reading the thumbnail sketches that follow, be aware that organizational details aren't what is important. What is important is learning about the developing applications of ISDN technology.

Signaling

This working group had the task of harmonizing the views of the major equipment manufacturers and the major telephone-company service providers to establish an interoperable set of signaling specifications that everyone would follow. One of the earliest groups to start working, this trailblazing group found it very difficult to agree to implementation statements for interoperability. (Many of the people involved in this group came from the one organization (the Bell system) that had centrally planned the progression of the telephone industry to interoperability and virtually dictated interoperability specifications to the industry. But a Bell system background did not guarantee their success in gaining industry consensus.)

Only after a great deal of leadership by the chairs of the group and by some key participants was progress made. Finally, this working group reached initial agreements toward the end of 1990. These basic signaling agreements laid the groundwork for the NIUF; they were absolutely essential to an interoperable ISDN.

ISDN Conformance Testing

To verify that the equipment manufacturers in fact complied with the implementation agreements, the *ISDN Conformance Testing (ICOT) Working Group's* mission was to develop objective tests. They dealt with developing a *protocol implementation-conformance statement (PICS)* and an *abstract test suite (ATS)* needed by the test-equipment manufacturers to build the testers (see Chapter 8). Various participants from industry and NIST cooperated to produce these tests. Without such objective tests, manufacturers would have continued to provide their own widely varying tests. Even given the standard ISDN signaling, different tests and testing procedures would have made it much more difficult to verify and implement a standard ISDN.

Application Software Interface

This group specifies *application software interfaces (ASI)*, which provide a common gateway from the popular computer operating systems (and architectures) to a wide variety of *terminal adapters (TAs)*. Terminal adapters are the equipment and software (often implemented as cards inserted into a personal computer) that adapt the computer to use ISDN services. The ASI common gateway encourages production of application software because the software can be used with a wider variety of TAs. Having the ASI interface provides end users with more software choices and saves software producers the costs of developing programs for each different TA.

ICSW (ISDN CPE and Software Workgroup)

As the previous section clearly demonstrates, there is an ever-growing need to make sure that *customer-provided equipment (CPE)* is planned and provided for in concert with the planning and provision of ISDN itself. After all, what good is ISDN without end-user equipment such as computers, workstations, and telephones? Each of the subcommittees listed below focuses on a particular aspect of ISDN that CPE vendors want to address. Collectively, they form the ICSW.

National ISDN CPE Subcommittees and Working Groups   At the national ISDN CPE subcommittee meetings, the authors of the national ISDN documents from Bellcore interact with end-user equipment vendors to ensure that equipment meets end users' needs. Representatives from telephone companies who have agreed to deploy equipment and provide these services are also present, as are key individuals from network-switch manufacturers. These representatives work together with equipment vendors to enable thorough planning and coordination.

Basic Rate Terminal Subcommittee   Many of the basic rate terminal issues are different from ISDN-primary-rate issues; a separate group of end-user equipment vendors meet to discuss and resolve these basic rate terminal issues. For example, on a basic rate interface, many terminals can be connected to a single interface (called a *passive bus* or *multipoint configuration*). Protocol details to support this configuration are very complex. As a second example, electronic key-set features also aren't relevant for most ISDN terminal equipment on a primary rate interface. This subcommittee deals with issues facing the basic rate terminal manufacturer. These issues must be treated separately because the end user might be a homeowner or a small business person as opposed to a telecommunications specialist in a large business who might be arranging for the installation, wiring, and powering of a telecommunications suite on their premises (a PBX).

PBX Subcommittee   Much of the work in ISDN has centered around the *basic rate interface (BRI)*. This is the 2B + D that most of us envision using in our homes and small businesses. However, many large organizations will be using PBXs to obtain telephone service. So this subcommittee is addressing many issues for the *primary rate interface (PRI)* of ISDN. Although BRI and PRI share many commonalities, the PBX subcommittee works through concerns and considerations specific to PRI. For example, one subcommittee objective is to provide a means to construct an enterprise network of PBXs and Centrexes.

Wiring and Powering Subcommittee   Analog telephone service allowed considerable latitude in wiring. Just about anything worked. In the ISDN era, however, more careful techniques will be needed. The Wiring and Powering Subcommittee is working on guidelines for ISDN wiring techniques and materials. Unlike analog telephones, ISDN terminals need a source of local power to operate. Typically, they plug into the wall to draw power, just as a TV or a computer would. But end users are accustomed to being able to use a telephone during a power outage. So this group is addressing powering in both normal circumstances and power outages.

Security Working Group

This group works on assuring security at the level of military communications requirements, dealing with specially designed telephones, encryption techniques, and other sensitive security considerations. Also, today's competitive environment prompts proactive behavior to ensure that reasonable precautions are taken with sensitive information.

Network-Management Working Group

End users want to be in control of their ISDN service. Sometimes this means verifying the performance of a circuit or equipment; at other times, it means actually controlling an aspect of performance. End users bring their requirements to this group, which in turn works to meet them.

Wireless Working Group

Recently, there has been a lot of interest in wireless technology. Wireless ISDN seems appropriate for LANs, PBXs, cellular communications, personal terminals, and satellite communications. This group compares various NIUF end-user applications to determine which ones would be appropriate in a wireless environment.

Satellite Working Group

Many implementors are involved in satellite technology and believe satellites have a role in providing and using ISDN. This group is looking at ways to take advantage of the strengths of this technology for ISDN applications.

Application-Analysis (and Catalog) Working Group

This group is, in some ways, the one that is closest to the end users in the NIUF. When the IUF approves a user-stated application, the Application-Analysis Group is the first IIW group to examine it. Preliminary analysis suggests whether the application is feasible with ISDN technology; the application is then routed through the IIW for further work. Because much of the work at the NIUF is spontaneous and decentralized, sometimes end users bypass the applications-analysis phase.

Prior to TRIP '92, this group also took on the task of producing an application catalog (aka "cookbook"), which presents a comprehensive array of ISDN solutions. The book was so well received that a second edition was prepared; since then, much of the effort of this group has shifted to catalog preparation.

Enterprise Network-Data Interconnectivity Family Working Group (ENDIF)

Although formally a part of the IUW, this group has worked to provide interoperability between ISDN LAN bridging and routing equipment. ENDIF has adopted methods agreed upon by the IETF and is experimentally implementing them to test for interoperability. At the June 1994 NIUF meeting, seven major vendors demonstrated interoperability using the *point-to-point (PPP)* protocol for bridging and routing. Future work will focus on test results for using multilink methods (simultaneously using more than one B channel for higher bandwidth) and compression methods (getting more effective throughput from ISDN connections).

Profile Teams

Even after the expert (technical) working groups write the necessary implementation agreements, they must be grouped together to speak to end-user application requirements. The profile teams start with the end-user application requirement statement and determine which implementation agreements are needed. Since these implementation agreements often concern a layer of protocol, the combination of the agreements results in a *protocol stack* of standards and related implementation agreements.

But the profiles are more than simply a stack of protocols. Typically, in addition to pointing to protocols, a profile describes possible architectures of equipment and services that meet the stated requirements. The profile cites conformance criteria as appropriate. To provide guidance to the user, the profile restates the application and describes and charts processes. To provide linkage to the standards process, diagram logic used by standards bodies is used to describe processes.

Call-Management Profile Team

This team works on a family of applications that manage calls—typically incoming calls, and usually via the *calling line identification (CLID)* information element. Imagine calling your insurance agent, who then pulls up your policy information on a screen by the phone. Your agent can then talk to you knowledgeably because the details of your policy are displayed on the screen. This is the type of call management application profiled by this group.

Messaging-and-Answering Profile Team

Sometimes when we introduce new technology we tend to overlook the basics. This profile team works to assure that our ISDN telephones will provide basic capabilities. Even with ISDN, we will still want phone coverage, message retrieval capabilities, and all of the normal capabilities that we enjoy today with our existing telephone systems.

Beyond the basics, this group also examines issues such as unifying messaging and answering. Most of us have used voice mail and electronic mail; many people even use multiple electronic and voice-mail services. Wouldn't it be handier if there was a common way to obtain messages from all of the messaging sources at one time? For example, wouldn't it save time if you could get voice messages from the terminal you use for e-mail, or if you could pick up e-mail messages on the phone you use to retrieve voice messages? Some progress is being made in unifying messages for end users.

Multimedia Profile Team

Most of us dream of the time when we will be able to electronically meet with others. While there will always be times when the advantages of being physically present will make that the preferred meeting style, electronic meetings will allow many of us to participate more regularly at meetings within our industries. This group focuses on multimedia issues with an eye toward taking full advantage of a ubiquitously available ISDN to bring this capability to everyone's conference room, desktop, and home.

CPE Capabilities and Compatibilities Profile Team

This group works on end-user equipment requirements. It's important that the ISDN CPE, or end-user equipment, provides the capabilities that end users want. For example, one requirement is that developers integrate workstations and telephones so end users can converse with others while viewing the screen or entering information from a keyboard.

9.2   OTHER USER GROUPS

Perhaps inspired by the NIUF or perhaps because the time is ripe, other user groups have formed to focus on ISDN and related communications infrastructures.

California ISDN Users' Group

Officially coordinating with the NIUF, the *California ISDN Users' Group (CIUG)* involves users in California. Because most of the NIUF meetings are held in Gaithersburg, Maryland, the California users are spared the expense and time of attending these East Coast meetings by having a local group.

The California group focuses more on practical and market aspects of ISDN that are outside the scope of NIUF activities. Often the group invites vendors to speak about their specific products so users can learn what is available and how they can use different pieces in combination to achieve a desired result. The CIUG even approaches regulatory bodies in California to promote ISDN availability.

Mid-Atlantic ISDN Users' Group

Originally begun as the Bell Atlantic ISDN Users' Group, the group consists of ISDN users from New Jersey, Pennsylvania, Maryland, Virginia, the District of Columbia, Delaware, and West Virginia. It is a fairly small group of end users who already have ISDN and want to share ideas and concerns with each other. While members are willing to contribute to helping potential ISDN users in forums such as the NIUF, the Mid-Atlantic ISDN Users' Group offers its members a smaller, more informal setting in which to learn how to better use ISDN and solve mutual and individual problems.

The group often meets at end-user locations to see first-hand how ISDN is used and to better understand how an application works in a particular environment. Various vendors and service providers demonstrate their capabilities and describe future plans so end users can improve their planning. Group members have traveled to the Johns Hopkins Medical Institute in Baltimore, Maryland; to West Virginia University in Morgantown, West Virginia; to the Bell Atlantic Tower in Philadelphia, Pennsylvania; and other locations throughout the region. In addition to conducting meetings at various end-user locations, the group also organized one meeting of tours of Bell Communications Research (Bellcore) and the AT&T Bell Laboratories, where attendees got a preview of various research efforts.

Washington-Area ISDN Users' Group

Started late in 1992, the *Washington-Area ISDN Users' Group (WAIUG)* provides a forum for Washington, D.C.-area ISDN users and potential users. By attracting users within a 30-mile radius of D.C., the group can offer more frequent, informal, and shorter meetings that typically last half a day. WAIUG also establishes a user base that can more readily provide mutual assistance, since logistical barriers are minimal.

The first WAIUG meeting in December 1992 consisted primarily of presentations. The C&P Telephone Company presented ISDN deployment and tariff plans; two D.C.-area end users discussed their experiences with using ISDN services and equipment; and a representative from the University of Maryland presented issues of telecommuting, for which ISDN seems well suited.

Subsequent meetings have ranged over a wide number of topics. In the fall of 1993, the WAIUG put on a presentation and discussion with three major IECs (AT&T, MCI, and Sprint) and the LEC (Bell Atlantic) addressing the issues of providing ISDN beyond the local area.

Various special-interest groups have formed to address specific interests and concerns. An applications subgroup has made presentations on several occasions to its membership on just how ISDN is used and justified in various representative organizations. The WAIUG encourages frank discussions of problems and issues to help newcomers avoid the pitfalls and understand the costs as well as the benefits of using ISDN.

European ISDN Users' Forum

About two years after the inception of the NIUF, the *European ISDN Users' Forum (EIUF)* was formed. In some ways, it is patterned after the NIUF. However, it deals with European needs and issues, which require cooperation from about a dozen different countries within the European Community (EC). The plan is to provide a common ISDN throughout Europe to create one big trading area. This is part of the larger plan to create a common European community, a process that is well under way.

The EIUF end users have requested that their service providers deliver an ISDN that interoperates with the national ISDN provided in North America. The service providers in Europe have agreed to provide a common ISDN within Europe (*Euro-ISDN*), and some have indicated a willingness to provide interworking from Europe to North America.

Asian-Pacific ISDN Users' Forum

As of January 1993, there has been discussion about forming an organization that might have this or a similar title. At the Pacific Telecommunications

Conference in 1993, various countries that border on the Pacific Ocean heard from NIUF and EIUF representatives. The interest and focus of the various Asian and Pacific telecommunications representatives was extensive. Some, such as the Japanese service providers, already have extensive deployments of ISDN. Others are only now planning for it. This is similar to the North American scenario, where some regions have large deployments of ISDN and others are still planning for it.

Once all the major areas of the world are represented by ISDN user groups, we can focus attention on making ISDN applications globally interoperable. Even though the CCITT standards were written with global interoperation in mind, many of the implementations don't interoperate. Interoperability issues become even greater among different countries and between different regions of the world. These problems stem from a combination of technical and political issues that are perhaps best addressed by end users who are willing to express their concerns and needs to the manufacturing stakeholders.

Other ISDN Users' Groups

There is no central user group responsible for planning or controlling these users' groups. Therefore, it's not possible to know with accuracy all the other user groups that might exist. It's likely that others exist or that new ones will emerge. Local groups will, no doubt, emerge to deal with issues that are indigenous to their areas, to provide local support, and to facilitate more frequent gatherings at lower expense. Sometimes user groups will form but have very short lives, so don't be surprised if you hear of one but can't find it.

9.3   OTHER RELATED USER GROUPS

Having seen users at the NIUF promote and guide ISDN technology, end users championing other technologies have tried to emulate the NIUF in forming their own groups to get their needs and requirements met. Each of these groups has its own style; while they seem to have been inspired by the NIUF, they are not necessarily patterned after it.

Frame-Relay Forum

This group focuses on the *frame-relay* technology. Although this service was first proposed as a bearer service for ISDN, it has since been first offered outside the context of ISDN. It now has its own forum. Many data-communications end users prefer frame-relay technology and feel they can obtain it much sooner than ISDN.

Although an independent group, its members have consulted with the NIUF for conformance testing methodologies and formed a working group within NIUF to develop PICS and ATSs.

ATM Forum

Asynchronous transfer mode (ATM), the fundamental architecture for *broadband ISDN (BISDN)*, is the technology focus of this forum. (In Chapter 14, this technology is discussed in some detail.) Prior to deployment of BISDN, this technology is being used for high-speed data communications. Informal discussions between NIUF members and ATM Forum founders and leaders have helped to establish this forum.

9.4 SUMMARY

The ISDN end users have found a powerful way of expressing their needs to stakeholders who have the ability to provide services and equipment that meet those needs. Fortunately, these industry stakeholders are not only able but willing to respond to these end users. Both users and implementors benefit from this arrangement.

The first ISDN user group was the NIUF. Others soon followed—to address a particular geography, a particular technology, or a particular emphasis. The success of TRIP '92 showed that the ISDN industry listens to and supports end users. Vendors and carriers spent millions of dollars to provide demonstrations and showcases of ISDN technology. TRIP '92 resulted in accelerated industry cooperation and activity as well as user understanding and acceptance of ISDN. That's a major accomplishment spurred by the ISDN end-user community.

9.5 IMPLICATIONS BEYOND ISDN

The NIUF and other similar groups have shown us new ways of solving new problems. Complex social, technical, political, governmental, and legal considerations are involved in creating and deploying the new technologies. Existing methods of providing technology infrastructure no longer apply. New paradigms, such as the one provided by the NIUFs, are needed to overcome barriers and help provide new infrastructures for these technologies. To date, user groups seem to be the best approach to doing that.

The table below identifies the characteristic work styles and attitudes of users and implementors that, in combination, have made the NIUF productive. This mix of perspectives is one of the keys to the NIUF's success and holds promise for user groups in other areas.

As the ISDN technology matures, the NIUF may not need to work solely on ISDN issues and applications. Accordingly, early in 1994 the organization chose to declare an expanded mission—to be a user-requirement focus group for the national information infrastructure efforts that have been publicized in the news media.

The success of ISDN user groups like the NIUF suggests that this user group model may be a successful way to develop infrastructures for other

End Users	Implementors
Focused on useful results (applications)	Focused on the process
More pragmatic	More purist, perfectionist
Less patient	More patient (longer time horizon)
Less willing to commit resources	More willing to commit resources
Want fewer meetings	Willing to have more meetings
Want entertainment at meetings (e.g., product demonstrations or even shows)	Willing to believe it will work without actually seeing it work
Enjoy interaction with implementors (providing input to get results)	See value in interaction with users (consider requests and suggestions)

new technologies—even major social programs such as health care. If such groups do proliferate, and if they follow the patterns already observed, they will be fairly effective. Absent a central hierarchy, the groups find it in their own best interest to coordinate with each other. This seems to be a description of bottom-up planning. Intuitively, most of us would prefer a top-down, structured approach. Yet the bottom-up method has worked well for the ISDN end users.

As a cofounder and longtime worker in the NIUF, I have found that working in the organization is professionally worthwhile and personally rewarding. It has also been very interesting to be forming an approach to making ISDN real, while at the same time being an organization that is a prototype for so many others. I find that the mix of users and implementors is beneficial.

Potential Uses for ISDN

There are more different views of how ISDN might be used than there are people to express them. This chapter is a personal view of how ISDN might be used in our information-age environment. It presents a brief review of the evolution of computing and telephony to provide a framework for understanding how ISDN might fit into evolving organizational structures and how ISDN might satisfy communications needs.

A recurring theme throughout this chapter is that organizational structures are losing their rigidity and so are communications requirements and applications. Offices without walls, or virtual offices, are becoming the norm for large enterprises. But this phenomenon need not be limited to large businesses; it can occur in small businesses, schools, health-care facilities, and in our homes. And ISDN can help groups, work teams, and individuals collaborate to achieve productive results in this new environment.

During the first few years of ISDN commercial availability, most applications were focused on voice telephony. Even in the ISDN era, we still want to speak with other people. Today, ISDN voice services are largely compatible with the older analog voice services. The most probable evolution of ISDN voice services is a direct extrapolation from the changes of recent decades.

Increasingly, data applications of ISDN are used and discussed. Popular opinion suggests the use of data applications will increase much faster than voice applications. Although that may be correct, data communications has evolved in a very discontinuous fashion, due mostly to the introduction of radically variant technologies. If data communications continues to evolve in discontinuous ways, its future will be more difficult to predict.

10.1 ISDN FOR DATA MOVEMENT

Information used by and moved between computers is usually thought of as data. But there are many different types of computers and applications supported by computer-based solutions. Traditionally, mainframe computers were the backbone of enterprise computing and, at first, were connected only to local terminals. Later, remote terminals were connected via communications channels. This evolution continues toward a more completely distributed set of computing platforms and terminals, deployed and connected wherever there is a need to move information.

Traditional Data Users

The earliest uses of computers were for mathematics computations supporting cryptography (code-breaking efforts) and for science research. But the first large-scale use of computers was for mainstream business applications such as managing the enterprise payroll system. This type of computing architecture became known as *mainframe computing*, which relied on large, centrally located computing machines. It started as computing only; users brought information to it via punched cards and computer tapes. Information was also extracted from these computers via cards and computer tapes and by printing data onto paper. A *computer console* (at first, an electromechanical *teleprinter*) was connected directly to the mainframe computer via an electrical cable. The computer console operator could key information into the computer via the keyboard and could receive information from the mainframe by reading what was printed on paper.

Printing output on paper at consoles gave way to displaying output on screens. These devices, known as *computer terminals*, were moved further and further away from the mainframe. To provide the electronic equivalent of an electrical extension cord, communications lines were used. A simplified configuration is shown in Figure 10.1.

The transmission pipes in Figure 10.1 are the *multipoint data communications lines* needed to connect the remote terminals to the main computer, or mainframe. Almost always, these multipoint lines are *leased lines* that stay permanently in place. Regardless of whether the end user needs to move information, these leased lines are always connected and ready for use. Typically, applications for these architectures are such that you can predict very accurately how much information you will need to move as well as when you will need to move it. After all, for every payroll run, the same people need the same checks.

Since most of the applications using these systems require high volumes of data traffic, leased lines provide an affordable way to communicate (as measured by cost per data bit moved or payroll check printed), even when the leased lines themselves are expensive. As these systems grew, they

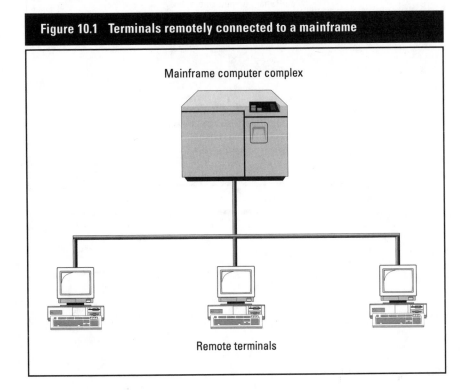

Figure 10.1   Terminals remotely connected to a mainframe

Mainframe computer complex

Remote terminals

became more complex but were still fundamentally centered around the mainframe and hierarchical in nature. (See Figure 10.2.)

Curiously, looking at the structure of the mainframe architecture diagram above, you can see a remarkable resemblance to the basic structure of the organization charts of the same era. A CEO or chairman of the board was typically at the top of most organization charts as a chief honcho (CH). (See Figure 10.3.) In real organizations, a number of assistants report to the CEO, generally with titles such as president, executive vice-president, vice-president, assistant vice-president, and so on. They are represented in Figure 10.3 as assistant chief honcho (ACH). This layering continues until you reach the lowest level in the organization—where the actual (tactical) work gets done. This is represented in Figure 10.3 by the grunt (G), who of course must be supervised

Figure 10.2   A more complex arrangement to connect many terminals to a mainframe to a mainframe.

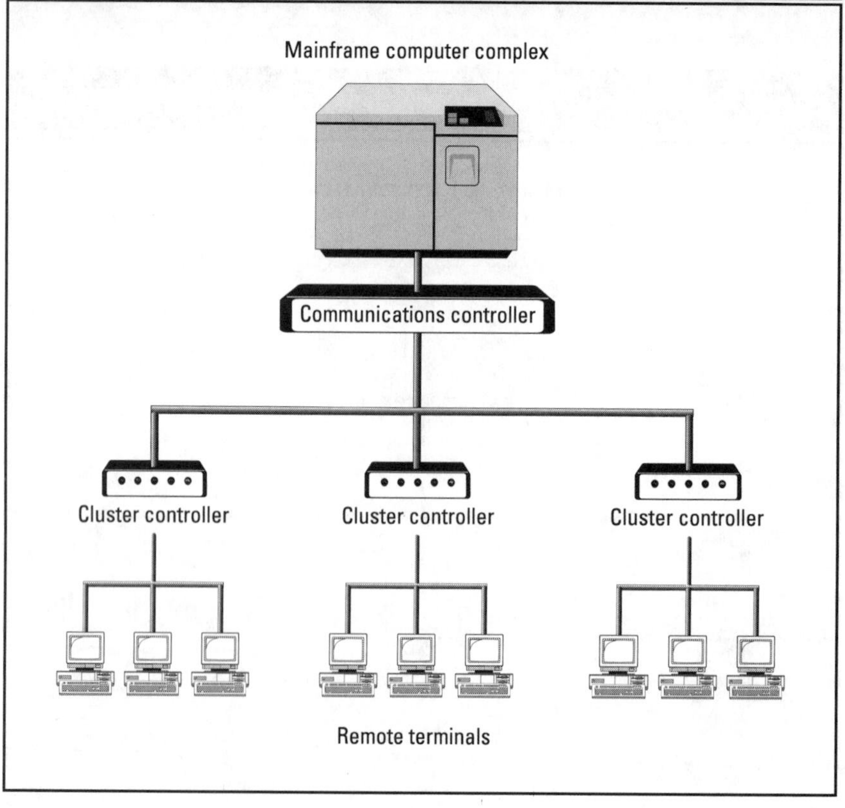

Mainframe computer complex

Communications controller

Cluster controller   Cluster controller   Cluster controller

Remote terminals

(S). Perhaps this hierarchical similarity of structures is not accidental—after all, the data network of its time was well suited to the organization of its time.

Both the organizational structure and the data-networking structure were hierarchical in nature and driven from the top. The chief honcho was the master of the organization, just as the mainframe computer was the master of the organization's data network. Implicit in the idea of being top-down driven is that the designer of the data-communications network has a great deal of knowledge about the information to be moved in the data network. A top-down network designer would typically know how much information needed to be transferred, to whom it was to be transferred, the urgency of the information, and all the other information attributes described in Chapter 3. Indeed, samples of actual data, such as payroll details, might even be available to the network designer. As these factors are predictable, data-network planners could select hardware, software, and communications technology, knowing it would be optimized for the upcoming tasks.

In those days, the tasks and needs of the grunts, and the terminals they used to perform their tasks, were well understood, predictable, and

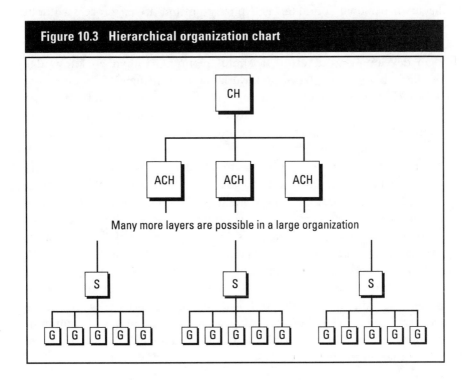

Figure 10.3   Hierarchical organization chart

CH

ACH   ACH   ACH

Many more layers are possible in a large organization

S   S   S

G G G G G   G G G G G   G G G G G

quantifiable. In a top-down organization, these work units followed directions and repetitively performed tasks. Generally, CHs and ACHs did not accept suggestions for changes in routines and work processes from the grunts; all the changes and ideas originated from the top. The situation was very orderly, predictable, and stable.

Postindustrial Information Users

Modern data-networking structures are driven as much from the bottom to the top as they are from the top to the bottom. This is particularly manifest in the *personal computer (PC)*. PCs were introduced into the corporate world during the mid 1980s. At that time, there were no connections between the various PC machines except via *sneakernet*—a pseudonetwork that involved moving data by physically transferring computer disks from one machine to another (wearing sneakers, of course, to allow you to move information faster).

Note that unlike the top-down model of the mainframe environment, the PC environment, in which every individual independently uses his or her own personal computer, is a purely bottom-driven process without overall organizational structure, guidance, or constraints. This environment evolved on an ad hoc basis to meet actual needs as they materialized rather than developing as a result of careful planning. Individual knowledge workers obtained a degree of empowerment in using their PCs but were not able to easily obtain information from others in the organization. Although corporate-culture vendors were advocating personal empowerment, responsibility, and accountability, they probably never intended to encourage Lone Ranger behavior.

The next step in the evolution was to connect locally adjacent computers and printers to share information and resources such as printers. After all (the thinking went), think of how much money the corporation could save if it didn't need to purchase a separate printer for every end user! Partly as a by-product of sharing equipment resources, people gained the major benefit: sharing information among adjacent end users. The *local area network (LAN)* was perhaps the most popular way to connect workgroups of geographically adjacent users' *workstations* (i.e., personal computers, computers, or similar but more powerful equipment that is used by knowledge workers). But data sharing still had an ad-hoc quality to it, and communicating with others in the organization continued to be difficult if they were not connected to the same LAN.

Soon, *teamwork* was increasingly emphasized in postindustrial corporate behavior and indirectly emphasized in organizational structure. Teamwork, in this sense, means working with others to achieve a shared vision. But implementing teamwork inevitably has a profound effect on corporate structure. In such an environment, each individual knowledge worker in the organization is simultaneously on a number of different *workteams* (or *matrixed-managed workgroups*). Participation on each of these workteams is often outside the reporting structure of the classical organizational chart. For example, a technology planner may be a member of a product team (or two), a member of a management team for *research and development (R&D)* projects and resources, a member of the standards team for a particular technology, a member of a corporate quality-improvement team, and perhaps others, too. Participating on as many as five or more workteams has become typical for many of today's knowledge workers.

Communications techniques and technologies are emerging to support this relatively new organizational development. Just as individual knowledge workers must cross lines of organization, so must individual information be shared across the islands of communications (often LANs for each workgroup) throughout the organization. *Wide area network (WAN)* technologies have entered the picture to connect together LANs. And since many knowledge workers now participate on workteams that involve many different organizations throughout industry and government, an even newer requirement has arisen to connect LANs of different organizations.

While the need for connectivity seems apparent, obtaining it can be confusing and difficult. Individual LAN technologies can be complex, and combinations of fundamentally different technology solutions supplied by many different manufacturers pose even greater complexities. In the same way that individual workers once selected their own PCs to meet their needs, each individual workgroup now typically selects its LAN technology independent of any other workgroup to meet its own particular needs. Attempts to connect these very different LANs have often run into compatibility problems.

As the structure of communications begins to mirror the structure of organizations, just as it did in the past, there is a strong resemblance between the organizational structure shown in Figure 10.4 and the communications structure shown in Figure 10.5. Although Figure 10.4 is labeled as an organizational structure, it could just as easily be a data-communications layout if

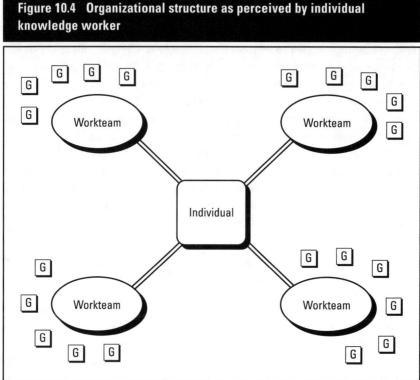

Figure 10.4   Organizational structure as perceived by individual knowledge worker

you simply relabel some pieces showing each collocated group of workers with access to a LAN. Just as there are workteams or virtual workgroups in the postindustrial organization, so too is there communications connectivity from any one worker to other workteam members via some *virtual network* within the corporate network. Typically, this connectivity is not provided via separate, dedicated LAN facilities to provide communications capabilities for each separate workteam because the needs change so rapidly.

Unlike the top-down situations described earlier, the postindustrial knowledge worker often has to perform ad-hoc work, focused on a particular goal, that may bear little relation to what was done yesterday or will be done tomorrow. More difficult still, there is frequently little or no notice of such changing work goals. And such knowledge workers are more likely to need or want sophisticated, nontraditional modes of communications such as images, video, or even *multimedia* (combinations of modes providing simultaneous information to more than one of the senses).

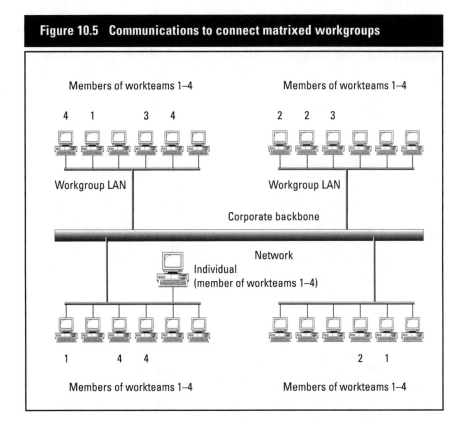

Figure 10.5   Communications to connect matrixed workgroups

Because the nature of workteams can change overnight, dedicated communications networks specifically tailored to a workteam aren't feasible. Further, the volume of information needed by the knowledge worker is variable. Although sometimes large quantities of data are needed, at other times much less data is needed. Consequently, even if a dedicated solution could somehow be correctly estimated and placed, the varying volumes of data moving between knowledge workers would often make such a network unnecessarily expensive. These requirements seem to suggest the need for a communications network that is available to everyone and from everyone (since we can't know in advance the makeup of workteams that will be needed) with a robust capability to carry volumes ranging from low to high (since we can't know how much volume will be required by workteams before they materialize).

By now, it should become obvious that we need ISDN. It allows you to quickly establish connections when you need them, and it can economically carry large or small amounts of data. ISDN allows individual workers to speak to others, to remotely access a LAN, and to transmit images and even video to other members of a workteam. And because it is on the verge of being deployed as widely as telephones are today, it will be available to knowledge workers just about anywhere they happen to be when they need access to the workteam.

10.2 VIDEO APPLICATIONS

For years, especially while sitting in airports or enduring long air flights, we have dreamed of meeting and working with others electronically to avoid the expense, inconvenience, and, most of all, the time it takes to travel. Beginning in the late 1970s, a select few were able to meet via videoconferencing from a special conference center, usually located in the nearest large city. Later, in the 1980s, many were able to use such a video-conference center right in their own office building.

But if this capability is to become truly integrated, we need to be able to use it right from our desktops. At least several manufacturers are currently working on an affordable PC-based video-conferencing capability. Early implementations show great promise—and they work over a basic rate ISDN service. Some use the entire 128 Kbps for video, with the voice mixed in as a composite signal. Others use one B channel for voice and the other B channel for video. Because of the impending ubiquity and affordability of ISDN basic rate service, it seems that videoconferencing from our desktops is finally within our grasp.

These systems consist of a very small external video camera that produce the image and a card that inserts into the PC to trigger the signal processing—both for receiving and transmitting. The modern PC already has adequate capacity to render images and motion, and sound can be rendered by using the appropriate sound cards or an associated telephone.

In one instance, you may decide to meet with a colleague who is geographically distant from you, and your work patterns might be very similar to the way you interact when you are in another person's presence. In other cases, you may decide to "attend" a convention or larger meeting, but keep half an eye on the proceedings while doing your main job. You would likely size the video window to small and stick it in a corner of the screen. As you work, you can hear the meeting progress and occasionally check the activities. While you are working, if your interest is aroused and you want to listen more intently, you may want to resize the video screen to full. You might choose to participate in this segment of the meeting by making suggestions or questioning speakers. As the meeting moves on to matters of less interest to you, you can resize the window to a small corner of your screen.

10.3 TRADITIONAL VOICE TELEPHONE USERS

Going back in history, end users of telephones once demanded that the operator connect them to the desired party. Later, people began to dial their calls for local destinations, then for anywhere in the world. At one time, incoming calls in business offices were answered by an attendant who would screen the calls. Later, machines were introduced to route incoming and outgoing calls.

Incoming-Call Management: Large Volumes

Traditionally, large volumes of incoming calls to a central source were managed with the help of technology labeled *automatic call distributors (ACDs)*. An ACD will route each incoming call to the next available agent. You encounter them when you make a reservation at a hotel or ticket center or when you call a "help desk" concerning a product you purchased. You have undoubtedly encountered the *queueing* feature of these ACDs when you have been instructed to wait for the next available agent.

ISDN capabilities work well for ACD services in obtaining calling statistics, routing calls to the next available agent, and other functions that are essential to managing large volumes of incoming traffic. Pre-ISDN ACD services required separately provided data channels and different arrangements for different ACDs. The standard features of ISDN allow simpler installation as well as geographical dispersion of the ACD equipment and software.

Incoming-Call Management: Office Environment

Traditionally, office environments have provided call coverage for incoming calls with *key equipment*. These phones have buttons that are keyed to the various telephone numbers within an office. You may have used a telephone with buttons that were used, for example, for picking up a call on line 2 or putting a call on hold. In its original form, the six-button key set had a row of illuminated buttons along the bottom, with the leftmost red button used for placing a call on hold and the other five buttons for selecting one of the incoming lines. Over the years, monstrously large versions of these telephone sets emerged; the newer ones have small *light-emitting diodes (LEDs)* that provide a pinpoint of light, often color coded, to indicate whether a particular line is ringing, busy, or on hold.

Often, the early key equipment was hidden out of sight in a *wire closet.* This enclosed area was used for making various connections in addition to housing and powering the equipment that provided key features on individual telephone sets. End users had to provide an environmentally suitable location for this equipment and, directly or indirectly, pay to acquire, install, and maintain it.

ISDN versions of the key telephone set eliminate the need for special equipment in the office and the office wire closet. The functions of call appearances, hold, and so on can be performed within the ISDN network; messages are sent from the network to the ISDN telephone to illuminate a button or even to display characters. In addition to eliminating extra equipment and bulky wiring in the office, the ISDN versions of the key telephone service often cost the end user less than the pre-ISDN versions.

10.4 CHANGING WORK STYLES THROUGH ISDN

In addition to allowing workteams to focus on common goals, ISDN connectivity allows geographical dispersion of teams. A workteam member can choose to attend a meeting either electronically or physically. What was once a single decision (to attend or not attend the meeting) becomes two separate decisions — whether to attend the meeting and where to be at the time of the meeting. In a broader sense, we may be able to apply these choices to where we work and where we live. Such an expansion of choice can add to the quality of life and add to the availability of time in a society that places great emphasis on both.

Increasingly, we read articles and stories about *telecommuting,* which usually emphasize that the individual worker can avoid the time, expense, and unpleasantness of commuting yet remain in touch with his or her workplace. In an ISDN environment, workers can be connected to others on their workteams almost as effectively as if they were in a well-connected work environment. Often, being able to send electronic mail and files to others on a workteam is all that is needed.

Ideally, an electronic group meeting would allow each worker to see and hear the meeting details. Audioconferencing was common in pre-ISDN electronic meetings, but seeing the meeting is a new concept. A video of the meeting moderator or the person currently speaking simulates the real meeting. Another goal is to provide a shared (viewgraph or slide) image capability so that each attendee at an electronic meeting can follow along as a person presents or discusses a point. Also, each attendee will want to be able to ask questions and raise issues.

For working meetings, a shared whiteboard capability might be a better approach as teams need to work collaboratively. With a whiteboard, each attendee at the working meeting would be able to enter text, drawings, images, or markings, and all attendees would be able to see the sum of the entries. Group ideas and directions could be captured to define a problem, gain consensus, and assign pieces of tasks for review at the next electronic group meeting.

Using ISDN to attend meetings and work collaboratively is not limited to telecommuting. Most of us work with others who are not conveniently close to our office. Perhaps one of the people you need on your team is located in a branch office in a different city. Maybe another team member is currently traveling, but can be available on the day and time of the meeting. Increasingly, workteams within industries require meetings and cooperative work from people in different organizations.

Perhaps the term *virtual office* is a more accurate way of characterizing this separation of physical presence from meeting attendance or collaborative work efforts. As long as you have computer equipment and can access your workteam via ISDN, you can create a virtual office wherever you are. It's appealing to think of being able to join a wide variety of workteams during the course of the day. If travel were required to each one—whether a few steps, a short drive, or an airline flight—the time and financial investment would diminish considerably.

It's also appealing to think that we might be reaching a point where we can express more freedom of choice about where we want to live and work. Our personal lives can now influence this choice. We can consider being with our families more (e.g., children, elderly parents, sick or invalid relatives), or choose to live in the mountains, at the seashore, or in a small community. Various ISDN possibilities and opportunities offer the potential to increase the quality of our lives while actually increasing the quality of our work efforts, too.

10.5 PROVIDING HEALTH CARE WITH ISDN

Whenever we think of moving information in the health care field, we think of transporting images for health diagnostics. It's easy to imagine a radiologist at home who receives an urgent call from the hospital to come in and examine an image and make treatment recommendations. ISDN can help radiologists work more conveniently—perhaps not even having to drive to the hospital for an emergency when they need to review images.

ISDN can transport images across the country or around the world almost as readily as across town. With ISDN, medical consults and second opinions would be readily available as images that could be sent very quickly to others for review. Perhaps more experts could review difficult or intriguing cases because access to the source images would be much greater. Images obtained over time could be stored and accessed by various health care experts who could review progress and change by reviewing a series of images and other information.

But case history review need not be limited to images. Some physicians already provide direct patient care via interactive video contact with patients. Patient gestures and conditions such as skin color can be key indicators in diagnosis and treatment. In health care, often a variety of health care providers are involved in treating a single patient. Each of these providers needs information on patient history and needs to be able to add to it. Taken together, this information can provide much greater insight than any one piece of information. A "holistic" health-care approach would mean having access to radiology images, EKGs, clinical data such as blood-work (pressure, cholesterol content, and so on), history of drug treatments and reactions, psychiatric assessments, and just about any other aspect of health care you can imagine. Having a more complete profile of a person's health would enable medical professionals to make better decisions concerning health care.

Considering the trend toward managed health care, managing records and providing appropriate access to them becomes increasingly necessary. Scheduling the use of health care resources is an effective and efficient way to maximize health service from physicians. Care could also be sequenced to provide more effective results. Vague complaints and difficult diagnoses could be considered from a number of different angles to avoid unnecessary tests and ensure that tests that are performed are effectively used.

Even in filing medical claims, ISDN can provide efficient, cost-effective solutions. Not only can text be transmitted quickly, but images can be transmitted much more quickly than on pre-ISDN circuits. Attaching images to medical claims can clarify issues for insurance carriers, avoiding follow-up calls to physicians.

As ISDN is used more frequently in providing health care, other applications will doubtless emerge. As in other endeavors in the post-industrial age, moving information is becoming more of a requirement in the health care field.

10.6   DELIVERING EDUCATION WITH ISDN

When parents review their children's educational environment, perhaps at "Back to School" night, one striking observation is how little things have changed. The academic subjects and techniques for delivering those subjects haven't changed much, either. It is readily apparent that school systems are very labor intensive and that the constantly increasing cost of education threatens to make it unavailable to some students. Unlike manufacturing or farming, where mechanization and labor-saving techniques have helped moderate or even lower unit prices, the proportion of income spent on education has constantly increased and, if not checked, will prevent many from obtaining an education. We don't yet have the educational equivalent of the manufacturing assembly line that provides affordable, high-quality products.

From a labor-saving perspective, computer-based instruction seems to offer the possibility of providing some relief. For some portion of the more routine parts of education and training, a computer delivery system may be appropriate. However, even if we deliver language and arithmetic drills via computer, we still need to learn how to integrate the skills of the teacher to deliver high-quality education.

In some geographic locations, particularly where student populations are relatively small, the scope of course offerings is constrained. Only one or two foreign languages may be offered. Advanced math or science courses may not be offered at all. Such schools find it impossible to fund courses outside the mainstream requirements. But by pooling resources and funds from a number of such schools, there is often a way to meet demand for additional foreign languages or advanced technical courses.

Using ISDN to allow a teacher to conduct lessons for students at several different schools could be part of the answer to economically meeting the need. Similarly, providing students with ISDN access to media or library resources at different schools would stretch specialized resources across a larger geographic area.

In addition to efforts at economy, new and more effective ways of teaching students are beginning to emerge. For example, using interactive video with ISDN access can facilitate teaching English as a second language. Because each student is effectively isolated from the rest of the class, he or she is forced to rely on the language to communicate effectively. In contrast, when physically grouped-together messages can be sent with a shrug, grin or a groan, spontaneous native language exchanges are also likely. Properly used, the technology may actually enhance the teacher's ability to guide the student.

Earlier in this chapter, the ideas of teamwork and workteams were introduced, with the observation that workteams could work together electronically over ISDN to achieve their ad-hoc goals. Since one of the results we'd like to see in education is preparation for the world of work, it seems logical to emulate the work pattern described earlier in our schools. Assigning tasks to groups of students and allowing them to work together electronically over ISDN to perform these tasks will develop skills these students will need later in life.

Other electronic applications seem worthwhile, too. Instead of spending an entire evening traveling to, attending, and departing a PTA meeting, a parent could join a meeting electronically from home, investing perhaps 1 hour or less of time that is directly useful. Instead of a once-a-year "Back to School" night during which a parent spends 10 minutes or less in each classroom, the school could electronically convene such an event four or more times per year so parents could be more proactive. A teacher, speaking electronically to all of the class parents as an electronic group, might ask for volunteers who are experts in a particular discipline to help prepare a special presentation or provide a field trip experience. Parents could readily converse among themselves to iron out any groupwide concerns.

Electronically tutoring students for some tasks and activities could be more effective and certainly more efficient than what we presently offer. One tutor could monitor the independent work of many different students. While one group of students is working, individual students could ask the tutor for assistance. A short burst of attention, including helpful hints and suggestions, might be enough to redirect a student who encounters a road-block. If each student is using a computer to do his or her supervised tasks, ISDN connectivity could allow the tutor to periodically monitor each student and proactively intervene with helpful hints and suggestions. Since each student would spend the majority of the time thinking through and performing tasks, the tutor's time would be effectively shared across the group.

Using computers and connecting them into electronic groups is still relatively new. Although we have only begun to experiment with combinations and applications of these technologies, we have already seen some successes. It seems likely that ISDN connectivity will play some part in lifelong learning in the information age.

10.7   SUMMARY

We have discussed various techniques and trends for moving information in organizations (illustrated from three different perspectives in Figure 10.6). Although earlier techniques such as voice communication and fixed main-frame data applications are not our current focus, they have not disappeared

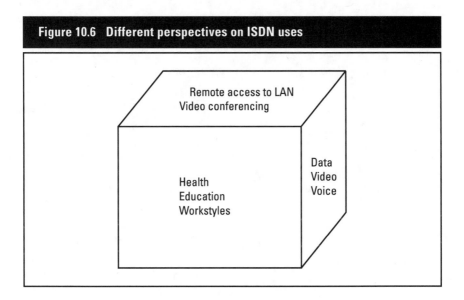

Figure 10.6   Different perspectives on ISDN uses

Remote access to LAN
Video conferencing

Health
Education
Workstyles

Data
Video
Voice

and perhaps never will. Rather, newer techniques, such as distributed computing, have been layered onto these earlier techniques.

ISDN technology is appropriate for many areas where information movement is required, enabling public access to information at relatively high speed, accuracy, and reasonable cost. When more bits are needed within a fixed time frame (such as in videoconferencing), higher bandwidths are available. ISDN technology is arguably the first affordable digital technology — available to virtually all of us — that has the capability to deliver in a multimedia environment. It could well be considered the on ramp to the digital information highway.

Providing ISDN

For ISDN to become a reality, it must be deployed and offered as a service by the network providers. For ISDN to be truly useful, its deployment must be widespread. In the previous chapter, we observed that data communications in the postindustrial world often requires ad-hoc responsiveness without much prior notice. Although most of us accept quick turnaround for voice communications, we are used to scheduling or planning our data requirements. But in the information age, users need to be able to send and receive data to each other on short notice.

This chapter provides an overview of what is involved in providing ISDN service. It's not simply a matter of the user buying pieces and getting ISDN services. Developers must resolve overall ISDN design issues before producers can provide the pieces. Once the pieces are available, we must resolve issues of interoperability and general network management. ISDN also requires a *lot* of capital. And there are lengthy legal, political, and regulatory considerations that impinge on ISDN implementation.

We will only skim the surface of these issues in this chapter. The numerous considerations make providing ISDN more like steering a boat than a sports car—with analagous response times. And the increasing complexities of other emerging technologies make providing ISDN an even more challenging task.

11.1   CREATING ISDN

From the beginning, ISDN was conceived as a standard set of broadly available services. Accordingly, the concepts were conceived, discussed, and documented in standards bodies—mostly the CCITT—before any deployment occurred. Providing this type of capability, instead of analog technology, promised more value to end users at reasonable costs to telephone companies.

However, for an evolution that seemed so logical and inevitable, getting from the analog networks of the early 1980s to the ISDN networks of the mid 1990s has been a longer and bumpier ride than expected.

Designing a Network

To provide an ISDN network, the various pieces must be identified, conceptually assembled into a complete construct, purchased, and deployed. Managing the ISDN network requires in-place methods, procedures, and computer-based management systems that are often different from pre-ISDN equivalents. First, only digital facilities and switches are acceptable to make ISDN digital from end to end. Transmission systems, SS7, and digital switches must be installed to carry ISDN service messages from end users to the network and application information between end users.

Today, many of the switches in existing telephone networks have not been upgraded from analog to digital. Even among the more progressive companies, it was only recently (about 1990) that these companies deployed digital switches in amounts equal to previously installed analog switches. Considering that there are probably over 10,000 switches in the United States, ubiquitous deployment of ISDN still requires a substantial commitment of time and money.

Obtaining digital switches to provide interoperable ISDN takes even more than time and money. Early ISDN switches were highly proprietary in nature. For example, an ISDN telephone that worked properly with a switch from vendor A would not work with a switch from vendor B. Further, within the network, the vendor A switch would not interoperate with the vendor B switch. The design question became: How can we make equipment for telephone companies that can become part of a whole network and that will work together to provide ISDN services? Even though these early switches were designed based on standards, they were not consistently produced by all manufacturers. National ISDN, announced in 1991, provided sufficient assurance of a unified effort to launch major switch-deployment programs.

Connectivity between digital switches requires that SS7 transport message-based signaling information throughout the ISDN network (and from network to network). Without SS7, each local ISDN switching office is an island without any messaging connectivity to other parts of the network. SS7 networks are new, and constructing them is complex. Only recently have designers achieved sufficient experience to appreciate the operational difficulties.

Even transmission facilities, largely digital since the 1960s, need to be upgraded or replaced for ISDN. The international and national standards specified 64 Kbps *clear-channel capability (CCC)*, which is different from the 56 Kbps systems used in the United States prior to SS7. These earlier digital facilities used some of the 64 Kbps transport capacity for signaling via a method known as "bit robbing." Periodically, some of the bits were "robbed" from the talking path for signaling purposes. These robbed bits were sufficient to provide the limited signaling capabilities required for pre-ISDN networks. The remaining bits (56 Kbps) were entirely adequate for voice calls; in fact, people couldn't detect a difference between bit-robbed and full bitstream. For data services, a bit-robbed signal still provided a sufficient 56 Kbps of data throughput. ISDN standards call for 64 Kbps for each B channel, but many existing transmission systems are not capable of going any higher than 56 Kbps. Fortunately, many recent transmission facilities were deployed in anticipation of ISDN requirements and can be reconfigured to operate at 64 Kbps.

Making It Work: Overcoming the Barriers

At one time, telephone equipment was centrally designed and planned to work together as a whole. Planning a network was (even then) a complex combination of considerations, but actually making the network work was fairly straightforward (though technically complex). The operational end of things is no longer straightforward. In addition to inherent technical complexities, there are competitive tensions that make it more difficult to directly address and solve the technical issues. Because ISDN is the first pervasive service offering since the breakup of the Bell System, the industry members have been challenged to cooperate to provide standards for the infrastructure at the same time they compete against each other for business. Progress has been made in achieving this balance between cooperation and competition, but success is incomplete and certainly has not been swift.

Making Network Equipment Interoperable

As mentioned above, one barrier to making ISDN work has been that each switch vendor offers products that can't be readily integrated into a whole network to provide an interoperable, consistent ISDN. Even if telephone companies buy all their equipment from one manufacturer, there are difficulties with using switches of different vintages. For example, services that operate in one way using a particular vintage of vendor A's switching equipment often operate somewhat differently on a later vintage of vendor A's switching equipment. End users can't obtain consistent services under these conditions.

Of course, switch vendors have their problems, too. One of the classic ways to maintain a desirable profit margin for products in a competitive market is to make the product unique so it cannot be replaced by a product from another manufacturer. This *product differentiation* strategy is often in direct opposition to the idea of an interoperable network, and it has proved to be a major stumbling block and slowing factor in the deployment of ISDN. Further, the m*odified final judgment (MFJ)* consent-decree prohibition against manufacture (resulting from the breakup of the Bell System) prevents telephone companies from designing or making compatible switches or even designing interworking units to promote interoperability between dissimilar equipment. Since there aren't many manufacturers who provide ISDN network switches, obtaining market share is crucial. Manufacturers who develop their own differentiated products may see it as a survival strategy in a competitive marketplace. Complying with a generic and interoperable requirement from the ISDN network providers may seem secondary in comparison. Needless to say, an incredible number of meetings over a period of almost a decade have helped to narrow the gap between noncompliance and compliance with generic requirements. Even now, different switching products make it challenging for ISDN service providers to operate an ISDN network and for end users to select terminal equipment to work with the network.

To the extent that vendors were willing to provide a generic, interoperable product, the ISDN standards weren't sufficiently complete to guide their efforts; clarifying implementation agreements and conformance tests have only recently emerged. As described in Chapter 8, these "poststandards" processes were being defined in the late 1980s and weren't available for use in planning ISDN. The standards development process is still not complete and perhaps never will be complete in the sense that every possible detail is completely specified.

Numbering Plans

Although weaknesses and failures in interoperable switching equipment and end-user terminal equipment were probably the major obstacles to deploying ISDN, another impediment was the numbering plan. Worldwide, this is described in CCITT standard E.164 (and E.163); each end user has an ISDN telephone number. In the United States, numbering is based upon the *North American Numbering Plan* (*NANP*), which is applicable to all of North America. It's the numbering plan that we all know: area code, then seven digits for the telephone number—10 digits in all. After divestiture, the federal courts appointed Bellcore as the NANP administrator. Whenever a telephone company needs more numbers, such as when the population grows, Bellcore assigns a block of numbers to the telephone company.

Now that competing network organizations in the United States wish to provide local ISDN service to end users, the networks all want to obtain phone numbers. But telephone numbers, particularly area codes, are scarce because the existing switching machines that route calls based on numbers can handle only certain types and quantities of digits. If numbering plans are changed by adding types and quantities of digits different than what has already been planned worldwide, then telephone companies will incur massive new expenditures to provide even *plain old telephone service* (*POTS*). This creates a dilemma—finding a way to provide the extra numbers for U.S. competitors without raising costs and rates for basic telephone-service end users within and outside of the United States. To complicate things even further, U.S. area-code changes and additions affect other countries in North America, such as Canada and Mexico, since they are also part of the NANP. For that matter, Mexico and Canada were directly affected in 1984 when the U.S. government appointed Bellcore to be the NANP administrator.

Tariffs for ISDN

Federal and state governments impose tariff requirements on ISDN providers. Whenever a local telephone company wants to provide a service, the service must be approved by one or more regulatory bodies. Usually known as the *public service commission* (*PSC*) or the *public utilities commission* (*PUC*), this local regulatory body ensures that the public interest is served. In the days before competition, regulatory commissions were essential to ensure that the public could obtain reasonable telephone service from a telephone company without competitors. As the United States heads towards complete competition, we will need to rethink the regulatory process to better support the new competitive environment. Meanwhile, whenever a telephone company wants to offer a new service, the company must convince the PSC that this new service is in the public interest and that the charges for it also are fair. In protecting the public interest, regulators encourage new services where they see value for end users. Many PSCs actively support ISDN as being in the public interest.

When telephone companies file ISDN tariffs at the PSC, the members of the public and competing service providers are entitled to comment on and intervene against them. In more complex cases, the PSC holds public hearings to consider a phone company offering a new service such as ISDN. For more straightforward filings, the PSC holds a consideration period (as little as a month in some jurisdictions) during which the PSC may ask questions and accept comments or testimony. If no significant obstacles arise, the tariffs are approved and become *effective* (can be used as a price and availability schedule). If you include the time needed to prepare the information the PSC requires, a straightforward tariff filing can take a few months.

It's hard to imagine this tariff process continuing unchanged in a fully competitive market. Can you imagine a grocery store requesting permission to sell particular products and requesting authorization to charge particular prices months ahead of time? The challenge is to find a way to protect the public interest while at the same time promoting competition. Many organizations and individuals are proposing solutions, but it's difficult to separate the sound ideas from self-interest. Decisions made now and in the near future will affect your ability to obtain ISDN and will shape the terms and conditions under which it is available.

Each stakeholder sees the pricing of ISDN services differently. End users want low prices and high functionality. Shareholders of the telephone companies and competing ISDN service providers want high profit margins and earnings and continued growth of earnings. Regulators want to protect the public interest and be politically successful. Because most existing telephone users use POTS, some argue these basic users should get lower prices. Usually this is wrapped in statements like "we need basic telephone services for the poor (or retired) person who can't afford higher rates." While there is truth in this statement, the strategy also favors obsolete technologies at the expense of newer ones. Over the medium and long terms, this is a losing strategy, and it is a strategic error that more competitive countries usually do not make. Advocates of full competition claim the marketplace resolves these pricing issues better than regulators.

Tariffs for ISDN are structured to allow end users to order the services they want at prices they are willing to pay. The end user subscribes to ISDN services by selecting the desired tariff elements; these comprise the ISDN services the users want. Each piece of the service is described and priced. In some areas, ISDN service is provided at a fixed monthly cost or *flat rate,* whereas, in other areas it contains usage-sensitive elements (more à la carte). Arguments can be made for either one of these basic approaches, but ultimately it comes down to what end users and regulators will accept. In practical terms, it is difficult to arrive quickly at a structure that society will support. Since tariffs for local ISDN service are approved by different PSCs, end users must deal with a wide variety of structures, prices, and even names.

Many local telephone companies first released ISDN tariffs as additions to their Centrex tariffs. That meant that an end user had to first purchase Centrex services to purchase ISDN. Many small business and residential users who didn't want Centrex service were not pleased; as a result, additional tariffs were filed to provide ISDN to those subscribers who didn't want Centrex service along with their ISDN.

Another concern often heard from end users is that they don't like paying a per-minute usage fee for circuit-switched data calls, especially if they can obtain circuit-switched voice calls at prices that are not dependent on the duration of the call. Since end users perceive the two ISDN services as very similar, it's understandable why this is perceived as an inequity. This raises still another question—how do we equitably price ISDN and other telecommunications services? Should end users who only occasionally make short calls pay the same rates as end users who make frequent and long calls? This is the net effect of flat-rated service. Perhaps the most equitable pricing plan is to have a fixed monthly fee plus a *small* per-minute usage fee on all circuit-switched services—both voice and data, both ISDN and pre-ISDN. This combination approach seems to match the costs of production more closely to price. But, this is a very unpopular proposal with users who are used to a flat-fee plan; they fear their rates will rise. Regulators are very sensitive to user concerns and do not want to displease them by introducing usage-sensitive pricing for existing services. But what results instead are tariffs for ISDN circuit-switched data services, which end users perceive as inequitable when compared to circuit-switched voice services. Some observers believe these tariffs will lead to a whole new industry of equipment for sending "data" messages over circuit-switched voice-mode ISDN connections to avoid the per-minute usage charges. That's the danger of short-sighted regulation—dysfunctional economic consequences.

Operations Support

After network equipment is deployed, there are ongoing needs to provision, administer, maintain, and support ISDN services. Telephone companies must make sure the ISDN network continues to operate correctly and must be able to repair it when it doesn't perform properly. Telephone companies must process service requests so that satisfied end users use their ISDN services. To accomplish these and other administrative tasks, a vast array of network measurements and monitoring techniques are conducted within the telephone community. These processes are referred to collectively as *operations, administration, maintenance and provisioning (OAM&P)*. Using these systems, phone companies can track the usage and performance of millions of pieces of the network; isolate and repair faults; and send bills to tens of millions of customers. Obtaining, dispersing, and operating on the basis of this information requires significant data networks and computer centers. (This OAM&P network is used by the telephone company to service the ISDN network and POTS networks that provide service to end users.) Operating a telephone company is a complicated, large-scale task.

Before applying mechanized systems to manage a network, the management systems must be conceived and designed. A whole system of data architectures, computing architectures, and methods must be planned and integrated into the manufacture of network switches and other network equipment and designed into protocols as they are developed and standardized. After creating the construct, still more planning and deployment goes on to create a computing infrastructure to manage the network information.

Because of the digital nature of ISDN and its enhanced use of messages, the potential capabilities for ISDN operations-support systems appear to be much greater than for previous systems. This is partly because digital systems lend themselves to more complete performance monitoring without intrusion on services delivery. It is also due to the messaging nature of the network and the access loop. Queries, commands, and status can be sent to controlling locations. Even raw data (for example, retransmission histories) can be sent to control locations to indicate transmission quality.

In fact, the protocol for ISDN access was constructed to provide a great deal of information to the network as well as to the end user. Not surprisingly, the OAM&P for ISDN is not nearly as completely developed as the same functions for pre-ISDN services, which have been developing over the last 100 years. Deployment of these OAM&P systems is gradually beginning, with some network devices, but is far from complete.

For OAM&P, we have a mixed outlook. The potential for obtaining network information and control is much greater than with POTS. Ultimately, such systems will promote more reliability, smoother operation, and greater ease in ordering and obtaining ISDN. But today, it is not as mature a system nor as completely deployed. The ISDN support systems are catching up and will likely surpass the value of existing ones. This is one of the reasons for the claim we made in Chapter 4—over the long run the production costs for ISDN may well decline. But in the near term, while OAM&P systems are still being crafted and implemented, the costs will be high.

Obtaining Modernization Funds (Capital)

Extrapolating information from several annual reports, the largest 10 to 12 telephone companies have an average of approximately 30 billion dollars invested in their current networks. Each year, these companies typically invest about 8 percent—or almost $2.5 billion—of their assets in new telephone-plant assets. Simple arithmetic yields about a 12-year turn-over rate for equipment. Actually, turnover takes longer than that because growth accounts for some of the new spending (which adds to, but doesn't actually result in, *retiring* existing plant). Government regulation of accounting rules, most notably depreciation, also constrains the rate of modernization.

For those of us who have only a nodding acquaintance with accounting techniques, it works something like this. Suppose a telephone company buys a $10 million switching machine and deploys it in the network. Suppose further that the company expects it to last for 20 years (that is, it should provide telephone services that generate revenue for the company over the next 20 years). Rather than record that $10 million as an expense in year one, expenses should be charged over the entire useful (revenue-producing) life of the equipment (20 years) for a more acurate view of profit performance. Ignoring inflation and other complications and assuming an equal distribution of the capital costs over the useful life of the switch, $500,000 is thus diverted from each year's revenue stream and designated as *depreciation* (the fraction of the total capital expense attributable to the given year).

But suppose the switch doesn't produce revenue over the entire 20-year period? For example, if the switch only produces revenue for 10 years, the depreciation rate will have been too low. If that happens, rates for services can be kept below long-term sustainable levels during the useful life of the switch, which looks attractive to end users at first. But when it comes time to replace the switch, it will not be fully depreciated. Usually the switch must be replaced anyway, since the company must provide services to obtain revenue. Now, the new switch is depreciated over the years of its useful life, in addition to the remaining undepreciated amount for the old retired switch. Since there are now two depreciation "expenses" for the same revenue, profits are really depressed. So are the stockholders and employees. Inadequate depreciation rates cause newer services such as ISDN to be introduced much more slowly because expenses for old equipment continue to be incurred. Over a period of time, when depreciation rates are too low, everybody suffers.

What if the depreciation rates are too high? If that happens, rates for services can be kept above long-term sustainable levels, which at first looks attractive to telephone companies. The high depreciation rate provides a larger pool of capital to enable rapid deployment of new technology. When depreciation rates are too high, the new switch is fully depreciated even while it is still capable of generating revenue. Prices for services are higher than they otherwise need to be to run the business at a reasonable profit level. Ratepayers are paying more than if depreciation rates were lower.

It's difficult to arrive at the "best" depreciation rate. It needs to be high enough to allow timely modernization but not so high as to price services at artificially high levels. Paradoxically, sometimes increasing the depreciation level will actually lower telephone rates in the long run— *if* the money thus gained is used to provide productivity-producing improvements.

When telephone service was provided without competition, regulation of depreciation rates historically mitigated this possibility. Historically, telephone companies have had depreciation schedules of 20 or more years for switches. This means that if every switch is replaced every 20 years, ISDN would be available in 20 years if *every* replacement switch was made ISDN capable. Regulators have addressed the issue by allowing faster depreciation. Looking forward to a fully competitive environment, it appears that even more flexibility in and acceleration of depreciation will be needed to establish equity with the newly emerging telecommunications providers. In the future, full competition will be the brake that prevents any company from overcharging its end users.

11.2   PUBLIC OR PRIVATE FINANCING FOR THE ISDN NETWORK

In the United States, telephone infrastructure has been built using investment capital rather than tax dollars. Investors have purchased telephone company stocks and bonds to provide for their retirement needs, their children's college educations, and other future financial requirements. Historically, when telephone companies are financially strong and growth is high, capital is attracted to the industry. In such a climate, new communications services such as ISDN can be provided in a timely fashion. Looking at Figure 11.1, note that investors fund the telecommunications companies, which in turn provide products and services to end users. Revenue from these sales rewards the investors and the companies.

The costs of providing ISDN everywhere in the United States are huge. A rough estimate of total capital costs for all of the central offices in the country would be several hundreds of billions of dollars. Modernizing *all* the switches for ISDN (and replacing many of them) would cost a staggering amount of money. These are the kinds of numbers we are used to seeing only as figures in the budget of the federal government.

Historically, the costs to provide telephone service were borne by the investors (shareholders and bondholders) in the telephone companies. In exchange for such huge investments, the regulatory bodies reduced the

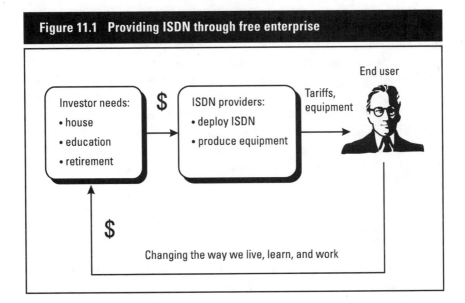

Figure 11.1   Providing ISDN through free enterprise

Investor needs:
• house
• education
• retirement

$

ISDN providers:
• deploy ISDN
• produce equipment

Tariffs, equipment

End user

$

Changing the way we live, learn, and work

risk of those investments by prohibiting direct competition within a franchise area. In return, the franchise holder assumed certain obligations to the public and accepted regulations so that monopoly profits could not be made. A popular misconception was that the industry was guaranteed profits. But even without direct competition, if end users were unhappy with the services provided, telephone companies could (and did) lose money on these services.

Currently, as we migrate from a regulated environment to competition, the trend is toward relaxing regulation of exisiting telephone companies and increasing permissiveness vis-à-vis new competitors. Existing phone companies often are constrained to offer services only with permission of regulatory bodies at terms and conditions that these regulatory bodies consider to be in the public interest. In the competitive extreme, competing companies offer whatever services they wish at almost any terms and conditions and do not even provide public notice. In this totally unregulated example, competing companies can charge some customers much higher rates than others. Regulators and legislators will almost certainly equalize conditions so that investors in either traditional or newly competing companies face similar risks and rewards. The table on page 227 provides a historical context for the successful implementation of ISDN under three regulatory environments.

As a society, we have a choice of financing the information infrastructure— and ISDN—either publicly (through taxes) or privately (through investment). There doesn't seem to be any moral basis for choosing one over the other. Rather, the choice is based upon which will be more effective. Telephone and power services traditionally have been funded with free-enterprise investments. Water, roads, and mail service traditionally have been funded by government taxes.

While the examples above illustrate that either method can be successful, the free-enterprise model seems more appropriate for future telecommunications companies to pave the information superhighway. In 1984, divestiture of the Bell system resulted in separate competing companies. The only reason for disaggregating the telephone system was to create a competitive environment and reap the rewards go along with competition. Only free-enterprise financing makes sense in a competive paradigm.

11.3 NATIONAL IMPERATIVES

The current administration, particularly Vice President Al Gore, has frequently and clearly championed the idea of a digital information highway,

Regulatory scheme	Full regulation	Full competition	Unequal regulation
Historical precedent	Bell System	Personal computer	Surface transportation
Cost structure	To best provide: • reliable service • universal service • basic research	To best provide: • innovation • new capabilities	Railroads: more regulation, higher taxes Trucks: less regulation, lower taxes, road costs subsidized by taxpayers
Business entry	Limited to telephone service and a single provider	Unlimited markets and entrants	Railroads forced to carry unprofitable passengers while trucks permitted to carry only profitable freight
Consumer prices	Regulated to be "reasonable"—prices similar throughout the country	"Invisible hand" of competition: "reasonable"—prices similar throughout the country	Prices in some areas much higher than in others
Results	Successful: • one very good provider • most (not all) consumers pleased	Successful: • many very good providers • most (not all) consumers pleased	Unsuccessful: • some railroads fail; assets acquired by government • some markets not served • fewer consumers pleased

or a *national information infrastructure* (*NII*). We often hear that just as the industrial age needed physical highways and transportation systems, we, in the information age, need the NII to be competitive with other countries, provide jobs for our citizens, and reach a higher standard of living. Although news coverage focuses mostly on the far future, to the time when these highways may be fiber based and very high bandwidth, perhaps ISDN is the next step in the evolutionary path. Like the on-ramp for the interstate highway, ISDN access will be the access path for most of us to the information highway.

Regulation

We need to decide what we want in terms of regulation. Do we want a competitive telecommunications environment? We seemed to want one in the early 1980s when we dismantled the Bell System. If competition is what we want, regulation should be structured to encourage it. Even in competitive markets, regulations apply to weights and measures, safety, and other matters of public welfare. However, in competitive markets, regulations typically do not *forbid* companies to enter markets for the reason of *promoting* competition. Rather, competitive forces themselves are supposed to guide the prices, products, and other terms and conditions that end users select.

It is logical to expect that regulations that govern who competes in what markets will be phased out so that all organizations are encouraged to fully compete. It is also reasonable to expect that regulations setting prices and other market-based terms and conditions will also be phased out so that market forces can control prices. Nevertheless, we can still expect to see regulations governing business ethics in order to assure honest trade and acceptable behavior.

National Goals

What sort of a telecommunications infrastructure do we want as a nation, and how do we obtain it? The shared vision is that we need a communications infrastructure appropriate to the postindustrial age. If we don't have one, we won't be globally competitive.

We as a nation need to decide on what we want and how we want to get there—public or private, competitive or regulated—then proceed toward achieving these network goals. Aiming at multiple goals along a variety of paths will only result in deployment of bits and pieces that don't add up to much.

If you are under 35, you probably don't have first-hand experience with obtaining services from a centralized, planned, and coordinated telephone-service provider like the Bell System. Although it worked well, we concluded a still better arrangement would be a fully competitive system. The emerging competitive companies claimed that for them to be successful in such a fully competitive market, they would need to be protected and to receive more favorable regulatory treatment than established companies. For more than 10 years, they have been protected. Now it seems time to migrate to full competition so users can get the additional benefits that were promised more than 10 years ago. Otherwise, we may as well restore a centrally planned telephone network.

11.4 SUMMARY

Providing a ubiquitous ISDN is complex. It requires a lot of systems planning, capital investment, and time. Under the best of circumstances, ISDN could not be provided in a few months or years. Still, it seems that ISDN is slowly proceeding and succeeding.

Collectively we need to know what we want in terms of competition, telecommunications financing, and telecommunications capabilities. In our current disaggregated environment, many individual organizations provide ISDN. Without a central planning process, however, it takes longer to provide ISDN; there is no guarantee that *any* telecommunications service will be deployed everywhere. Perhaps the very idea of providing national telecommunications is past history.

But it appears that the mood of the country is to create a more fully competitive environment and to use private capital to build the networks. Still not answered are questions of how we will make the services pervasive so all end users who want to can obtain ISDN services.

12

Implementing ISDN Applications

mplementing ISDN applications is best approached from the point of view of arranging for a complete solution that relies upon ISDN connectivity. Only after you understand what it is you are trying to accomplish and what equipment and services are required to meet your requirements can you order ISDN services with any confidence that you will actually benefit.

Fortunately, many hardworking people in the ISDN community have prepared an *Applications Catalog* that describes a large number of solutions. Each application is described, a typical set of equipment is listed, and the configuration of the equipment set is described. To connect the equipment, various ISDN services (both bearer and supplementary) are also suggested to implement the solution. Solutions in this catalog that speak to your needs will help you plan your equipment and ISDN selections for maximum benefit.

It is also useful to review descriptions and presentations of solutions that are actually installed, working, and providing end-user benefit. Such presentations are sometimes offered at ISDN user-group meetings, as articles in magazines, and in expositions at trade shows. For example, at inCITE '94 in Nashville, Tennessee, various ISDN solutions for distance learning were demonstrated and described by the end users who had been using them to teach. Interacting with such end users helps you clarify the important aspects of your solution.

At the end of this chapter, we provide two very brief examples of how end users were able to "obtain" ISDN services by obtaining assistance from others. In one case, the end user is not even aware of this, and in the other case, the end user is only vaguely aware of it. Many of us will begin using ISDN solutions provided by the same service organizations (often within our own enterprise) we rely on today.

12.1 VISUALIZING THE SOLUTION

An overall plan to achieve the benefits of information technology requires an understanding of what information you need and the various attributes of information as described in Chapter 3. Sometimes this analysis is so straightforward you will not need to document the information flows. But when it is desirable to document, you can select from tools ranging from simple flowcharting to structured information-flow diagrams. These diagrams allow you to visualize your solution in the same way that an architect visualizes a building by looking at sections, elevations, and plans.

Once the information requirements have been identified, you will want to have a view of the overall architecture of the solution, including the types of equipment you need and where you need them. At this point, you should be able to sketch the solution in at least as much detail as the sketches that appear in the *Applications Catalog*. As your plans progress, you will need to identify more precisely the interfaces between the pieces of equipment and between the equipment and the ISDN network.

You will also need to identify the various software elements required to achieve the solution. Some of it will be systems software (operating systems, communications programs, and so on). Other software elements will be at the applications level (such as word processors and database programs). Taken together with ISDN and other telecommunications services, a combination of computer software and hardware forms the basis for a useful information-technology system.

Next, identify all the ISDN services you need for the solution you have chosen. If voice-bearer services are needed for the solution, you will find a large number of supplementary services to enhance their capabilities. Perhaps circuit-switched data services are appropriate for your solution, and you also need the *incoming calling line identification (ICLID)* supplementary service for security. Or perhaps a packet-mode solution is best for you. A careful reading of the catalog will provide examples of solutions and a lot of insight into how to weave them into your plans.

At some point in this visualization process (but well before starting to implement it), you will probably want to seek advice. Generally, the more research you have done before seeking help, the better you can articulate your requirements and make use of the help you get.

If you are having trouble with the visualization process, you should study complete solution packages, as provided by a single vendor or group of vendors, to understand how the solution achieves the goal. Also review existing implementations used by other end users and described in the *Applications Catalog*. For those of you who choose to rely more completely on the guidance of a complete solutions provider (a specialist who provides all the "pieces" of a problem as a "total solution"), make sure your information requirements are well understood and that you have at least a general understanding of how the proposed architecture meets your information requirements.

12.2 IMPLEMENTING THE SOLUTION

Arranging to fulfill the visualization of your solution takes some detective work on your part. You first need to consult vendors of various equipment, or perhaps you can consult with an expert who will guide you through the selection process. Your selection of a software and hardware mix will be constrained, at least in some ways. Perhaps the software you need only runs on a particular platform (such as a DOS machine or an Apple computer). Or perhaps the existing architecture you want to access (such as a LAN) constrains your choices of hardware and software.

If you do not have the advice of an expert, identify one or more of the vendors listed in the catalog; many of them are capable of providing the guidance you will require. Since many of the useful ISDN solutions involve some sort of distributed computer arrangements and require successful interaction of products and services from a number of vendors, this systems integration phase can be complex and rigorous.

Ordering ISDN Services

Ordering ISDN services is probably easier than what went before, but it will require knowing what you want. The main difficulty you will have is communicating your generic ISDN requirements to a service provider. Because ISDN service is so flexible in its capabilities, the details of implementing it are complex and voluminous. Your general reading (including this book) is simply not sufficient to guide you in ordering service to support specific product names and groupings of products.

To simplify your (end-user) participation in this process, the NIUF and COS has produced a set of procedures and documents, known as the *order simplification process*, which describes groupings of interfaces and services. By the time you read this, this NIUF and COS work should be finished and supported by the ISDN service providers. Your equipment or software vendor will include instructions along with the product to instruct you on how to conveniently place your ISDN order. In general, vendors instruct you to order your service using specific ISDN ordering codes.

Some combinations of manufacturers and telephone companies have already cooperated to make it simple to order ISDN services that interoperate with end-user equipment. One of the earliest examples of this cooperative spirit is the instruction sheets included in Intel products. Right in the sheets is the instruction to order the "Intel Blue" configuration for ISDN. This seems to be a harbinger of the type of ISDN ordering code you will begin to find routinely packaged with ISDN products.

Powering Considerations

Using ISDN equipment requires power, just like operating a radio or a television set does. This is significant because it is different from what you have experienced with pre-ISDN telephone service. For simple telephone service, pre-ISDN service ordinarily supplies power to your telephone set over the telephone wires. During commercial power failures, you are still able to use your telephone because of the power delivered from the telephone network over the subscriber pair of wires through your telephone. This will not happen with ISDN. (If your pre-ISDN service involves switching equipment or other powered equipment, you are already familiar with the need to plan for power outages.)

In part, ISDN equipment is not powered from the telephone line because it consumes a great deal more power than pre-ISDN telephone sets, making network-delivered power unfeasible. Perhaps even more importantly to this power issue is the future trend toward using fiber cable for part or all of the subscriber loop. Although fiber is a fine medium for carrying high bandwidth (optical) signals, it is not capable of delivering electrical power to your equipment.

From a practical perspective, you must provide a commercial power source for normal operation and plan for what you will do during a commercial power failure. Exactly what you plan to do during power failures depends on your needs. If you are using a computer-based ISDN application and don't plan to provide power to it during power failures, you will not be able to use your computer. But not having ISDN connectivity when you can't use your computer anyway may not be a problem for you.

On the other hand, if you absolutely must be able to communicate during a power failure, you will need to provide power during that period of time (for example, by providing battery power to an ISDN phone or by providing some sort of *uninterruptible power supply (UPS)* for your computer-based ISDN solution). Again, the *Applications Catalog* contains information on suppliers of UPS equipment.

Wiring Considerations

Whatever your circumstances, you need to be aware of the possibility that you may need to focus on the wiring that runs inside your building. ISDN signals operate at much higher frequencies than pre-ISDN services, which makes their transmission somewhat trickier. Some existing wiring was not manufactured with the capacity to carry ISDN signals, and when it was originally installed, pre-ISDN installation techniques were used.

Sometimes, existing wiring in your home or office is entirely adequate for ISDN services. In these cases, it's only necessary to provide appropriate jacks and plug the equipment into them. This scenario is most likely with houses and small offices wired in the last 10 or 15 years, especially for applications where ISDN service is terminated directly and to only one end-user equipment location. In other cases, you may need to devote special considerations to your wiring. You may run into problems if the existing wiring is very complex, such as office wiring that was originally installed for key telephone systems, with many connections, extensions, and terminations. Also, you may run into special wiring considerations if your applications require multiple ISDN terminals to be terminated to a single ISDN line.

At the NIUF, work is progressing on a generic wiring guide for use in your house or office building. Also, you may find specific instructions packaged with equipment or software you purchase for your solution.

12.3   EXAMPLE: WORK AT HOME

This particular example is based on a real-life case. The names and some details have been changed to protect the guilty and the innocent. The technical arrangements and details are accurate and true. (Actually, some are implemented and some are planned.)

A staff worker named George decides that it suits his purposes to work at home on a regular basis, perhaps as much as 30 percent of the time. George has discovered that there are certain capabilities he will need to function effectively as a work-at-homer. He has discussed the idea with his supervisor, Rodney. Rodney also has certain requirements that George must meet, even when working at home.

When George is working at the office, he normally uses a PC to produce reports with a word processor. When he needs to make presentations, he uses a different software product on the same computer. Occasionally, he needs to perform calculations (using a spreadsheet software product). He contemplates using other software products, such as databases, when needed. At the office, George regularly accesses a LAN to send and receive email to others in his organization. Using a graphical user interface, George clicks on icons to select programs from his personal computer or from the LAN and to access e-mail (from the LAN).

Visualizing the Electronic Solution

George wants to provide these same capabilities so he can work at his residence in the same way that he currently works in his office. He wants to purchase a computer and printer similar to the ones he uses at the office so he can work effectively at home. He also needs to access email and other programs from the LAN. He has discovered that he can remotely access the

LAN using ISDN. If possible, he would like to operate his computer at home just like he operates it at the office.

George and Rodney agree that George will purchase, own, and completely control the equipment he uses at his house. Rodney will purchase and receive bills for the ISDN service to George's house so George can access the office LAN. Rodney will also purchase the bridge and the ISDN service at the office, which George (and several others on Rodney's staff) will need to access the LAN.

Rodney voices his concerns to George about how to deal with impromptu situations where small groups of workers confer in the office to work on group projects. Currently, a small group often gathers around a whiteboard to work collaboratively. Group members list considerations onto the board, and sometimes one member of the group draws on the board to convey an idea or a configuration. How will George be able to work in such a mode when he is at home?

George surveys the available hardware and software and finds that several vendors provide collaborative software packages to allow people to work in a shared whiteboard-like environment. Some even offer video capabilities as part of the desktop conferencing suite. Rodney agrees that with such electronic capabilities, collaborative work can progress electronically even if George is not actually in the office on that particular day.

Implementing the Work-at-Home Vision

George obtains an ISDN LAN *terminal adapter (TA)* from a vendor he saw listed in the ISDN *Applications Catalog*. It is on a printed circuit card, which he inserted into his computer. (See Figure 12.1.) Power is provided to the adapter from the computer itself, so George needs to take no additional steps to arrange for power. (If George wants to provide power to the PC and the adapter during a power failure, he can obtain a UPS from his PC supplier for about $150. But since he only rarely loses power at his house, he chooses not to provide power backup to his PC workstation.) The particular adapter he selects has an NT1 mounted right on the board. There is a telephone jack on the back of the card. George supplies a telephone cord, which he plugs into that jack; he plugs the other end into the ISDN service jack in the wall. Because he is using only one ISDN terminal and connecting to the U interface, he finds the existing house wiring is adequate to carry the ISDN signals.

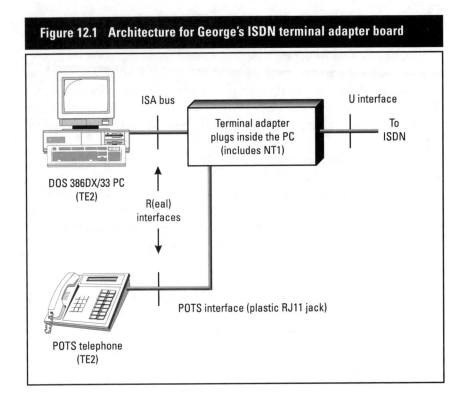

Figure 12.1   Architecture for George's ISDN terminal adapter board

The ISDN service that George orders is one basic rate service (2B + D). The vendor who supplies his ISDN LAN adapter instructs George that he needs alternate voice and data on each of the two B channels. Packet services are not required by this particular vendor's product. Because George will primarily use this product for data access to the LAN, he requests no ISDN supplementary services.

The particular ISDN LAN adapter that George selects has additional telephone jacks to connect pre-ISDN analog telephones. These jacks are provided so if George decides he wants to speak over one of the B channels, he can use an ordinary phone to do so, while transferring data over the other B channel. He also selects that capability so he can connect his fax-modem card to it for compatibility with other staff workers who still communicate via pre-ISDN services.

When George works collaboratively with coworker Paul, he establishes a direct connection to Paul's PC. Paul has the mirror image of George's arrangement—the same type of PC, an end-to-end compatible

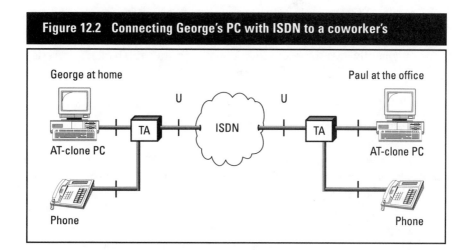

Figure 12.2   Connecting George's PC with ISDN to a coworker's

ISDN terminal adapter, and a conferencing system (consisting of shared whiteboard software and video capabilities). (See Figure 12.2.)

Back at the office, George confers with the LAN administrator to provide an ISDN bridge for the LAN. This ISDN bridge is compatible with the ISDN LAN adapter in George's PC back at his house. The LAN administrator also arranges for the ISDN line to connect to the ISDN bridge. (See Figure 12.3.)

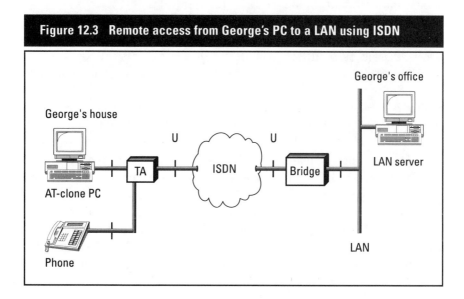

Figure 12.3   Remote access from George's PC to a LAN using ISDN

George keeps his existing analog (pre-ISDN) residential telephone service for his own personal use and for the use of other family members. In this way, family members can use the phone during George's workday without interrupting him or vice versa.

Using the Work-at-Home Solution

George is an early riser, starting his day at about 5:00 A.M. He typically starts his day by drinking a cup of coffee, listening to softly playing chamber music, and reading for 30 to 45 minutes. He usually has to hurry to leave the house by 6:30 A.M. so he can drive to the carpool location to commute to the office. Because he rides in a carpool that satisfies the *high-occupancy vehicle (HOV)* requirements, it usually only takes about 1 hour for him to arrive to work.

On days when George's workload and calendar demands are conducive, he works at home. Typically, this is 2 days a week or less, but it does vary depending on office commitments. He also has the capability to travel to the office on short notice if an urgent need can be satisfied in no other way (for example, an unexpected meeting with a client). He cannot remember the last time he had to travel to the office unexpectedly, but both he and the others at the office are much more relaxed about George working at home because they know that he can arrive there in less than one hour (since non-rush hour traffic means reduced travel time).

Usually, George prefers to start working early when he stays home. At about 6:30 A.M., he scans his e-mail and voice mail to see if there is anything urgent that needs attention. (The details of how he does this are virtually identical to how he does this when he is at the office.) George has scheduled himself to work on a project for the first 2 hours of the day, so he works without contacting anyone during that time. Using ISDN, George is able to obtain all of his previous work on the project (word-processing files) from his PC at work. He can also obtain similar files from others by accessing the LAN. Although he plans to work mostly in solitude, he is accessible to others if they need to contact him by phone or email or need to work collaboratively with him.

At about 8:30 A.M., George refreshes his coffee while he again scans for voice and email messages to see how the day is unfolding. He makes a few calls, mostly leaving messages for others. It isn't until about 9:00 or 10:00 A.M. that George returns a lot of calls, since he has learned that he can often reach people at that time.

During one of these conversations, he and Joe, a colleague from another company, plan on how to conduct an upcoming industry meeting scheduled for the following week (they are chair and vice-chair of the group). They use the arrangement illustrated in Figure 12.2 to review the agenda and discuss how to approach each item. Joe sends George a copy of a baseline text document that the group is using, and suggests changes to George. Both George and Joe see these changes on their screens at the same time they are discussing the changes. After a few iterations, they agree, and they each retain a final copy of the agreement. They electronically send a copy of the document file to everyone else who participates on the committee, so they can think about how to make the most of their meeting time when they all travel to the meeting next week.

In the afternoon, George finds an email message from a person in his own company whom he has never met (Cris). Cris has been told that George has done some work in a particular area and may have some knowledge that could be useful to her. George calls her and, during their discussion, realizes he made a presentation to an industry group about 6 months earlier that would help Cris. He forwards the presentation to Cris by attaching it to an email response. Since it is in the native program format, Cris receives it into her presentation software and can make changes and additions. She is able to create her product by making changes to the one that George has already used. In 3 hours, she is finished; she was concerned earlier that it might take several days to do the research and another day or more to prepare her report.

On the personal side, George decides to walk and jog through the neighborhood during his lunch hour. On other work-at-home days, he meets friends, neighbors, and colleagues at his favorite lunch spots. He finds that many of his acquaintances, also working at home on some days, appreciate the socializing during the middle of the day.

Late in the afternoon, George decides he needs a break from desk work and prepares a casserole dinner for his family's return. Forty-five minutes later, the dinner is cooking in the oven; it will be ready in one hour. While sipping a predinner burgundy, George quickly scans his voice and e-mail to make sure no critical messages are waiting. He also plans his workday tomorrow.

Often, George quickly scans for voice and e-mail messages late in the evening. Occasionally, he finds that the news he hears can help him. If a meeting has been suddenly cancelled or created, he can alter his plans for the following day because he has advance warning.

During the days George works at home, he avoids the aggravations of commuting for more than 2 hours (total). He can concentrate with fewer interruptions, while at the same time remaining accessible to coworkers within the company and outside it. He can also act on his aerobic-exercise New Year resolution and prepare a dinner so his hardworking wife is spared.

The results are so beneficial, George is now dreaming of telecommuting from a cabin in the mountains or from a beach house at the ocean. Wouldn't that be great?

12.4   EXAMPLE: TRANSACTION PROCESSING

As John Dough drives along one day, he notices that his gas gauge is reading nearly empty. As he drives by his neighborhood gas station, he pulls into the pump station to get gas. It's raining but the fuel pumping station is covered; John will only get wet if he needs to go into the office.

John inserts his credit card into a machine, which prompts him to wait. About 3 seconds later, the message on the screen changes to instruct John to begin pumping. At this point, John pumps his gas as he would at any other self-service gas station. After John replaces the filler nozzle into the dispenser machine, the screen prompts John to wait for his receipt. A few seconds later, a receipt is dispensed, which John removes from the machine and saves. He notices that it contains the date and location of purchase as well as the quantity in gallons and the price per gallon. Still dry, John drives to his destination with a full tank of gas.

If John had been curious, he could have inquired how this system worked. If he had been interested in the system rather than in simply getting gas and staying dry, he would have found out that the pumps are connected to the credit-clearing locations via a point-of-sale system using ISDN. But frankly, John didn't care. He never did find that out. But he did stay dry, and he didn't have to stand in line to make his payment.

12.5   EXAMPLE: AGENT AT HOME

Sally works for an electric utility company called City Power, which provides electrical power to your house or business for a fee. Prospective customers call City Power to initiate their electrical power service. Sally has always traveled to a City Power business office where she is the one who answers those calls. She discusses various terms and conditions of the service with potential customers, checks their credit rating, and generally makes sure that both City Power and its customers understand and benefit from the business arrangements. While talking to her customers, Sally checks service and payment details from a PC on her desk.

Sally works with about 12 other colleagues, who collectively form a pool of service representatives to answer incoming calls. A telephone system called an *automatic call distributor (ACD)* distributes the calls to the various agents in Sally's group. If more calls come in than the agents can handle, the incoming caller is informed that there will be a short wait until an agent becomes available.

Recently, the *management information services (MIS)* group within City Power has found that a new type of ACD, which allows geographical scattering of agents, is available. Using ISDN, the various pieces of the ACD system can be connected together so that all of the functionality that City Power has obtained in the past can be provided to the houses of individual agents. Agents who work at home can still use a PC to access customer records. (See Figure 12.4.) The pieces of the system installed at City Power can still track calling statistics (such as number of calls received and average time per call) and provide a service-assurance capability (call monitoring by supervisor).

City Power has informed Sally that if she wishes, she can work at home. She has elected to do that, because she prefers to work fewer hours per week and avoid the commute. She can then meet other personal obligations while continuing to provide needed income for her family. She has also offered to be available on short notice for emergency and unusually busy times so City Power can meet customer needs even during unexpectedly busy periods.

12.6 SUMMARY

From an end user's perspective, obtaining ISDN services can be quite involved (as George found for his work-at-home solution), fairly simple (as Sally saw when the MIS department set up her solution for her), or so simple and easy that the ISDN dimension is not even obvious (as John Dough found when he purchased gasoline with a credit card).

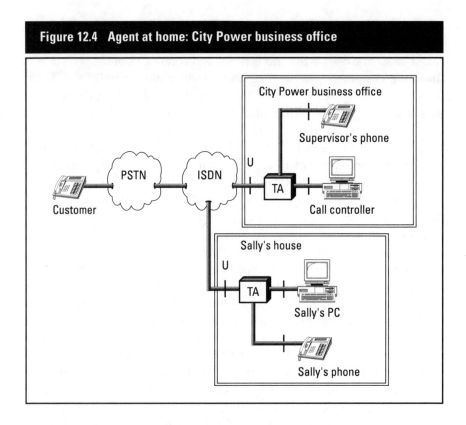

Figure 12.4   Agent at home: City Power business office

If you are in the business of running a credit-card process or an MIS department, you will have to do the same kind of planning, in even greater detail, that George had to do to set up his work-at-home system. But this should be only a difference in details for you—setting up systems from a series of piece parts is something that you have done before.

If you are the end user, sometimes you will need to get involved in the solution, sometimes not. Regardless of the level of detail you ultimately master, you need to understand the possibilities that using ISDN presents so you can take advantage of it to improve your productivity and well-being. As with many other things in life, from getting your car fixed to having a house built, you will probably find it worthwhile to have a speaking fluency and a basic understanding of the key ISDN elements and operational issues so you can convey your requirements fully to the people who are trying to help you with ISDN solutions.

13

What Could Go Wrong?

O ften, office buildings have no thirteenth floor. Perhaps the builder or architect was superstitious and didn't want to invoke any mishaps. It's fitting, therefore, that in this thirteenth chapter we explore potential snafus—ways in which ISDN could be delayed, derailed, or otherwise kept from end users.

ISDN seems like a good idea—capable of so many applications that it seems almost inevitable. But there are many ways in which the success of ISDN could elude us. Even though it seems like the most reasonable and desirable way to move information in the near future, barriers to obtaining ISDN are formidable.

You will notice that the discussion of possible problems or barriers is fairly long. If things do go wrong, ISDN will be delayed (in fact, it has already been delayed longer than most of us would have predicted, even a few years ago), or ISDN will be modified so that it's less capable or standardized than it could be.

The good news is that we are already overcoming or mitigating many of the barriers discussed here. The prognosis is positive. Problems that are still to be overcome include replacing existing telephone plant (switches, cables, and so on) with newer plant compatible with ISDN; reaching a common understanding among the large number of relatively disparate stakeholders; and obtaining constructive government support (or at least preventing unnecessary barriers).

Do not allow the seriousness of the barriers to ISDN overwhelm you. The ISDN public network provides an all-purpose, ubiquitous, and digitally capable infrastructure, which we need in the information age. In the near future, there is no competing alternative that offers such a combination of benefits. We must—and will—find ways to work through each barrier to ISDN.

13.1 DEPLOYMENT BARRIERS

Obviously, to effectively provide ISDN services, network providers must deploy the necessary physical plant. As you will recall, one of the five key attributes of ISDN is that it is digital, from end to end. Therefore, the various service and equipment vendors must provide digital telephony, end to end. In addition, message-oriented signaling mandates the deployment of SS7. And network providers have only partly addressed issues concerning ISDN network management. Network providers need to obtain and deploy the necessary capabilities—computer-based systems supported by appropriate methods and procedures—to offer the ISDN services that end users require.

Digital Switches (Central Offices)

Clearly, telephone network switches, if not already digital, need to be replaced. What may be less clear is the magnitude of doing just that. In the United States alone, perhaps 10,000 switches provide telephone service. Each of these offices can cost millions of dollars to buy and install. Tens, even hundreds, of billions of dollars are invested to provide central offices.

Even if such huge sums of capital were instantly available to replace these switches, it would be difficult to supply sufficient switches and the manpower to install them rapidly. Rather, a continuous program of modernizing existing U.S. telephone networks is more realistic and practical.

On a more positive note, as more central offices become digital, it becomes much easier to provide the ISDN-controlling software globally. Thus, the continuous modernizing of digital switching offices facilitates providing ISDN for end users. Many network providers have already converted significant numbers of their switches to digital operation.

Interoffice Facilities

Although, as we discussed earlier, interoffice facilities deployed since 1960 have been largely digital, even this digital conversion is more complex than it might seem. Early digital facilities are not directly suited to ISDN because some bits are "robbed" for signaling; they support only 56 Kbps, not the full 64 Kbps capability specified in standards. Transmitting any pattern of data bits at the full 64 Kbps rate is called *64 clear channel capability (64 CCC)*.

To accommodate 64 CCC, a special coding system, *B8ZS*, is used. This coding system avoids synchronization problems otherwise encountered when not using the "bit robbed" signaling and certain patterns of user data. Newer systems have this capability, but it can't be used in the POTS network with inband signaling. Rather, B8ZS can be selected by toggling a switch on the transmission equipment so that it can be used in an ISDN network. Otherwise, network providers must purchase new facilities. Even if newer facilities are obtained, and the switch is thrown to implement B8ZS for ISDN, it's fairly expensive for a large company to just keep track of which systems have which capabilities and use the appropriate systems for the correct applications.

At least one large telephone company has reportedly declined to deploy 64 CCC trunks and offers only 56 Kbps links. Perhaps future connectivity requirements will influence the company to conform to the 64 CCC norm.

Access Loops

Most of us are connected via loops of copper wire to a telephone company switch. To provide ISDN, network providers need to provide special electronics equipment at each end (NT1 at the customer end and the corresponding LT at the telephone switching machine). Even if each LT only costs tens of dollars, providing enough for the large number of subscriber loops represents a capital investment of billions of dollars. Furthermore, each end user incurs additional expense providing his or her own NT1 (currently priced at a few hundred dollars each).

This scenario, however, assumes that network providers will not need to take any extraordinary steps to provide the digital access loop. In some cases, customers will be out of range (further than about 3 miles) from the central office. This will require additional equipment, such as special

ISDN loop repeaters or ISDN subscriber-loop carrier systems, and special administration to give these customers the access loop for ISDN. Also, some subscriber-loop cable that is within range needs to be *groomed* (administratively selected or physically improved) to provide ISDN. Extraneous parallel sections of cable (*bridge taps*)—useful in providing conventional telephony—will often have to be removed. Analog-transmission enhancement devices such as *load coils* will need to be identified and removed to provide ISDN digital access. Network providers will probably incur heavy administrative and labor costs. Until we gain more experience installing and maintaining ISDN, we can only guess at the problems in the access loops and the expense of providing ISDN universal service.

SS7 Deployment

SS7 is crucial to providing the out-of-band, message-oriented signaling used in ISDN. However, it is quite expensive to deploy. U.S. court rulings have required SS7 deployments in every LATA, which has made the deployment more expensive than if the marketplace, investors, and technical decision makers only considered benefits, costs, and technical issues. Because of this court-mandated cost penalty, some telephone companies will delay its provision in many areas, slowing down the connectivity of ISDN.

While it might not seem to make much difference to the end user, SS7 provides much faster connection setup times. End users have actually measured connection times at 1 to 2 seconds for an SS7 circuit-mode digital ISDN call approximately halfway across the United States. In contrast, these users measured connection time at 15 or more seconds for an inband 56 Kbps connection that did not use SS7. With a lengthier setup time, ISDN cannot be used for some private line replacement applications and for some remote-access-to-LAN applications. In addition to a lengthy setup time, using conventional in-band signaling precludes the possibility of conveying messages across the network from one end user to the other.

Deploying SS7, however, is less a matter of whether and more a matter of when. Even in areas where it is not foreseeable, it will ultimately be deployed. And increasing pressure from end users, stockholders, and regulators will cause companies to deploy sooner than they otherwise might have.

OAM&P Deployment

Each company that wants to provide ISDN to its end users must make a substantial commitment to the procedures, methods, and computer-based systems that support ISDN. End users are very unforgiving of procedures and systems that make it difficult to order ISDN. And they are even less forgiving if the systems cause improper provisioning of an installed ISDN.

Although preliminary evidence suggests that ISDN could be more reliable than POTS, network providers still must maintain it and monitor its performance to assure quality of service. Many companies are reluctant to make such huge investments until the demand for ISDN actually materializes. Of course, when the demand does materialize, support systems will be needed immediately.

13.2 INDUSTRY-COMMITMENT BARRIERS

When the Bell System was dissolved, so also was the central mechanism for telecommunications research, development, planning, and deployment that had served the country so well in the past. In the decade since divestiture, new paradigms have begun to replace the central planning function, but a plan to ensure universal coverage, consistency, and compatibility is still lacking.

Competing organizations often take positions that appear to be winning strategies, even when they know that collectively such strategies in the industry will lead to failure. Thus, while one telephone company deploys a particular technology, another company deploys a slightly different incompatible version of the same technology. And yet another company deploys an altogether different technology. Equally problematic is the fact that equipment and transmission suppliers work hard to differentiate their products — which would otherwise be compatible and interoperable—from other products. Collectively, we end users may wind up with hash rather than a harmonious national telephone system.

Lack of Standards

As discussed in Chapter 7, standards are written by volunteers in the standards organizations. But with competitive telecommunications companies, it may no longer be necessary, or even desirable, for an individual company to voluntarily supply the writers to craft these standards.

Traditionally, the existing larger companies have been expected to provide the leadership and bear the largest expense for writing standards. Unfortunately, upstart companies, many of which emerged over a decade ago, have provided few (and often absolutely zero) resources to help fund standards-development efforts. While this might have been acceptable for the first few years of a company's existence, it is no longer. The same argument can be used for incumbent switching-equipment manufacturers. Why should they show new and foreign manufacturers how to compete more effectively for lower-profit-margin business?

Even when all volunteer parties work hard to achieve quality standards, the market demands of timeliness, simplicity, and functionality often cannot be met. For ISDN, most of the basic standards have been written and agreed upon. For successive technologies, however, the volunteer process of public standards making is open for debate.

Inadequate Implementation Agreements

As discussed in Chapter 8, after standards bodies produce, standards users usually need implementation agreements to help interpret the standards. First, users must determine which of the many standards are applicable. Generally, so many standards are available that even agreeing on which ones apply is a big step toward interoperability.

In addition, users must address issues of options, parameter values, and ambiguous text. For ISDN, National ISDN (NI-1, NI-2, and NI-3) deals with the most basic issues; these agreements are almost identical to the agreements in the NIUF. Further, National ISDN is being widely deployed in the United States to support the need for a common ISDN.

Nonetheless, many proponents of proprietary ISDNs are pushing constantly to slow the impact of National ISDN so they can promote their own differentiated products. This is, no doubt, a natural byproduct of the procompetitive paradigm within the telecommunications industry.

For ISDN, it appears that the pendulum is swinging toward National ISDN. It's not clear whether similar support for implementation agreements will be forthcoming for successive technologies. Manufacturers and telephone companies do not want to suffer the time delays again that have plagued ISDN because of its emphasis on interoperability. Rather, these companies may decide it is competitively more advantageous to quickly deploy noninteroperable systems.

Lack of Reliable Conformance Testing and Certification

As seen in Chapter 8, if ISDN equipment is certified as successfully conformance-tested, it is more likely to operate properly within ISDN networks. But competitive pressures often mitigate against such a system of testing and certification.

Many of the ISDN telephone and terminal vendors do not want to participate in such a system. They have no desire to spend time and money on additional testing, which they believe will not directly result in a salable product. Since vendors do test their products with existing implementations of ISDN, they believe their products will perform properly. What is not yet known is whether these products will continue to operate properly with ISDN networks as they evolve. If they do, these vendors will have successfully avoided costs while providing a quality product.

If these vendors are incorrect in their assumptions, end users will begin to insist that ISDN terminal equipment be tested and certified for conformance with National ISDN. But the infrastructure to support such a testing and certification program is very slow to evolve. This is, in part, similar to the standards effort—it is a volunteer effort that many companies don't equitably support. And in cases where testing organizations have mobilized for profit, they have found very few vendors anxious to pay the fees to obtain their services.

Motivation Barriers for ISDN Industry

Many of the barriers stated previously could be restated as problems of motivation. Each industry member needs to commit to making ISDN happen. Each industry member relies on other industry members for ISDN success. In fact, it takes a fairly large number of committed organizations to achieve results. Human nature being what it is, most wait to see if others are going to commit before committing themselves; competitive pressures accentuate that tendency. While many organizations are stepping up front to make ISDN happen, still more commitment is needed to achieve ISDN success.

Another (related) issue is that the industry is producing goods and services that are essentially public in nature (that is, goods that are available to anyone, regardless of whether they paid for them, such as standards, ordering and provisioning aids, and applications advice). In a competitive environment, how can the industry produce these required public goods? Not only do we need to answer this question for ISDN, we need to answer it for future technologies, which are the fast lanes of the information superhighway.

13.3   GOVERNMENT INFLUENCE

Increasingly, our government affects commerce. This has a beneficial side: ensuring honest weights and measures and providing currency to support commerce, for example. In many other ways as well, our national and local governments support commerce to the benefit of end users and businesses alike. It seems unlikely that elected and appointed officials would deliberately undermine technological and commercial progress. It is still possible, however, that they might impede the success of ISDN because of a lack of business or technological acumen. Still, a variety of legal and regulatory considerations may keep ISDN from being as successful as it might otherwise be.

Legal Trammels

Historically, telephone service was provided in the United States by the Bell System. It was a unique system that allowed one company to provide telephone service to the vast majority of the country. The undesirable aspects of monopoly were mitigated through the process of regulation. When the Bell System was dissolved to resolve a lawsuit, a legal document known as the *Modified Final Judgment (MFJ)* was written. It contains the details of how the Bell System would be dispersed. It is an agreement between AT&T (the parent company of the Bell System) and the U.S. government.

The MFJ mandated that the divested local-exchange carriers (telephone companies known as *regional Bell operating companies (RBOCs)*) not provide long-distance telephone services between LATAs. The RBOCs were also prevented from manufacturing any products and providing information services. In the early 1990s, however, this constraint (not to provide information services) was removed from the MFJ.

Generally, these constraints work (and have worked) to delay or derail the provision of ISDN. SS7 is delayed because of the increased expense of providing massive, expensive equipment for every LATA (even without any appreciable demand for ISDN). Interoperability is affected by the manufacturing constraint that prevents RBOCs from designing or developing the equipment that provides the services they sell. Also, RBOCs have lost interest in basic research because it is well known that manufacturing is the way to significantly profit from any laboratory breakthroughs. Why invest money in research if there is no way to profit from success?

Regulatory Trammels

In a variety of ways, both local exchange carriers and interexchange carriers are regulated by various sectors of government. In the old Bell System environment, regulation enabled a single carrier to provide a ubiquitous, homogenous telephone service without extracting monopoly prices and conditions from its customers. Many of our current regulatory practices are holdovers from this earlier era.

Traditionally, telephone companies have been regulated by *rate of return*. Regulators fix a rate of return for telephone companies, then allow the telephone companies to charge certain rates for certain services with the expectation that, at projected sales levels, the companies will achieve a rate of return on their invested plant that is sufficient to attract investment capital.

A popular misconception is that telephone companies are guaranteed to earn their authorized rate of return. In fact, if a telephone company earns less than its authorized rate of return, it is not allowed to raise rates unless a lengthy series of hearings can demonstrate that the company does not deserve low earnings due to poor performance. Should a telephone company do exceptionally well by introducing a new service or technology and earn more than its authorized rate of return, it must refund the extra earnings to consumers.

In today's competitive environment such regulation obviously tends to stifle any risk-oriented investment. Investors are not likely to invest money in ventures that are susceptible to loss when their successes result in money going to others who don't share in the risk.

From the regulator's point of view, the public generally wants ubiquitous service at the lowest possible rates. Appointed or elected terms are generally only a few years in duration. Even ruinous regulatory policies often don't take full effect until after regulators have left office. So why not satisfy consumers now? Most regulators do, in fact, sincerely try to balance constituent needs and are receptive to new and beneficial ways of doing business in today's competitive marketplace. Investor analysts frankly identify which regulators excel and which ones don't.

For ISDN, key regulatory issues involve the regulation of prices. If the price is too high, end users won't be able to afford ISDN. End users can't obtain the benefit they seek, and risk capital is lost. If ISDN prices are too low, however, the return on risk capital is too low, and critics claim that other rate payers of pre-ISDN service are subsidizing ISDN. Regulators attempt to regulate the prices for optimum results, so end users can afford the service to obtain its benefits, and the return on investment is sufficient to attract enough capital to complete ISDN deployment. (Proponents of competition claim that market forces are the most efficient way of setting prices.)

When trying to determine optimum pricing structure, there are two fundamentally different ways to evaluate the costs of providing ISDN. In the traditional, regulated rate-of-return environment, average costs were often used to establish a base to calculate the rate of return. In competitive environments, marginal costs are used to determine where risk capital can be directed for maximum return on investment. The tension between the average-costs and marginal-costs approaches is at the root of many disagreements. The financial aspects get quite complicated in the rate-setting process.

The most procompetitive position would be simply to end regulation of rates and services altogether. In such an environment, any company could offer any services it wanted to provide, at any price it chose to set. A company would be successful or not depending on how much end users purchased the offered services at the prices the company set.

In the meantime, prior to fully competitive pricing, many regulators have approved rate-cap regulation, which caps the rate, using an agreed formula, but allows the service provider to increase margin by reducing costs and increasing sales (to earn a higher return on fixed costs). This system rewards prudent management while protecting consumers from the dangers of uncontrolled prices.

13.4 SUMMARY

As suggested in the beginning of this chapter, ISDN is not inevitable. It could be delayed or even derailed if we don't overcome enough of the barriers.

Events over the last few years suggest that we are overcoming these barriers and that ISDN will be successful. But for end users, ISDN doesn't seem to be happening as fast as we would like.

One very encouraging sign is the use of digital-overlay deployments to provide ISDN anywhere in a telephone company serving area. If this trend continues, we may all be able to obtain ISDN at affordable rates much sooner than we might have expected. Another encouraging sign is the recognition by various governments and regulatory bodies of the inherent worth of ISDN: its ability to make our businesses more competitive with those of other countries. Many of the issues in this chapter are actually being addressed in the political and regulatory arena.

In addition to its regulatory role, government has been the source of funding for public services, including standards such as traffic regulations and applications such as advice as provided by agriculture extension agents. Will the government ultimately be the source of telecommunications public goods and services, providing an interoperable and ubiquitous infrastructure? If so, will this result in speedier availability of telecommunications? Or will the private sector continue to work in a volunteer manner with minimal governmental support or subsidy?

On a final note, although anxious end users sometimes get discouraged because ISDN hasn't happened overnight, be aware that there is virtually no alternative to ISDN. It has to happen. There are no alternative digital services planned for ubiquitous general-purpose use over the telephone networks. ISDN is the only game in town when it comes to new and advanced digital services for individual end users. If ISDN does not succeed, end users will be able to access their data sources only with POTS capabilities. This is so unacceptable in our postindustrial information age that ISDN seems *almost* inevitable.

Broadband ISDN

A s time goes on, users need, or at least want, more bandwidth. This is consistent with the trend to increase information storage capacity in other systems: ever-increasing memory on computer systems, increasing disk-storage capacity for those systems, and more bookshelf space in libraries. When it comes to moving these larger stores of information, bandwidth must necessarily increase to keep the transfer times about the same as on earlier systems. But many users now want even shorter transfer times while the amount of transferable information is steadily increasing.

When we speak of *broadband ISDN (BISDN)*, we really mean bandwidths of more than 1.5 Mbps — the capacity of a *primary-rate interface (PRI)* for a narrowband ISDN. In fact, the industry has coined the term *narrowband ISDN (NISDN)* to differentiate it from BISDN.

One of the prime motivations for developing BISDN is to provide *high-definition TV (HDTV)*. This service, which requires perhaps 140 Mbps, captures the imagination not only of technologists but of politicians who believe they can lead us to an HDTV nirvana. The picture quality of HDTV is roughly equivalent to that provided by a 35 mm slide projection. Like a slide projection, this image can be magnified to huge proportions without losing much quality. It's possible that an entire wall could be used as a projection screen—perhaps even more than one wall to achieve a wrap-around effect. Imagine camera perspectives that allow football game coverage to show close-up and panoramic views of the offensive and defensive lines. This is a far cry from today's close-up shots of the running back holding the ball. Not only would such a TV service be a big improvement over today's services, but you could obtain it by simply "dialing" for it over the BISDN telephone network. You could select any number of different service providers to view detective movies, basketball games, or tutoring services on a wide variety of subjects.

14.1   IS IT REALLY ISDN?

To assess whether this new capability is really ISDN or something entirely new and different, we need to have some sort of a test. Recall from Chapter 1 the five-attribute test. If BISDN satisfies these five criteria, in some definitional sense, it must be ISDN.

End-to-End Digital Connectivity

If the service is digital from one end to the other with no analog links or conversions, it satisfies the first criterion. BISDN is truly digital end to end, although it is, in many ways, different from the way NISDN is digital. For example, the digital line codes are different, and even the digital multiplexing techniques are different. This is due in part to the higher bandwidths, which require or suggest a need for a different set of methods, and it is due in part to other technological advances that provide greater capabilities than were available when NISDN was first constructed.

Although details are still sketchy, the current view is that there will probably be about four channels of 140 to 150 Mbps each. This will allow an end user to select up to four HDTV channels simultaneously or perhaps 3 HDTV channels and over 2000 B channels.

Integrated Access

When you use NISDN, you can request any of the available services over a single access loop. This is also true for BISDN, but there will be more services to summon. All of the services you can get over NISDN will likely be available over BISDN; but many additional services, such as HDTV and many of the high-speed data services, will also be available. And all of them will be available over a single access loop.

But the integration story doesn't stop at the access loop. Inside the network, for the first time, there is the possibility of integrating all services into a single switching fabric and a single network transport. This integration opportunity is due to the method of multiplexing selected for BISDN—*asynchronous transfer mode (ATM)*. This method of multiplexing seems to be capable of providing the wide variety of services currently contemplated for an ISDN of narrow- or wideband capabilities. This increased level of integration is illustrated in Figure 14.2. (Compare it with Figure 14.1—a lower level of integration.)

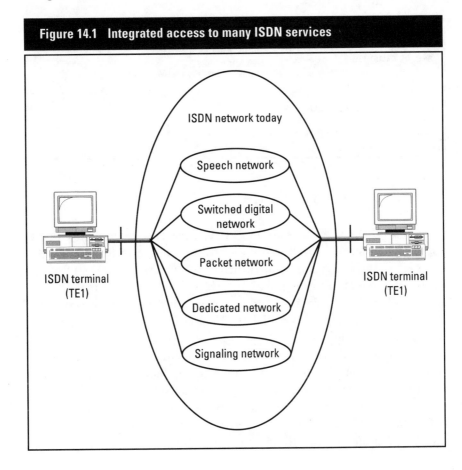

Figure 14.1   Integrated access to many ISDN services

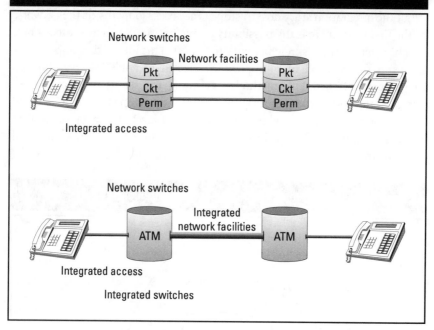

Figure 14.2   ISDN today (top): integration of network services in the access loop. Future ISDN (bottom): complete integration of services in network switches, facilities, and access loop

Small Family of Standard Interfaces

Although BISDN standards are not yet complete, standards developers are intent on minimizing the number of services and interfaces without sacrificing the desired capabilities. In fact, tremendous effort is going into developing a global interface for one universal BISDN access (plug, line encoding, and the messaging to provide services). History suggests that this will be difficult to achieve, but many are struggling valiantly.

As mentioned above, it looks like the standard interface will be about 600 Mbps and will be divided into four equal channels. Developers are selecting the actual numbers so BISDN channels can accommodate all of the existing NISDN interfaces used in various parts of the world (BRI, PRI at 1.5 Mbps, PRI at European line speeds of 2 Mbps) an integral number of times to promote the smooth transition from NISDN to BISDN.

Message-Oriented Signaling

As in NISDN, the BISDN end user will converse with the network using messages. Many of these messages will be the same or similar to the ones we saw in NISDN because basic needs really haven't changed. But because there are a wider array of possible services, BISDN will have new message elements, new service descriptions, and new *code-points* (binary encodings that uniquely refer to these services). It is already being called *DSS2* (*digital subcriber signaling system 2*).

The channel over which the signaling occurs will also be different. In BISDN, it appears likely that the signaling channel will be derived in ATM fashion just as the bearer signals are derived. Hence, a predetermined bandwidth (for example, 16 Kbps for BRI in NISDN) will not have to be set aside for signaling. Only the actual bandwidth required for signaling will be used.

Customer Control

End users will still want to select services and control bandwidth, among other things. Inherent in the ATM construct is more precise control of bandwidth than is possible with NISDN. With greater bandwidth available for signaling and bearer transport, you can construct a richer set of messages, which will allow for increased control.

14.2 EVOLUTIONARY STAGES

It has taken us over 10 years to achieve NISDN, and here we are already plotting to replace it with BISDN. Shouldn't we just wait for BISDN and skip NISDN altogether? End users—and even some people in the industry—are asking these and similar questions. The short answer to these questions is that although we are now beginning to deploy technology for BISDN, at best, it will take many years to have ubiquitous deployment of fiber optics and BISDN switches to provide service. On the other hand, we can now provide NISDN at affordable (most people agree) costs. It appears that it will be at least 20 years before NISDN is crowded out by BISDN, which suggests that we should aggressively pursue NISDN now.

Another question end users ask is: Isn't ISDN just an interim technology? The answer must certainly be: "Of course!" All technology is interim technology. The key is to use it as productively as possible. If we always wait for the next technology, we'll never use any.

Another view is that BISDN deployment will be different from NISDN deployment. For NISDN, network providers deployed capabilities exactly as they had deployed telephone service—everywhere. Network providers assumed that if NISDN was deployed, it would be used. But with the very high cost of BISDN deployment, perhaps it will not be pervasively deployed. It may make more sense to deploy it only where there is customer demand. If there is demand everywhere, the results will be the same and the distinction academic. But if there is demand only in certain areas, BISDN may never be available everywhere.

Synchronous Optical Network (SONET)

Synchronous optical network (SONET) digital hierarchies were constructed to provide economies of scale and to directly multiplex and demultiplex the various levels within the hierarchy. This direct access to even the lowest level of the hierarchy (64 Kbps DS0) provides economical transport for today's telephony services while at the same time seeding the network with capabilities that will be needed in the BISDN era.

In telephone networks, there is a hierarchy of digital transport, as introduced in Chapter 4 (see the table on page 63). At the lowest level, a DS0 has a bandwidth of 64 Kbps. Hence, 64 Kbps was chosen for the B channel because 64 Kbps can be conveyed across the network on a DS0. The next higher level in the digital hierarchy, DS1, has a bandwidth of 1.5 Mbps and contains 24 DS0s.

The DS3 stream, at 45 Mbps, has also been widely deployed. It contains 28 DS1s and 672 DS0s. As described in Chapter 4, the bundling of DS0s into DS1s and DS3s is not altogether simple. First, the DS0s are combined into the DS1; then DS1s are bundled into a DS3. The "extra" bits of bandwidth that are left are used for various purposes such as synchronization. If a DS0 signal is needed at some point in the network, the DS3 signal must be demultiplexed into DS1s; then the appropriate DS1 is dissolved into 24 DS0s. The needed DS0 is selected, and then everything else is packaged back into the DS3 to travel along the network. This process is slow, awkward, and expensive.

But SONET allows direct selection of DS0s because of its straightforward multiplexing arrangement. In addition to meeting the needs of today's telephone network and NISDN, SONET enables easy identification of larger bundles of bandwidth without having to divide the bundles into smaller pieces. This will allow the use of very large channels for HDTV as well as for many channels for DS0s, each of which can be easily selected and removed from the bitstream.

Formats in the SONET hierarchy are defined by OC-1 through OC-48. (Actually, in principle, there is no upper bound.) These are optical specifications; there are corresponding electrical specifications at the same rates. OC-1 is at 51.48 Mbps, corresponding to the DS3 rate of 45 Mbps (plus, some extra overhead bits for maintenance and coordination of concatenated systems). OC-3 is at 3 times that rate, OC-4 at four times, and so on. As you can see, there is room left for growth.

Although these bitstream hierarchies were developed for use within the network, they are also useful for defining user-network interfaces. It seems logical, desirable, and cost-effective to select rates for BISDN that are also used also in the network. In fact, a good deal of the wrangling in the standards-setting process has been over which rates would be suitable for both contexts within the network as well as at the user-network interface.

Metropolitan Networks

We often hear about *local area networks (LANs)*. We know that they connect computers, printers, and servers that are located within a small geographic area—typically, a floor of an office building. A *metropolitan area network (MAN)* is similar in function, but its scope is typically an entire city or community. The scope can be much greater: a state, a county, or even the globe. The technology of BISDN allows LAN-like methods to be used over much larger areas. MANs can be used in place of a LAN or they can be used to connect a number of LANs.

Today, various service providers are beginning to offer ATM services so end users can create MANs by connecting their LANs and other data resources. These ATM services provide high-speed data movement at OC-1 rates (and higher) using the native ATM cell format. It seems likely that in time other user-network interfaces will be offered so that NISDN, frame relay, and other data formats can be conveyed over ATM services.

Probably, this ATM service is the beginning of the path to BISDN. These early services provide *permanent virtual connections (PVCs)*, which are intended to replace private-line services. This service provides connectivity over fixed paths of known requirements, but the next stage in the evolution of these services will be *switched virtual connections (SVCs)*. BISDN, however, is still a long way from that future state.

Standards for BISDN

Participants of the standards body T1S1.3 were actively working on early BISDN standards during the mid to late 1980s. Most of the work then was focused on defining the cell structure for BISDN (that is, the ATM cell structure). At the same time, T1X1 was defining SONET, and IEEE 802.6 was working on cell-relay data service. Internationally, CCITT was working to agree on standards for universal rates, formats, and interfaces. Many organizations made valiant attempts to harmonize and synchronize all these efforts so that the industry could deploy high-speed data networks that would gracefully evolve to BISDN later. Unfortunately, certain parameter selections that optimize data performance seem to be suboptimal for conveying images or video. So choosing the basic cell structure involved technical compromise and political agony. It was a trying time for these organizations, but without their efforts we would not have the degree of commonality we can now enjoy.

For signaling, standards groups are extrapolating the protocols used for NISDN into service to provide BISDN signaling. The name for that protected suite—DSS2—is also extrapolated from NISDN service (DSS1). From the user-network interface, the Q.931-like protocols form the basis of signaling, much as described in Chapter 6. Standards groups are proposing SS7-like signaling within the network, although it may be transported over ATM cells rather than separate 64 Kbps channels, as is done today.

14.3 ATM—THE UNIVERSAL MULTIPLEXING FORMAT

In this section, we will examine just what ATM is and why it is effective in telephony networks. We will also see why it promises to be a universal multiplexing format, suitable for circuit-switched services, packet-mode services, and even channel-mode services. It takes advantage of what the network does well and uses network resources cleverly to provide a wide variety of services.

How ATM Works

ATM is the multiplexing method selected by standards bodies to provide high-bandwidth services such as BISDN. It has aspects of both synchronous and asynchronous transmission. To really understand how ATM works and why it seems to offer an advantage, we need to briefly compare it to *time-division multiplexing* (*TDM*), which is the way narrowband ISDN transfers data today.

A basic rate interface has a 2B + D channel structure. One B channel is allocated 64 Kbps, the second B channel is allocated 64 Kbps, and the D channel is allocated 16 Kbps. (Another 16 Kbps not directly seen by the end user is used to maintain, test, and generally administer the basic rate interface.) These bit allocations are fixed. If an end user wants to transmit 46 Kbps of information over a 64 Kbps circuit-switched B channel, 18 Kbps of capacity are left. Similarly, if an end user wants to transmit 72 Kbps over a circuit-switched B channel, the information won't fit. Perhaps the latter implementation will select a second B channel and use part of it to provide the needed throughput capacity.

Ideally, the channel sizes would adjust to fit the end-user requirements. Then channel capacity wouldn't be wasted by not fully using allocated channel sizes. The downside is that the network operates better with synchronously transmitted, fixed-size blocks of data bits than with random sizes of data blocks sent whenever the end user needs them.

The appeal of ATM is that it combines those two requirements: the network requirement for fixed-size, synchronous data-block transmission and the end user requirement for an interface that allows selection of bandwidth in varying amounts. But processing costs will necessarily increase to construct the ATM data blocks (called *cells*) and route those ATM cells through the network. Today, the extra processing power seems worth the added cost.

Accordingly, the actual "buckets" (the cells) that hold the bits of data are generated *isochronously* (with the regularity of a drummer in a marching band) or *synchronously* (if the timing source is centrally located in the network transmission system). But these cells are only used as they are needed, which is, in general, not regular with time. Thus, the service to the end user (and the actual use of the cells to convey bits of data) is said to be *asynchronous* (not regular in time; whenever needed).

Each ATM cell has a fixed-length size of 53 *octets* (8-bit groups). Since the cell size is fixed and the interface transmission rates vary, cells are generated isochronously, often enough to occupy the entire bandwidth of the channel. Although the ATM's 53-octet size might seem odd, recall that it has to be serviceable for data, images, video, and other services. It also has to accommodate the wide variety of existing multiplexed bandwidths that are used around the world today.

The 53-octet cell is split into two pieces: 5 octets for the header and 48 for the user data. Any information the user wants to send can be inserted into the 48-octet payload part of each cell. Since end-user data is often larger than 48 octets, the user data is *fragmented* (or *segmented*) to fit into the cells. At the receiving end, the 48-octet pieces are reconstructed to form the original information the user sent. Computers and computer-oriented transmission systems can readily (easily and cheaply) carry out this fragmentation and reconstruction of data.

The header performs two functions: it indicates the destination (address), and it indicates the channel associated with the particular cell. This channel association is what provides the multiplexing capabilities of ATM. Whenever an end user wants more bandwidth (in 48-byte increments), his or her equipment selects additional cells for a particular channel going to the desired destination. At the very high speeds of ATM (50, 150, or 600 Mbps), cells whiz by so fast that (as a practical matter) there are always more of them available. If availability becomes a problem, newer, higher-speed interfaces can be defined to make more cells available.

Not only does this cell header association provide the mechanism for creating various bandwidths, it also provides a mechanism for transporting various types of bearer services. As discussed below, the cell-head association transports bearer services by selecting the cells using a time pattern and transport rate that emulates the bearer-service capabilities.

Providing Circuit-Switched Services with ATM

Often, we want to send information using a circuit-mode (circuit-switched) bearer service. Suppose we want to use ATM techniques to replicate the circuit-switched digital mode at 64 Kbps, just as we have today on the basic and primary rates for NISDN. We can achieve the circuit-switched bearer service by using ATM techniques to select cells to provide transport at a *constant bit rate (CBR)*. Every cell of 48 octets contains 384 bits of user data. When the user selects a cell every 6/1000 of a second—or an average of 166 cells per second — 64 Kbps flow across the network isochronously. (There must be a time-regular transmission of data for this bearer service; the simulated NISDN service is one continuous, constant-rate bitstream.)

Of course, there are fragmenting, buffering, and reassembly issues to be addressed, but assuming the implementation makes sense, the end user will work with the same 64 Kbps data stream that he or she sees today with NISDN.

When ATM provides circuit-switched services, a *circuit* is not actually established — as with NISDN. (Recall that in today's ISDN, a path connects the sending end of the network to the receiving end of the network, and the 64 Kbps bitstream is transported across that network.) In the case of ATM, the selected cells are segregated from the others, and the header is used to route each cell to the distant end. The 48-octet contents are extracted and combined to produce the original bitstream. From an end user's perspective, the service appears the same as circuit-switched service on NISDN. All of the other cells in the ATM cell stream are available to provide other services. (At DS3 rates, every 672nd cell is assigned to emulate a 64 Kbps circuit-mode bearer service; the other 671 cells—out of every 672 — are available to provide other services.)

So the ATM system offers benefits for circuit-mode services that today's ISDN does not offer. First, ATM techniques can be used on bitstreams of any speed (the header does the associating), whereas today's ISDN is only appropriate at fixed, predefined BRI and PRI bit rates. Also, the ATM allows any bitstream to provide various channel bandwidths. If the user wants a higher bandwidth channel, such as the H_0 channel size of 384 Kbps, the user (actually, the user's equipment) must select a cell every 1000th of a second and associate it with the channel. If you need a lower bandwidth circuit-switched channel, select a cell every 24/1000th of a second to associate with your channel. At this point, you will have created a 16 Kbps channel. Depending on the speed of the bitstream and the fractional number of cell associations, you can create almost any channel bandwidth (subject to the limitation of NX48). At bitstreams of 50 to 600 Mbps, this granularity seems fine enough for most applications. (Just as the staircase with many steps in Figure 1.4 seems to have enough granularity to represent a ramp.)

Providing Channel-Mode Services with ATM

The only difference between providing channel-mode (permanent and semi-permanent) services and circuit-mode services is the duration of the connection. The cell associations are created in the same way to achieve similar bandwidths. But implementations must achieve suitable economies. (Since the processing overhead could continue for years, it can't be excessively expensive to the network provider or to the end user. Recall that in today's NISDN implementation, such capabilities are not yet available at an economically viable cost. We will see whether BISDN implementations, using ATM, will be able to meet this need economically.)

Providing Packet-Mode Services with ATM

In Chapter 5, we introduced packet-mode services (pages 83–87 and Figures 5.5–5.7). In many ways, packet mode is similar to ATM. In both, logical channels are identified from bits in the header. End-user data bits are grouped (into a variable-sized packet rather than a 48-octet cell); where necessary, the original end-user data is fragmented to accommodate the maximum allowable size of the packet. There are so many similarities between ATM and packet mode that ATM is often considered to be a packet-mode service and is sometimes called one of the *fast-packet* services.

But there are also differences. ATM has a pool of synchronous cells available for selection. In X.25 packet service, equipment only forms packets when end-user data requires one (from an available pool of synchronously generated bits). Also, the length of packets in packet service usually varies to accommodate needs. Although there is often a maximum size, smaller packets may be transmitted across the network. On the other hand, for ATM, the cells are quite uniform in size, structure, and timing.

You probably have noticed by now that packet formation is an asynchronous event (occurring when needed for end-user data transport). To transport end-user packet data across an ATM network, the end-user packets must be fragmented into 384 bit chunks and each chunk must be inserted into an available cell. Since time regularity is not needed for packet service, the only other requirement is for the receiver of the far end to sequence the packets correctly when they arrive.

Impact on Switches and Trunks in Network

In the preceding sections, we have seen that all of the bearer services of ISDN (and BISDN) can be conveyed on the common infrastructure of ATM. This process is very different from what we have on today's networks, where packet switches are separate from circuit switches, which in turn are separate from channel switches and from frame-relay switches and from fast-packet switches. Using ATM, once the end users access a variety of services from the integrated ISDN or BISDN channel, they will be routed to the one and only network that provides all of the desired services instead of being routed to separate networks. (See Figure 14.2.)

Integration in the ATM-based BISDN will be present in the network as well as in the access link, as it is today in NISDN. Perhaps this integration will provide sufficient economy to allow more affordable high-bandwidth services. It certainly will make it far easier to design, provision, and administer networks. Interoperability issues will also be minimized, because the one network will only have to be able to work with other networks that are simply replicas of itself.

14.4 WHAT GOOD IS BISDN?

Sometimes, it seems new and faster products and services are introduced without any real justification other than that they are possible. For BISDN, however, this is probably not the case. The wide variety of service possibilities will add value to end users who want better entertainment, education, and work-life arrangements (for example, working without having to travel to a distant work location).

Video Services

With newly improved video-encoding algorithms (for example, Motion Picture Experts Group (MPEG)), video services can now transmit at about 1.5 Mbps at a quality level essentially equal to that of a videocassette recorder. Higher quality video services require more bandwidth, which is one of the primary reasons why BISDN is so attractive.

Broadcast-quality video services currently need approximately 45 Mbps of bandwidth for accurate transmission. This quality is better than what you ordinarily see on your television set; it is the quality of a high-performance studio monitor. It has sharp images and vibrant color that does not bleed. You don't see defects like fringing and herringbone effects, which you sometimes see on a television set receiving a local broadcast channel.

High-definition TV currently requires approximately 140 to 150 Mbps of bandwidth to transmit an image. In return for requiring three times the bandwidth of broadcast quality transmission, HDTV offers substantially improved images. First of all, the images are proportioned differently — they are more rectangular than conventional TV images — more like the Cinemascope picture you see in movie theaters. As the picture is enlarged (by projection), it stays clear, sharp, and colorful like a projected photographic slide. It is probably adequate for projection in movie theaters and is certainly adequate for large-screen (perhaps 8-foot-by-12-foot) TV in the home. It might even be unsettling to be so "close" to and surrounded by some scenes, such as the chariot race in *Ben Hur.*

Future video services might even include three-dimensional TV, which could make the chariot race in *Ben-Hur* quite unsettling. Virtual-reality constructs could conceivably use such three-dimensional projections for more realistic entertainment or training.

Avoiding Traffic Jams

Imagine if we could quickly and easily create additional roads for our automobiles so we would never have a traffic jam or a parking problem. Just such an opportunity is available with broadband ISDN for our information traffic. We don't have to suffer information traffic jams, because the costs, in the era of ubiquitous fiber-optic cable, don't appear to be excessive.

Naturally, we can't expect to avoid all information traffic jams. After all, whenever new roads are built (or new transportation systems are developed), new demands arise that exceed the original capability. Remember, when NISDN was first developed, data transmission was mostly at 1200 bps, with 2400 bps just becoming available. NISDN, as it was first conceived, provided 25 to 50 times the bandwidth, on just one B channel, with much better performance (many fewer errors) than earlier systems. Yet before NISDN was widely deployed, the industry began carping about how it was inadequate to carry data.

Peering cautiously into the future, we can see a much greater bandwidth on fiber-optic cables than we currently have standardized in BISDN. Each BISDN interface (perhaps at 600 Mbps) is conveyed using a stream of light that is gated on and off. In *high-density wave-division multiplexing* systems, many different wavelengths of light (that is, different colors) can be carried on the same optical fiber. Transmitters and receivers can "tune in" to the various wavelengths just as we tune in to various radio stations today. Some researchers speculate we could convey as many as 1000 channels over each fiber, each one of which might be capable of providing 1 gigabit (1000 Mbps) of information. From today's perspective, it doesn't seem possible that we could find ways of using all that bandwidth.

Obtaining Bandwidth Support for Expanded Services

Considering that we will have four channels of 140 to 150 Mbps with BISDN, many different kinds of services are possible. Not only will HDTV be the first service to receive a lot of attention, it will make many other possibilities into realities. If you were to have four HDTV channels at real-life projections on your office walls, you could conduct video conferences with five people (including yourself) almost as though each person was in the same room with you. You could telecommute or conduct small-group meetings while each individual stayed in their office. This type of conference or meeting service is different in kind from the groupware document sharing that was described for NISDN. Although many of us may be satisfied with groupware, others will insist on a heightened sense of reality before conducting telecommunications meetings. This HDTV-style service would probably satisfy almost everyone.

Another example of its usefulness is in document retrieval and imaging. If you needed to research a topic at the library, you could retrieve documents and project them on a large screen, wall, or desktop so you could examine them in detail. Written documents, original music scores, color photographs, video excerpts, and audio recordings all could be transmitted to such a workstation. Imagine searching through any library in the world, to your heart's content, and seeing and hearing the original as well as if you were actually in the stacks. You could read in bed with a projection of text on the ceiling. Naturally, it would be sized and focused to accommodate to your vision.

14.5 SUMMARY

Communications technology continues to evolve, and the pace of its evolution seems to be quickening. As with computers, price-performance capabilities promise us a future where we will continuously be able to obtain sophisticated services at affordable prices. Having peered into the future in this chapter, we can see possibilities.

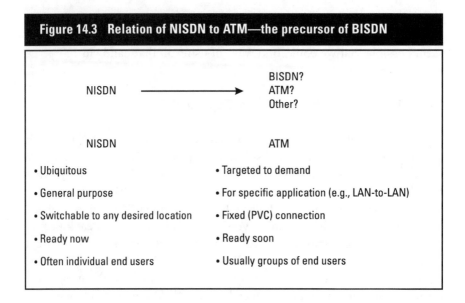

Figure 14.3   Relation of NISDN to ATM—the precursor of BISDN

In the meantime, NISDN is available now and offers perhaps ten times the capability of pre-ISDN services at roughly twice the cost. End-user equipment purchased now and used to provide ISDN solutions will almost certainly provide benefits for many years before ISDN is replaced by BISDN. But in all likelihood, BISDN will not be widely available a decade or two. Since end-user PCs and similar equipment that might be used to provide ISDN solutions probably have a useful life of only 2 to 5 years, there is little or no risk associated with investing in ISDN now—even though we all understand BISDN is coming.

There is also a fundamental difference between the way BISDN will be deployed and the way NISDN has been deployed. The telephone company has deployed NISDN ubiquitously, so everyone can obtain it. This has been characterized as a "build it and they will come" strategy. The industry is taking a much more cautious approach, however, to deployment of BISDN, which is consistent with the fact that BISDN will require much larger sums of money than NISDN. In particular, ATM cell-relay data service has been deployed only in response to specific customer demand, in cases where end users are willing to pay the thousands of dollars a month that it now costs. Perhaps someday, as the price continues to drop and the demand increases, BISDN will also become pervasive. But it's anybody's guess when this will happen.

ISDN Information
Sources

L ike the personal computer, ISDN has increasingly made its way into
many aspects of our lives. In this chapter, we point to sources that
contain or refer to ISDN-valuable information, and we offer tips to help
you spot ISDN information in similar sources. By keeping ISDN in mind,
you will be able to spot ISDN-related information, which appears frequently
in the media. Try to do this in moderation, or your friends will begin to find
you boring.

Understand that ISDN technology and issues change so rapidly that only you
can to be sure the material you use is in fact current and up to date. Even recent
electronic or verbal information could be from a dated source; even seemingly
ultimate sources, such as standards, can often use some freshening up.

Also, be aware that no one source of information will be complete. There
is always another application, another option for signaling, an unusual
condition that might occur, a new service, a new kind of equipment
produced, and so on. It is unreasonable to expect to obtain comprehensive
and complete information in this rapidly changing world. But if you achieve
a reasonably complete composite of information from a variety of sources,
you're doing well. You will not want to try to understand every aspect of
ISDN. It's not worth it. Rather, start with your needs. Add more detail until
you are satisfied.

In summary, look for ISDN-relevant information in the ordinary information sources you normally use, and be cautious about completely accepting the validity and accuracy of any one source of information. Get substantiation.

15.1 TEXTS

As with any new technology, it is difficult to find texts that address the subject of ISDN. But you will find a number of texts listed in the bibliography. Some of these texts are so dated they have only historic value. Others rehash pre-ISDN technology and append some ISDN information. Some are focused on certain technical aspects of ISDN. You should glance through them at a bookstore or library to find out if any of them are appropriate for you.

15.2 PERIODICALS

Many magazines and newspapers provide information on ISDN. Special-interest magazines and targeted newspaper sections aimed at trade, professional, or technologically literate audiences have informative articles. While reading a professional studio-recording journal, one reader noticed an advertisement for an equalizing device that used ISDN to allow geographically separated musicians to make recordings together. The article described how the user could make that kind of recording and how to correctly specify and order ISDN service.

Trade Journals

In the telecommunications industry, many publications strive to keep people informed as to what is happening. Some titles include *Communications Week*, *InfoWorld*, *NetWorld*, *Datamation*, *Telephone Engineer and Management (TE&M)*, *Telephony*, and probably a dozen others that have started between the time this book was written and the time you begin to read it.

These magazines and newspapers are aimed primarily at the practicing professional industry member. However, because their target audience is usually fairly broad (for example, users and administrators as well as manufacturers and designers), introductory material is often included.

Nevertheless, the articles in these journals tend to be slanted toward someone who already knows a great deal about ISDN and who is following along to see what has developed. Consequently, the reader generally will be expected to know many acronyms, history pertinent to a particular issue, and so on. Journals often provide explanatory information for new developments, but such information generally compares new to existing technology, which may not appeal to the newcomer unfamiliar with existing technologies.

Generally, these journals are good sources for learning about current events in the telecommunications industry. Sometimes journalistic emphasis on a particular topic or service will actually shape industry planning and direction, as more and more readers become interested and knowledgeable. Every publication aims for a slightly different audience, but there is a large overlap. For example, one publication is primarily geared toward telephone-plant construction techniques. Another is geared toward private networks; another toward public networks and services. Still another is geared toward computing capabilities and solutions. But virtually all of these publications touch on all of the topics mentioned above over time. The best way to determine what you need is to skim a large number of these journals, searching for information that speaks to your need. Gradually, you will find that you are looking regularly at only a few of the publications. If you are an industry member, most of these publications are available free of charge if you fill out an application form.

These journals are very good sources of information on new products: new ISDN telephones, ISDN workstations, PBXs, network equipment, ISDN service capabilities, and so on, appear regularly in many of these journals. Reader service cards and telephone numbers are readily available so users can contact suppliers.

Popular Newspapers

Surprisingly, daily newspapers are an excellent source of up-to-date ISDN information, especially indirect information (that is, *not* detailed technical articles about new products and their capabilities). A reader might see a supplement section explaining the basics of ISDN and how it might affect the home or business. It is very easy to imagine one of the more colorful papers having a supplement insert with diagrams, arrows, and conjectures about how ISDN will affect us all. The economic performance of ISDN-oriented companies are also often reported, often with mentions of technology or discussions of America's technological rise (or decline, depending on the perspective of the author).

More business-oriented papers such as the *Wall Street Journal* and the *New York Times* have, in recent years, focused more on technology and how it affects us. And, more and more, you will be reading about ISDN in these papers: about which telephone companies are deploying it, and about which states and cities have it. Many of these articles will also focus on how businesses can use ISDN to increase revenue and avoid costs. Be especially alert to articles that tie in ISDN to achieving business objectives. These insights can be extremely helpful to you when you think and rethink how you should run your business.

Interestingly, ISDN is popular with business owners who are *reengineering* their businesses. Although a rigorous definition is elusive, reengineering basically means rethinking how your business should be operated, without constraining it to what exists now in the way of equipment, procedures, or people. You can provide your business with an ideal or long-range target, which you can approach while still in transition. Look toward improved and less costly PCs, ISDN, universal product coding, scanners, smart cards, and other technology advances to achieve your desired end states. Use technology appropriately where it makes good business sense. For example, ISDN is appealing to many business planners who need to move information between geographical locations. Many news articles integrate concepts of business planning in their discussions of technologies such as ISDN.

Popular Magazines

Popular magazines are generally available at most news stands and news stand sections of bookstores, airports, and drugstores. Familiar titles include *Time, Newsweek, U.S. News & World Report, Business Week, The Economist, Forbes, Fortune, PC Magazine, Byte, MacWorld,* and *Consumer Reports.* Popular magazines that are likely to have the most ISDN and ISDN-related news are the general news magazines (particularly their business sections), the business news magazines (particularly their technology sections), the technology magazines, and the product-review magazines. Search out the types of information that speak to your needs by examining as many popular magazines as possible. Not only do you get factual information from these publications, you can also obtain a perspective that might help you use the information productively.

One advantage of reading these publications is that often they do not assume that the reader already understands the basic issues and that only an update of current events is needed. Rather, the reader is gently led to the point; these publications explore the social and personal impacts and potentials of new technology.

15.3 TELEVISION

Although no one admits to watching TV, some information on ISDN has been presented on television. So far, there has not been much on ISDN, and what has been broadcast has aired on shows that are not widely viewed.

Computer-Oriented Programs

As we use personal computers more and more, television inevitably has featured programs to help us use the machines. One such regular program is a series called *Computer Chronicles*. Each week, demonstrations on this program illustrate new products available in the field of personal computing. Recognizing that PC users need to communicate and that ISDN is ideal for facilitating effective PC communication, several programs in this series have been dedicated to ISDN. In addition to describing the technology, *Computer Chronicles* has taken us to other countries to see how they are deploying ISDN, and how people are using it.

The information in this and similar productions is presented from the perspective of a PC user. Little attention goes to communications in general, and less still to ISDN in particular. Unless you plan to watch these programs for other reasons, or unless you know that a particular story will focus on ISDN, television is a fairly inefficient way to learn about ISDN.

Science-Oriented Programs

Science programs such as *NOVA, Smithsonian World, In Search Of,* and other special shows may sometimes focus on a topic related to ISDN. Programs on the nature of information, new manufacturing or business techniques, and ISDN itself can show us how to apply information to solve business and social problems.

Business Programs

Programs such as *Wall Street Week* focus on industry fairly regularly. Programs dealing with the telecommunications industry will likely emphasize ISDN and other advanced technologies as key factors in the success of the companies highlighted in the program. Analysts may examine key success factors for companies such as manufacturers in terms of the technology they deploy to provide the products their customers want.

News Programs

During a major trade show held in January 1994, there were many product announcements and demonstrations. A local Washington, D.C., television station (WJLA) showed film clips of a desktop conferencing arrangement using ISDN. John Harter, a WJLA business reporter, correctly and capably described the ISDN service and the desktop conferencing equipment while showing how representatives from vendors were remotely making a photograph badge for him to use at the show. As more of these fancy new services and capabilities are introduced, film clips will highlight them on evening news programs. As ISDN becomes more feasible for the mainstream, it will become ever more newsworthy.

15.4 CONFERENCES AND SEMINARS

There is a whole industry growing up around the idea of providing training to people who need to know about ISDN and ISDN-related issues. These training firms advertise that they offer immersion in the subject matter over a very short period of time. They also claim that you can meet and converse with key players and prime movers in the industry. Some attendees feel they obtain the equivalent of a college semester course in a period of a few days at such a seminar or training session.

Industry Groups: Training Programs

One type of training program is a lecture or tutorial-style program that resembles a classroom but is held, typically, in a hotel environment. Usually, an instructor sits at a viewgraph machine and shows numerous overheads while lecturing. This can be very effective, especially if you are fairly new to ISDN and want to be able to interact with the instructor. Usually, these arrangements have small enough class sizes so you can ask questions and discuss issues, but you should inquire before signing up for one of these courses to make sure it meets your needs. It is not unusual for such training to cost several hundred dollars per day, exclusive of any travel expenses. Expect to pay over $1000 for a course lasting 3 days.

Another type of training format is the seminar. In this arrangement, a hosting organization arranges the entire production. Guests are invited to speak and are sought from various parts of the industry (for example, manufacturers, service providers, users who have particular applications, regulators, and legislators). It is not unusual to hear from people who are writing standards, producing products, and otherwise professing to have first-hand knowledge of the subject matter.

Typical formats for a seminar include a 2- to 3-hour session in which there is a moderator and three or four speakers. At the beginning of such a session, the moderator introduces the theme, the speakers, and the topics that will be discussed. Each speaker presents his or her information, usually with viewgraphs or slides along with a lecture. Usually, the audiences for a seminar are large, and there are few if any opportunities for interaction during the presentations. After all the speakers have made their presentations, a panel discussion often allows questions from the audience. One or more speakers may address each question, and sometimes, a question sparks additional discussion among the speakers.

Seminars can be extremely beneficial to those in industry who have some knowledge of a subject but want information on current developments or want more detail about a specific aspect of an ISDN topic. Another benefit to attending a seminar is that there are usually a great many attendees, and those of us who have been in the industry for some time meet many old friends and acquaintances and make new ones. It's amazing how just knowing who to call can often solve a specific problem or quickly answer a question.

Even when you provide that insight for someone else, you are exposed to what is on the minds of others and to what others are doing.

Industry Groups: Working Meetings

A number of groups that work toward particular ISDN goals or missions will allow you to participate. For example, the standards body T1 allows all interested participants to help write standards. Direct costs of membership are fairly low, but travel and the time required to participate can take their toll. Groups such as the NIU Forum also are available to the public. Other groups may be more difficult or expensive to attend.

These groups exist primarily for the purpose of achieving their goals (for example, writing a standard or promoting interoperability) but can be excellent learning environments. Participants who are genuinely interested and willing to help work toward the group goals are usually given enough information to understand what they need to know to participate. If you have no interest in helping the group achieve its goals but only want to learn about ISDN, do yourself and the group a favor by obtaining the information elsewhere.

Sales-Oriented Presentations

Depending upon your business affiliations, you may have the opportunity to attend a presentation by a potential supplier who wants your business. For example, if your business is a likely candidate to purchase a number of ISDN telephones or workstations, a manufacturer of these products might invite you to a seminar where an entire family of products are demonstrated in the context of plausible applications. Smaller candidate customers are often invited to a more general presentation, larger candidate customers to a special customized presentation. Telephone companies often present information to their customers in this way.

A sales presentation is an ideal time to ask questions and try out actual equipment. While talking with supplier representatives, you can soon determine how they can help you. Sadly, many potential customers focus on what these sales representatives cannot do. Sometimes people attending these seminars get very upset if technical questions remain unanswered. If these representatives are more sales oriented, they may not be able to provide technical or applications information, but they may be quite helpful when discussing terms and conditions of a sale or a trial. You will still need to obtain technical information, but you will have acquired very useful information nonetheless. Often, these sales people can direct you to others who can talk about the applications or technical aspects.

Don't forget to actually try some of the equipment. You need to make sure that it can do what you need it to do, with reasonable evolutionary prospects. Especially for equipment you will use directly, such as an ISDN telephone, make sure you like its look and feel. Don't just assume you will get used to the product in time; if an indicator is hard for you to see, it probably won't get easier with time.

15.5   STANDARDS PUBLICATIONS

National and international standards are generally available to anyone who wishes to purchase them. Unfortunately, acquiring them can be very expensive. For example, the complete set of CCITT blue books is thousands of dollars; individual ANSI specifications vary in price according to size but are often $10 or more for specifications consisting of 15 or more pages. For the casual reader, other sources of information will do just as well and are more enjoyable.

ANSI Documents

These standards and technical reports range from nuts and bolts, to photographic standards, to electronic and telecommunications standards. The ones we are interested in describe how ISDN is standardized in North America. These are not legal documents that obligate any individual or company to abide by their contents. Rather, they are agreed-upon standards that provide a benchmark for those who wish to conform. Accordingly, if a manufacturer offers a product and claims conformance to a particular standard, you can expect the equipment to conform to the document, which you can read.

CCITT Documents

These standards and technical reports deal with the entire scope of telephony and telecommunications. For ISDN, obtain the I series of standards (three fascicles in the blue books) and the Q series pertaining to access signal-ing.(You may also want those documents pertaining to the CCS 7). If these don't satiate you, you might consult the G series pertaining to μ-law encoding, and possibly some of the X series pertaining to packet services (especially X.31, which describes ISDN access to X.25 services). The X.200 and 400 series describe modeling and abstract symbolic notation.

ISO Documents

These standards and technical reports deal with the entire scope of computing and data communications. Much of this work has been adopted by the CCITT (for example, the OSI reference model has been adopted by the CCITT as X.200). Many of the computing capabilities that will use ISDN services are covered in the OSI standards. These capabilities include email or message handling, *electronic document interchange (EDI)*, and others. Conformance testing methodology (ISO 9646), which was devel-oped in ISO for use with OSI standards, has also been adopted by the ISDN community. The NIUF abstract test suites for ISDN protocols use ISO 9646 methodology.

15.6   THE NIU FORUM

As described in Chapter 9, the NIU Forum was created so that ISDN could be molded to meet user needs and promote interoperability in a multi-vendor environment. Although participation is open to anyone with an interest, the NIU also produces documents.

NIUF members have written introductory tutorials that describe the way the Forum operates and describe particular aspects of ISDN. These and other tutorials, typically presented on the day before the opening Forum plenary, are reproduced in a bound volume distributed to all persons attending the meeting.

NIU implementation agreements are highly technical documents that pro-mote the interoperability of ISDN. Regardless of whether you participate in the NIUF, these technical documents can help technically sophisticated people understand what parts of the standards are currently being imple-mented and what options are currently being selected. This information helps equipment manufacturers, service providers, and ISDN users plan for the availability of ISDN and know what applications might be planned for those same time frames.

Application profile documents describe the use of ISDN to meet end-user-stated applications. They include end-user context in addition to all the relevant layers of protocol. These documents provide both users and implementors with guidelines for achieving the benefits the end user wants. Hence, the end user can purchase products and services that actually achieve those results. These documents also guide the implementor community to provide the desired equipments and capabilities to the user.

The *Application Catalog* is the most popular document ever produced by the NIU. Thousands of copies have been distributed. It's fairly easy to read, has a lot of good ideas about how to derive benefit, and includes a list of contacts for obtaining services and products to implement the applications. Reading the catalog will help you envision possibilities. It also can help in developing a vision from a vague idea to a sketched-out architecture.

Wiring and powering documents published by the NIU can help you understand wiring considerations within your building. You may simply decide to read the instructions packaged with the ISDN products that you have purchased. Chances are the instructions will either be based upon the NIU documents or derived from them.

15.7 WORKSHOPS: OSI WORKSHOP

Like the NIU implementation agreements that promote interoperability for ISDN, these agreements promote interoperability for *Open Systems Inter-connection (OSI)* products. Like the standards for ISDN, standards for OSI also include options, unspecified parameters, and ambiguous text, which implementation agreements address. (These documents are intended for technically sophisticated readers.)

15.8 THE CORPORATION FOR OPEN SYSTEMS

This organization spawned the ISDN Executive Council, which was largely responsible for TRIP '92, National ISDN, and (being planned as of this writing) ISDN Solutions '94. Each of these activities has resulted (or will result) in a variety of publications (such as the *Atlas* during TRIP '92 and the *Solutions Guide* for 1994). COS also publishes results of inter-operability tests and conformance tests and publishes a list of certified ISDN test equipment.

15.9 PURCHASE SPECIFICATIONS

Why would you want to see someone else's purchase specifications? Why not just write your own or purchase by selecting from what is available? Large organizations write purchase specifications that can provide you with insight to help you make your own determinations.

Many large users don't shop the way individuals and small businesses do. Rather than simply shop for what they want, they specify how they want it developed. Because of their large purchasing power, they can sometimes literally create a market for such products. These products then become available for individuals and small business people to purchase. In fact, many of these manufacturers will indicate right on their product that it meets a certain purchase specification. This phenomenon is not unique to ISDN. In the world of public-school textbooks, the requirements of just a few of the largest states result in textbooks that are used by the entire country. Similarly, the requirements of a few large and early ISDN users may well steer the development of ISDN services and terminals.

Federal Information Purchasing Specifications

One of the largest of the large users is the U.S. federal government. The *federal information purchasing specifications (FIPS)* are vehicles to describe the products that government agencies want to purchase; typically, many manufacturers go to great lengths to provide products that satisfy these requirements. Because of relatively recent attempts by the federal government to buy products like those in the commercial sector whenever appropriate, many users feel that government specifications might even provide a guide for their use. Government specifications that are consistent with commercial specifications can result in greater availability of products and lower costs for both government and commercial users.

Bellcore Technical References

Bellcore's *Technical Reference (TR)* documents are used primarily by manufacturers planning to develop equipment for use in public ISDNs and equipment that will operate with those public ISDNs. These TRs provide what the guidance manufacturers need to ensure they meet operational requirements and can interoperate in a multivendor environment. End users will not normally read or be aware of these documents but will know of the results of Bellcore TRs via designations such as National ISDN, which is a convenient way of describing an ISDN that complies with a large number of TRs and therefore provides a particular array of services.

Manufacturers' Specifications

For products from automobiles to high-fidelity audio equipment, manufacturers will frequently produce specifications. It is reasonable to expect that these specifications for ISDN equipment will be just as useful as those published for other products. Don't overlook them when you are doing your "R&D" (reading and dreaming).

15.10 SALES INFORMATION

Sales information can also be useful to the user. Many sales proposals contain useful application ideas. For medium and large users, vendors may provide specific recommendations based upon needs for the particular enterprise. Finding communications solutions to business problems can be a winning strategy for everyone. Proposals will often contain cost information, revenue-impact estimates, and consequent-profit results. Often vendors will obtain the raw information used in these proposals directly from you or your organization. It is in everyone's best interest to provide information that is as accurate as possible to contribute to the value of the final proposal. Users who are not fortunate enough to receive such custom proposals (or who choose not to entertain them) will need to examine potential solutions on their own using much the same methodology.

15.11   ELECTRONIC-INFORMATION SOURCES

Perhaps the most widely discussed form of electronic access is the Internet. There are news groups on the Internet (such as newsgroup group comp.dcom.isdn) that frequently post questions, answers, and discussions about ISDN issues and applications. Also, there are various electronic mailing lists that you can join. Some of these lists are intended primarily for developers who are working on products for ISDN; but other lists are more open to the lay person. The NIUF maintains a mailing list for the *Enterprise Network Data Interconnectivity Family (ENDIF)* of applications.

Also on the Internet are a wide variety of archive sites that contain information about ISDN. These archives contain *Internet Engineering Task Force (IETF)* recommendations as well as ITU-T information and summaries. Various NIUF workgroups have archive sites with meeting information and work-in-progress information.

Within the NIUF is a bulletin board. Since as of this writing it is undergoing change and reevaluation, you should get details on it when you wish to use it.

15.12   SUMMARY

You can obtain ISDN information from almost every traditional source of information. Of course, some sources provide better yields than others. Even where information sources don't yield a lot of specific ISDN information, the astute reader can read ISDN possibilities into the news.

After reading this book, perusing other documents, and attending user-group meetings, you will begin to become an expert yourself. You can then offer help and guidance to others who are newly emerging as prospective ISDN users.

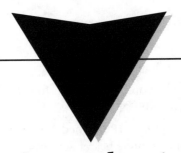

Appendix A
ITU-T I-Series
Recommendations in Force

This Appendix provides a list of I-Series recommendations that were in force on November 18, 1993. This list was obtained from the ITU-T via the Internet. To obtain a current list, gopher to info.itu.ch, which is the ITU archive for this and a great deal more information. Menus will guide you through your search.

ISDN: General Structure, Frame of I-Series Recommendations, Terminology

I.112 (1993) [Rev.1] [18 pp.] [Publication scheduled: December 1993]
   Vocabulary of terms for ISDNs

I.113 (04/91) [Rev.1] [18 pp.] [Published: August 1991]
   Vocabulary of terms for broadband aspects of ISDN

I.114 (1993) [New] [5 pp.] [Publication scheduled: December 1993]
   Vocabulary of terms for universal personal telecommunication

Description of ISDNs

I.120 (1993) [Rev.1] [2 pp.] [Publication scheduled: December 1993]
   Integrated services digital networks

I.121 (04/91) [Rev.1] [2 pp.] [Published: July 1991]
   Broadband aspects of ISDN

I.122 (1993) [Rev.1] [1 pp.] [Published: October 1993]
   Framework for frame mode bearer services

General Modeling Methods

I.130 (1988) [Blue Book Fasc. III.7] [Published: June 1989]
   Method for the characterization of telecommunication services
   supported by an ISDN and network capabilities of an ISDN

Telecommunication Network and Service Attributes

I.140 (1993) [Rev.1] [23 pp.] [Publication scheduled: December 1993]
   Attribute technique for the characterization of telecommunication
   services supported by an ISDN and network capabilities of an ISDN

I.141 (1988) [Blue Book Fasc. III.7] [Published: June 1989]
   ISDN network charging capabilities attributes

General Description of Asynchronous Transfer Mode

I.150 (1993) [Rev.1] [10 pp.] [Publication scheduled: December 1993]
   B-ISDN asynchronous transfer mode functional characteristics

Service Capabilities—Scope

I.200 (1988) [Blue Book Fasc. III.7] [Published: June 1989]
   Guidance to the I.200-series of recommendations—general aspects of
   services in ISDN

I.210 (1993) [Rev.1] [35 pp.] [Publication scheduled: December 1993]
Principles of telecommunication services supported by an ISDN and
the means to describe them

I.211 (1993) [Rev.1] [17 pp.] [Publication scheduled: December 1993]
B-ISDN service aspects

Common Aspects of Services in the ISDN

I.220 (1988) [Blue Book Fasc. III.7] [Published: June 1989]
Common dynamic description of basic telecommunication services

I.221 (1993) [Rev.1] [5 pp.] [Publication scheduled: December 1993]
Common specific characteristics of services

Bearer Services Supported by an ISDN

I.230 (1988) [Blue Book Fasc. III.7] [Published: June 1989]
Definition of bearer service categories

I.231 (1988) [Blue Book Fasc. III.7] [Published: June 1989]
Circuit-mode bearer service categories

I.231.1 (1988) [Blue Book Fasc. III.7] [Published: June 1989]
64 Kbps unrestricted, 8 kHz structured

I.231.2 (1988) [Blue Book Fasc. III.7] [Published: June 1989]
64 Kbps, 8 kHz structured, usable for speech information transfer

I.231.3 (1988) [Blue Book Fasc. III.7] [Published: June 1989]
64 Kbps, 8 kHz structured, usable for 3.1 kHz audio information
transfer

I.231.4 (1988) [Blue Book Fasc. III.7] [Published: June 1989]
Alternate speech/64 Kbps unrestricted, 8 kHz structured

I.231.5 (1988) [Blue Book Fasc. III.7] [Published: June 1989]
2 × 64 Kbps unrestricted, 8 kHz structured

I.231.6 (1988) [Blue Book Fasc. III.7] [Published: June 1989]
384 Kbps unrestricted, 8 kHz structured

I.231.7 (1988) [Blue Book Fasc. III.7] [Published: June 1989]
1536 Kbps unrestricted, 8 kHz structured

I.231.8 (1988) [Blue Book Fasc. III.7] [Published: June 1989]
1920 Kbps unrestricted, 8 kHz structured

I.231.9 (1993) [New] [7 pp.] [Publication scheduled: December 1993]
Circuit-mode 64 Kbps, 8 kHz-structured multiuse bearer service
category

I.231.10 (08/92) [New] [5 pp.] [Published: November 1992]
Circuit-mode multiple-rate unrestricted 8 kHz structured bearer
service category

I.232 (1988) [Blue Book Fasc. III.7] [Published: June 1989]
Packet-mode bearer services categories

I.232.1 (1988) [Blue Book Fasc. III.7] [Published: June 1989]
Virtual call and permanent virtual circuit

I.232.2 (1988) [Blue Book Fasc. III.7] [Published: June 1989]
Connectionless bearer service category

I.232.3 (1993) [Rev.1] [15 pp.] [Publication scheduled: December 1993]
User signaling bearer service category (USBS)

I.233 (10/91) [New] [1 pp.] [Published: April 1992]
Frame mode bearer services

I.233.1 (10/91) [New] [34 pp.] [Published: April 1992]
ISDN frame relaying bearer service; note—published with I.233

I.233.2 (10/91) [New] [18 pp.] [Published: April 1992]
ISDN frame switching bearer service; note—published with I.233

Teleservices Supported by an ISDN

I.240 (1988) [Blue Book Fasc. III.7] [Published: June 1989]
Definition of teleservices

I.241 (1988) [Blue Book Fasc. III.7] [Published: June 1989]
Teleservices supported by an ISDN

I.241.1 (1988) [Blue Book Fasc. III.7] [Published: June 1989]
Telephony

I.241.2 (1988) [Blue Book Fasc. III.7] [Published: June 1989]
Teletex

I.241.3 (1988) [Blue Book Fasc. III.7] [Published: June 1989]
Telefax 4

I.241.4 (1988) [Blue Book Fasc. III.7] [Published: June 1989]
Mixed mode

I.241.5 (1988) [Blue Book Fasc. III.7] [Published: June 1989]
Videotex

I.241.6 (1988) [Blue Book Fasc. III.7] [Published: June 1989]
Telex

Supplementary Services in ISDN

I.250 (1988) [Blue Book Fasc. III.7] [Published: June 1989]
Definition of supplementary services

I.251 (1988) [Blue Book Fasc. III.7] [Published: June 1989]
Number identification of supplementary services

I.251.1 (08/92) [Rev.1] [4 pp.] [Published: October 1992]
Direct-dialing-in

I.251.2 (08/92) [Rev.1] [5 pp.] [Published: October 1992]
Multiple subscriber number

I.251.3 (08/92) [Rev.1] [9 pp.] [Published: October 1992]
Calling line identification presentation

I.251.4 (08/92) [Rev.1] [16 pp.] [Published: October 1992]
Calling line identification restriction

I.251.5 (1988) [Blue Book Fasc. III.7] [Published: June 1989]
Connected line identification presentation (COLP)

I.251.6 (1988) [Blue Book Fasc. III.7] [Published: June 1989]
Connected line identification restriction (COLR)

I.251.7 (08/92) [Rev.1] [8 pp.] [Published: October 1992]
Malicious call identification

I.251.8 (08/92) [Rev.1] [6 pp.] [Published: October 1992]
Subaddressing supplementary service

I.252 (1988) [Blue Book Fasc. III.7] [Published: June 1989]
Call offering supplementary services

I.252.1 (1988) [Blue Book Fasc. III.7] [Published: June 1989]
Call transfer (CT)

I.252.2 (08/92) [Rev.1] [15 pp.] [Published: November 1992]
Call forwarding busy

I.252.3 (08/92) [Rev.1] [9 pp.] [Published: November 1992]
Call forwarding no reply

I.252.4 (08/92) [Rev.1] [11 pp.] [Published: November 1992]
Call forwarding unconditional

I.252.5 (08/92) [Rev.1] [9 pp.] [Published: November 1992]
Call deflection

I.252.6 (1988) [Blue Book Fasc. III.7] [Published: June 1989]
Line hunting (LH)

I.253 (1988) [Blue Book Fasc. III.7] [Published: June 1989]
Call completion supplementary services

I.253.1 (07/90) [Rev.1] [12 pp.] [Published: October 1990]
Call waiting (CW) supplementary service

I.253.2 (08/92) [Rev.1] [8 pp.] [Published: November 1992]
Call hold

I.253.3 (1988) [Blue Book Fasc. III.7] [Published: June 1989]
Completion of calls to busy subscribers (CCBS)

I.254 (1988) [Blue Book Fasc. III.7] [Published: June 1989]
Multiparty supplementary services

I.254.1 (1988) [Blue Book Fasc. III.7] [Published: June 1989]
Conference calling (CONF)

I.254.2 (08/92) [Rev.1] [10 pp.] [Published: November 1992]
Three-party supplementary service

I.255 (1988) [Blue Book Fasc. III.7] [Published: June 1989]
Community of interest supplementary services

I.255.1 (08/92) [Rev.1] [14 pp.] [Published: November 1992]
Closed user group

I.255.2 (1988) [Blue Book Fasc. III.7] [Published: June 1989]
Private numbering plan (PNP)

I.255.3 (07/90) [New] [9 pp.] [Published: October 1990]
Multilevel precedence and preemption service (MLPP)

I.255.4 (07/90) [New] [6 pp.] [Published: October 1990]
Priority service

I.255.5 (08/92) [New] [6 pp.] [Published: November 1992]
Outgoing call barring

I.256 (1988) [Blue Book Fasc. III.7] [Published: June 1989]
Charging supplementary services

I.256.1 (1988) [Blue Book Fasc. III.7] [Published: June 1989]
Credit card calling (CRED)

I.256.2 (1988) [Blue Book Fasc. III.7] [Published: June 1989]
Advice of charge (AOC)

I.256.2a (1993) [New] [12 pp.] [Publication scheduled: December 1993]
Advice of charge—charging information at call set-up time (AOC-S)

I.256.2b (1993) [New] [11 pp.] [Publication scheduled: December 1993]
Advice of charge—charging information during the call (AOC-D)

I.256.2c (1993) [New] [10 pp.] [Publication scheduled: December 1993]
Advice of charge—charging information at the end of the call (AOC-E)

I.256.3 (08/92) [Rev.1] [10 pp.] [Published: November 1992]
Reverse charging

I.257 (1988) [Blue Book Fasc. III.7] [Published: June 1989]
Additional information transfer

I.257.1 (08/92) [Rev.1] [16 pp.] [Published: November 1992]
User-to-user signaling

Network Functional Principles

I.310 (1993) [Rev.1] [21 pp.] [Publication scheduled: December 1993]
ISDN—network functional principles

I.311 (1993) [Rev.1] [41 pp.] [Publication scheduled: December 1993]
B-ISDN general network aspects

I.312 (10/92) [New] [37 pp.] [Published: May 1993]
Principles of intelligent network architecture; note—same as Q.1201

Reference Models

I.320 (1988) [Blue Book Fasc. III.8] [Published: July 1989]
  ISDN protocol reference model

I.321 (04/91) [New] [7 pp.] [Published: July 1991]
  B-ISDN protocol reference model and its application

I.324 (10/91) [Rev.1] [17 pp.] [Published: February 1992]
  ISDN network architecture

I.325 (1993) [Rev.1] [15 pp.] [Publication scheduled: December 1993]
  Reference configurations for ISDN connection types

I.327 (1993) [Rev.1] [12 pp.] [Publication scheduled: December 1993]
  B-ISDN functional architecture

I.328 (10/92) [New] [4 pp.] [Published: April 1993]
  Intelligent network—service plane architecture; note—same as Q.1202

I.329 (10/92) [New] [12 pp.] [Published: May 1993]
  Intelligent network—global functional plane architecture; note—same
  as Q.1203

Numbering, Addressing, and Routing

I.330 (1988) [Blue Book Fasc. III.8] [Published: July 1989]
  ISDN numbering and addressing principles

I.331 (1988) [Blue Book Fasc. III.8] [Published: July 1989]
  Numbering plan for the ISDN era; note—same as E.164

I.333 (1993) [Rev.1] [41 pp.] [Publication scheduled: December 1993]
  Terminal selection in ISDN

I.334 (1988) [Blue Book Fasc. III.8] [Published: July 1989]
  Principles relating ISDN numbers/subaddresses to the OSI reference
  model network layer addresses

I.335 (1988) [Blue Book Fasc. III.8] [Published: July 1989]
  ISDN routing principles; note—superseded by E.172

Connection Types

I.340 (1988) [Blue Book Fasc. III.8] [Published: July 1989]
  ISDN connection types

Performance Objectives

I.350 (1993) [Rev.1] [16 pp.] [Publication scheduled: December 1993]
  General aspects of quality of service and network performance in
  digital networks, including ISDNs

I.351 (1993) [Rev.1] [9 pp.] [Publication scheduled: December 1993]
  Relationships among ISDN performance recommendations

I.352 (1993) [Rev.1] [22 pp.] [Publication scheduled: December 1993]
  Network performance objectives for connection processing delays in
  an ISDN

I.353 (1993) [New] [9 pp.] [Published: October 1993]
  Reference events for defining ISDN performance parameters

I.354 (1993) [New] [9 pp.] [Published: October 1993]
  Network performance objectives for packet-mode communication in
  an ISDN

I.355 (1993) [New] [28 pp.] [Publication scheduled: December 1993]
  ISDN 64 Kbps connection type availability performance

Protocol Layer Requirements

I.361 (1993) [Rev.1] [15 pp.] [Publication scheduled: December 1993]
  B-ISDN ATM layer specification

I.362 (1993) [Rev.1] [3 pp.] [Published: October 1993]
  B-ISDN ATM adaptation layer (AAL) functional description

I.363 (1993) [Rev.1] [76 pp.] [Publication scheduled: December 1993]
  B-ISDN ATM adaptation layer specification

I.364 (1993) [New] [13 pp.] [Publication scheduled: December 1993]
  Support of broadband connectionless data service on B-ISDN

General Network Requirements and Functions

I.370 (10/91) [New] [10 pp.] [Published: January 1992]
Congestion management for the ISDN frame relaying bearer service

I.371 (1993) [New] [29 pp.] [Publication scheduled: December 1993]
Traffic control and congestion control in B-ISDN

I.372 (1993) [New] [12 pp.] [Publication scheduled: December 1993]
Frame relaying bearer service network-to-network interface requirements

I.373 (1993) [New] [20 pp.] [Publication scheduled: December 1993]
Network capabilities to support universal personal telecommunication (UPT)

I.374 (1993) [New] [8 pp.] [Publication scheduled: December 1993]
Framework recommendation on network capabilities to support multimedia services

General

I.410 (1988) [Blue Book Fasc. III.8] [Published: July 1989]
General aspects and principles relating to recommendations on ISDN user-network interfaces

I.411 (1993) [Rev.1] [8 pp.] [Publication scheduled: December 1993]
ISDN user-network interfaces—reference configurations

I.412 (1988) [Blue Book Fasc. III.8] [Published: July 1989]
ISDN user-network interfaces—interface structures and access capabilities

I.413 (1993) [Rev.1] [10 pp.] [Publication scheduled: December 1993]
B-ISDN user-network interface

I.414 (1993) [New] [4 pp.] [Publication scheduled: December 1993]
Overview of recommendations on layer 1 for ISDN and B-ISDN customer accesses

I.420 (1988) [Blue Book Fasc. III.8] [Published: July 1989]
Basic user-network interface

I.421 (1988) [Blue Book Fasc. III.8] [Published: July 1989]
Primary rate user-network interface

Layer 1 Recommendations

I.430 (1993) [Rev.1] [112 pp.] [Publication scheduled: December 1993]
Basic user-network interface—Layer 1 specification

I.431 (1993) [Rev.1] [45 pp.] [Publication scheduled: December 1993]
Primary rate user-network interface—Layer 1 specification

I.432 (1993) [Rev.1] [43 pp.] [Publication scheduled: December 1993]
B-ISDN user-network interface—physical layer specification

Layer 2 Recommendations

I.440 (1988) [Blue Book Fasc. III.8] [Published: July 1989]
ISDN user-network interface data link layer—general aspects;
note—same as Q.920

I.441 (1988) [Blue Book Fasc. III.8] [Published: July 1989]
ISDN user-network interface, data link layer specification;
note—same as Q.921 layer 3 recommendations

Layer 3 Recommendations

I.450 (1988) [Blue Book Fasc. III.8] [Published: July 1989]
ISDN user-network interface layer 3—general aspects; note—same as Q.930

I.451 (1988) [Blue Book Fasc. III.8] [Published: July 1989]
ISDN user-network interface layer 3 specification for basic call control;
note—same as Q.931

I.452 (1988) [Blue Book Fasc. III.8] [Published: July 1989]
Generic procedures for the control of ISDN supplementary services;
note—same as Q.932

Multiplexing, Rate Adaption, and Support of Existing Interfaces

I.460 (1988) [Blue Book Fasc. III.8] [Published: July 1989]
Multiplexing, rate adoption and support of existing interfaces

I.461 (1988) [Blue Book Fasc. III.8] [Published: July 1989]
Support of X.21-, X.21 bis- and X.20 bis-based data terminal equipment (DTES) by an integrated services digital network (ISDN); note—same as X.30

I.462 (1988) [Blue Book Fasc. III.8] [Published: July 1989]
Support of packet mode terminal equipment by an ISDN; note—same as X.31

I.463 (1988) [Blue Book Fasc. III.8] [Published: July 1989]
Support of data terminal equipment (DTES) with V-series type interfaces by an integrated services digital network (ISDN); note—same as V.110

I.464 (10/91) [Rev.1] [1 pp.] [Published: December 1991]
Multiplexing, rate adoption and support of existing interfaces for restricted 64 Kbps transfer capability

I.465 (1988) [Blue Book Fasc. III.8] [Published: July 1989]
Support by an ISDN of data terminal equipment with V-series type interfaces with provision for statistical multiplexing; note—same as V.120

Aspects of ISDN Affecting Terminal Requirements

I.470 (1988) [Blue Book Fasc. III.8] [Published: July 1989]
Relationship of terminal functions to ISDN

Internetwork Interfaces

I.500 (1993) [Rev.1] [6 pp.] [Publication scheduled: December 1993]
General structure of the ISDN internetworking recommendations

I.501 (1993) [New] [10 pp.] [Publication scheduled: December 1993]
Service internetworking

I.510 (1993) [Rev.1] [12 pp.] [Publication scheduled: December 1993]
Definitions and general principles for ISDN internetworking

I.511 (1988) [Blue Book Fasc. III.9] [Published: July 1989]
ISDN-to-ISDN layer 1 internetwork interface

I.515 (1993) [Rev.1] [15 pp.] [Publication scheduled: December 1993]
Parameter exchange for ISDN internetworking

I.520 (1993) [Rev.1] [13 pp.] [Publication scheduled: December 1993]
General arrangements for network internetworking between ISDNs

I.525 (1993) [New] [17 pp.] [Publication scheduled: December 1993]
Internetworking between ISDN and networks which operate at bit
rates of less than 64 Kbps

I.530 (1993) [Rev.1] [9 pp.] [Publication scheduled: December 1993]
Network internetworking between an ISDN and a public switched-
telephone network (PSTN)

I.540 (1988) [Blue Book Fasc. III.9] [Published: July 1989]
General arrangements for internetworking between circuit-switched
public data networks (CSPDNs) and integrated services digital
networks (ISDNs) for the provision of data transmission;
note—same as X.321

I.550 (1988) [Blue Book Fasc. III.9] [Published: July 1989]
General arrangements for internetworking between packet switched
public data networks (PSPDNs) and ISDNs for the provision of data
transmission; note—same as X.325

I.560 (1988) [Blue Book Fasc. III.9] [Published: July 1989]
Requirements to be met in providing telex service within ISDN;
note—same as U.202

I.570 (1993) [New] [9 pp.] [Publication scheduled: December 1993]
Public/private ISDN internetworking

I.580 (1993) [New] [25 pp.] [Publication scheduled: December 1993]
General arrangements for internetworking between B-ISDN and
64 Kbps-based ISDN

Maintenance Principles

I.601 (1988) [Blue Book Fasc. III.9] [Published: July 1989]
General maintenance principles of ISDN subscriber access and
subscriber installation

I.610 (1993) [Rev.1] [26 pp.] [Publication scheduled: December 1993]
B-ISDN operation and maintenance principles and functions

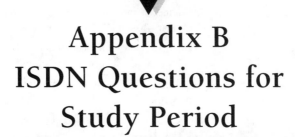

Appendix B
ISDN Questions for
Study Period

The following table provides a list of questions under study from 1993 through 1996 for Study Group 13 (formerly Study Group XVIII). This list was obtained from the ITU-T via the Internet on November 18, 1993, and should stay constant. To obtain this and other relevant ITU information, gopher to info.itu.ch.

Question Number	Title
1/13	Network capabilities for networks other than B-ISDN
2/13	Network capability description for support of B-ISDN services
3/13	Network capabilities for the support of multimedia services in 64k-ISDN and B-ISDN
4/13	Network requirements for B-ISDN signaling
5/13	ATM Layer
6/13	ATM adaptation layer
7/13	Requirements for OAM and network management in B-ISDN

Question Number	Title
8/13	B-ISDN resource management
9/13	Internetworking of B-ISDNs with other networks
10/13	Internetworking of 64k-ISDNs with other networks
11/13	ISDN frame mode bearer service (FMBS)
12/13	Refinements and enhancements to Layer 1 64 Kbps-based ISDN recommendations
13/13	Refinements and enhancements to B-ISDN customer access recommendations
14/13	Functional characteristics of interfaces in access networks
15/13	ISDN architecture and reference models
16/13	General performance issues
17/13	Availability performance
18/13	Security performance
19/13	Error performance
20/13	Performance for ISDN connection processing
21/13	Network synchronization and timing performance
22/13	Universal personal telecommunications (UPT) performance
23/13	Transport network architecture
24/13	Network applications of SDH
25/13	NNI and transport network internetworking principles
26/13	Vocabulary for general network aspects
27/13	Support of broadband connectionless data service on B-ISDN
28/13	Integrated video services (IVS) principles for B-ISDN

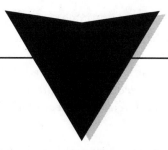

Appendix C
Obtaining IETF RFCs
from the Internet

T he following excerpts of IETF RFCs are for illustrative purposes only.
The list was obtained via anonymous ftp in November 1993 from a site
that no longer provides ftp service. As of press time, you can obtain a
current RFC index from the ftp site at ds.internic.net (via anonymous ftp;
/doc/rfc). Style, format, and content often change, so don't be surprised
if what you obtain is slightly different than what you see below. RFCs are
listed in reverse numeric order. RFC citations appear in this format:

> RFC Number   Title of RFC. Author 1.; Author 2.; Author 3. Issue date;
> Total number of pages (Format: PS=xxx TXT=xxx bytes) (Also FYI
> xxx) (Obsoletes xxx; Obsoleted by xxx; Updates xxx; Updated by xxx)

The format and byte information in parentheses follows the page information.
The format—either ASCII text (TXT), PostScript (PS), or both—is noted,
followed by an equals sign and the number of bytes for that version. The
example

> (Format: PS=xxx TXT=xxx bytes)

shows that the PostScript version of the RFC is xxx bytes and the ASCII
text version is xxx bytes. The (Also FYI xxx) phrase gives the equivalent
FYI number if the RFC were also issued as an FYI document.

"Obsoletes xxx" refers to other RFCs that this one replaces. "Obsoleted by xxx" refers to RFCs that have replaced this one. "Updates xxx" refers to other RFCs that this one merely updates (but does not replace). "Updated by xxx" refers to RFCs that have been updated (but not replaced) by this one. Only immediately succeeding and/or preceding RFCs are indicated— not the entire history of each related earlier or later RFC in a related series: for example,

> 1129   Internet time synchronization: The Network Time Protocol.
> Mills, D.L. 1989 October; 29 p. (Format: PS=551697 bytes)

Many RFCs are available online; if not, this is indicated. Paper copies of all RFCs are also available, either individually or on a subscription basis. In addition, RFCs may be requested through electronic mail. Details are available at the anonymous ftp site (at press time, these include ds.internic.net and wuarchive.wustl.ed among others).

The following are excerpts from the RFC Index (November 1993).

> 1463   FYI on Introducing the Internet—A Short Bibliography of Intro-
> ductory Internetworking Readings for the Network Novice.
> Hoffman, E.; Jackson, L. 1993 May; 4 p. (Format: TXT=7116
> bytes) (Also FYI 19)
>
> 1462   FYI on "What is the Internet?" Krol, E.; Hoffman, E. 1993 May;
> 11 p. (Format: TXT=27811 bytes) (Also FYI 20)
>
> 1334   PPP authentication protocols. Lloyd, B.; Simpson, W.A. 1992
> October; 16 p. (Format: TXT=33248 bytes)
>
> 1333   PPP link quality monitoring. Simpson, W.A. 1992 May; 15 p.
> (Format: TXT=29965 bytes)
>
> 1332   PPP Internet Protocol Control Protocol (IPCP). McGregor, G. 1992
> May; 12 p. (Format: TXT=17613 bytes) (Obsoletes RFC 1172)
>
> 1331   Point-to-Point Protocol (PPP) for the transmission of multi-
> protocol datagrams over point-to-point links. Simpson, W.A.
> 1992 May; 66 p. (Format: TXT=129892 bytes) (Obsoletes RFC
> 1171, RFC 1172)

Appendix D
Excerpts from the NIUF
Catalog

T he excerpts from the *Catalog* are presented here to give you an idea of
what it contains. The entire document is rather large, so if you want one,
you have to order one or obtain it via anonymous ftp from archive site
info.bellcore.com (/pub/isdn/catalog). Section 3.1.22 is the only application
from the *Catalog* included here. It corresponds to the illustrative example in
Chapter 12. These excerpts are from the second edition of the *Catalog;* the
third edition is currently being produced. The draft was voted stable at the October
1994 NIUF meeting and should be "final" after the February 1995 meeting.

NOTICE OF DISCLAIMER

This document is published by the North American ISDN Users' Forum
(NIUF) to aid the identification of ISDN applications and facilitate their
timely, harmonized and service interoperable introduction. This document
is subject to review and change, and superseding publications, if any,
regarding this subject matter may differ extensively in content and format.

The NIUF reserves the right to revise this document for any reason, including but not limited to, conformity with standards promulgated by various agencies, utilization of advances in the state of the technical arts, or the reflection of changes in the design of any equipment, techniques, or procedures described or referred to herein.

The NIUF, NIST, and the organizations contributing to the development of this document, including the information from suppliers, makes no representation or warranty, express or implied, with respect to the sufficiency, accuracy, or utility of any information or opinion contained herein. The NIUF expressly advises that any use of or reliance upon said information or opinion is at the risk of the user and that the NIUF, NIST, and the organizations contributing to the development of this document shall not be liable for any damage or injury incurred by any person arising out of the sufficiency, accuracy, or utility of any information or opinion contained herein.

This document is not to be construed as a suggestion to any manufacturer to modify or change any of its products, nor does this document represent any commitment by any organization to purchase any product or furnish a particular service whether or not it provides the described characteristics.

Readers are specifically advised that Section 4 of this document results from a survey of suppliers who claim to meet some or all of the functional requirements of the solutions of Section 3. This survey may not have reached the majority of suppliers who could assert such claims. The use of the supplier information, subsequent affairs with these suppliers, or subsequent investment in these products or services for achieving the solutions in Section 3 is solely at the risk and discretion of the user of such information.

Nothing contained herein shall be construed as conferring by implication, estoppel or otherwise, any license or right under any patent, whether or not the use of any information herein necessarily employs an invention of any existing or later issued patent.

The NIUF and NIST do not recommend products or services, and nothing contained herein is intended as a recommendation of any product or service to anyone.

If further information is required, please contact:

NIUF Secretariat	TEL 301 975 2937
c/o NIST	FAX 301 926 9675
Bldg 223 Rm B364	
Gaithersburg, MD 20899	

PREFACE

The NIUF is pleased to present the second edition of its *ISDN Solutions Catalog*. The purpose of the second edition remains the same as the first, to make it easier for vendors to develop and support ISDN applications and for users to understand and install them. The North American ISDN Users' Forum (NIUF) was formed in 1988 under the auspices of the National Institute of Standards and Technology. The mission of the NIUF is "to create a strong user voice in the implementation of ISDN and ISDN applications, and to ensure that the emerging ISDN meets users' application needs."

A team of experts from across the industry wrote the first edition of the *Catalog* in 1992. It was approved for publication by the NIUF at their February, 1993 meeting. The first edition included 34 solutions to the Forum's high priority applications using National ISDN-1 basic rate services, and 4 using primary rate, as a preview of National ISDN-2.

Demand for the first edition has been noteworthy. Since the fall of 1992, thousands of copies have been distributed by accredited sources. Since reproduction is permitted with proper acknowledgment, thousands more have been disseminated by others.

In February of 1993, the NIUF authorized work on this second edition. It provides a more robust set of solutions in Section 3, and adds Section 2 for the "decision maker," who must decide whether to use ISDN. Many other refinements were made. The scope is essentially the same as the first edition, with additional coverage of National ISDN-2. National ISDN continues to grow. New solutions in the *Catalog* cover National ISDN-2, especially primary rate. Of course, changes in products and services are tracked through an updated chapter of product information.

Subsequent editions of this document will depend on the commitment of contributors and the support of the NIUF. Following this page is a list of those who have made this edition possible. As Editors, we want to thank those who gave their time, energy, and expertise to complete the second edition; without forgetting those who provided the foundation in Edition 1. We hope you find the results useful.

Stuart Boose   Brajesh Mishrak
Editor   *Editor*

                  David LaPier
                  Editor
                  Chair, Applications Analysis Working Group

CONTRIBUTORS

Many people have contributed to the first and second editions of the *Catalog*. In addition to those suppliers who offered information about their products, the following individuals have contributed their time to write, review, comment or produce the second edition:

Steve Roberts	Ameritech
Cathy Simon	Ameritech
Grantley Nurse	AT&T
Greg Sturgis	AT&T
Carl Francolini	AT&T Bell Labs
Gerry Hopkins	Bell Atlantic
Bahman-Amin Salehi	Bellcore
Barbara Shaw	Bellcore
Bob Brillhart	Bellcore
Bobbie Rentko	Bellcore
Brajesh Mishra	Bellcore
Chin Chiang	Bellcore
Darnese Hill	Bellcore
David LaPier	Bellcore
Dick Khan	Bellcore
Janice Rathmann	Bellcore
John Mulligan	Bellcore
Lynn Case	Bellcore
Paul Roder	Bellcore
Paul Spraggs	Bellcore
Phil Patrick	Bellcore
Rhonda Cooperstein	Bellcore
Rich Beckman	Bellcore
Rich Nici	Bellcore
Robin Rossow	Bellcore
Stuart Boose	Bellcore
Tom Vanderwater	Bellcore
Zach Gilstein	Bellcore
Joy Maguire	Centigram
Sunil Dhar	Cisco
Robert Larribeau	Combinet
Ira Clark	DGM&S

Larry Horner	DGM&S
Steve Rogers	EDS
Eugene Chang	Extension Technology
Wunnava Subbarao	Florida International University
Richard O'Brien	Gandalf-Premier
Ed Dunlap	Gandalf-Systems
Bill Taylor	Hayes Microcomputer Products
Robert Ayres	IBM
Dorothy Mulligan	Jersey City State College
Stan Kluz	Lawrence Livermore
Lena Nilsson	LifeSoft
Mike Dunn	ManyLink
Chris Stacey	National Semiconductor
Randy Sisto	Network Express
Dawn Hoffman	NIST
Leslie Collica	NIST
Dan Stokesberry	NIST
Jennette Floyd	Northern Telecom
Daniel McCauley	NYNEX
George Peabody	PC Associates
Glenn Ehley	Siemens Stromberg-Carlson
Mark Haigh	Siemens Stromberg-Carlson
Robert C. Schickofke	Siemens Stromberg-Carlson
Stephen Hill	Tone Commander
Bryan Juliano	Univ. of Conn.
Robert Berger	Uranix Consulting
Thom McKay	US WEST
Michael Gawdun	USAA
John Menzel	Verifone
Farooq Raza	Verilink

TABLE OF CONTENTS [for *NIUF Catalog*]

1. INTRODUCTION

ISDN (Integrated Services Digital Network) makes it possible to send, receive and modify information using telephone lines in ways that were not previously possible for speed, quality and other reasons. ISDN is not an application itself; it's really just a technique that works to augment applications. For instance, work at home for some engineers is too slow even over 9600 bps modems, but 64 Kbps with a direct interface into their department LAN means that they can use the same software and have access to all the data as if they were in the office. Still and motion video pictures can now be sent between two or more parties without being in special conference rooms. Colleagues can jointly edit a report, graphics and a spreadsheet while talking on the telephone, despite being hundreds of miles away.

This document is a guidebook of solution sets that presents how ISDN is used to address common communications needs. It makes it easier for users, systems integrators and application developers to understand what ISDN components are needed to implement their applications and solutions. Thanks to an agreement by the major equipment makers called National ISDN, the building blocks for these solutions are now more standard than ever, which means more competition, better products and integral services by the telcos [telephone companies]. National ISDN is the first step toward making consistent ISDN services available across the country.

The authors of this *Catalog* do not pretend that these solutions are a *complete* list. They know that some things you need aren't here. And they know that some things here will be used in ways they could not have imagined. That's all to the good.

The authors offer this catalog in the hope that you will use it as a guide, a reference, and a point of departure for the imagination.

Please note that a Reader Response Form is provided at the very end of this document should you desire to contribute your impressions on the merits of this *Catalog*.

1.1. Organization of the Second Edition

This is the second edition of *A Catalog of National ISDN Solutions to Selected NIUF Applications*. It is again targeted to the community of systems integrators, application developers, and corporate telecom managers who want to learn how ISDN works — to solve their business communications problems and provide opportunities. However, the technical scope has grown to include both *National ISDN-1 (NI-1)* and NI-2, and the focus has sharpened on solutions.

Section 2, a new section for this edition, is for the decision maker who must decide whether or not to look at ISDN for solutions to meet his or her needs. It highlights the benefits of ISDN through simple examples of key applications. Tools are presented for analyzing the benefits and costs of an ISDN-based solution, and presents the status of ISDN-related interoperability.

Section 3 covers how ISDN can be used to meet a wide variety of business opportunities. The solutions show generically, but in detail, what end-systems are needed, and what network services are required. Each solution addresses a specific user need. Section 3 contains 40 solutions using *basic rate interfaces (BRI)*, with the features available under NI-1, and 4 BRI solutions that require the features available in NI-2. In addition, 17 solutions using *primary rate interface (PRI)* features available in NI-2 are included. There are, in total, 26 new solutions in the Second Edition. In addition, all the solutions in this edition have been written in a new style for ease of use.

Section 4 is a product compendium resulting from a new survey of vendor information. Products covered in Section 4 include ISDN terminal equipment, software, and services. However, neither the NIUF or NIST recommends or endorses products or services and nothing contained herein is intended as a recommendation or endorsement of any product or service.

Section 5 covers selected topics on ISDN in greater technical detail. A variety of topics are covered, including: call types, SPIDs, and TEIs; rate adaptation; lower-layer and higher-layer compatibility information elements; SS7; multiline hunt group; powering; configurations for high bandwidth applications; communication servers; parameter groups and interface groups; conformance testing; and signaling diagrams.

The *Catalog* is a rich source of information on ISDN. A Bibliography is included. If you are new to ISDN and want an introductory text, check the Bibliography for titles. The Index is an excellent way to explore specific topics. The Annex presents background information on the activities of the North American ISDN User's Forum.

There are as many ways to use this book as there are readers. If you are using this book to learn ISDN, a good place to start is the Table of Contents. The rest of Section 1 contains an introduction to ISDN technology. Section 2 can help you get started on the decision making process. In

Section 3, read those guides which look interesting to you. Look up the names of the various components necessary in the index, and find out where those products appear in Section 4. If you are already familiar with ISDN, take the time to flip through Sections 3 and 4 so that you know what is covered. Also look at Section 5, since there are several new topics discussed. Finally, the annex contains an overview of the activities of the NIUF. Also, please take time to complete the Reader Response form in the back of this document so that future editions of this document may be improved.

3. NATIONAL ISDN SOLUTIONS

This section consists of three parts, each containing application guides highlighting the features of a specific ISDN interface. Section 3.1 contains guides which use National ISDN-1 *basic rate interfaces (BRIs)*. Section 3.2 contains guides to illustrate the additional functionality of the National ISDN-2 BRI. Although they are not repeated here for space reasons, all the guides in Section 3.1 could also be implemented using NI-2 BRI. Section 3.3 demonstrates solutions using the National ISDN-2 *primary rate interface (PRI)*.

Each guide in the *Catalog* contains the following components (in order of presentation): an application description with potential benefits to the end user, the configuration of the example solution identifying alternate configurations, a short description of how the solution works, equipment required, and capabilities to be requested from the ISDN service provider. Each guide concludes with "technical notes" which provide further details about the operation of the solution and possible options. Additional implementation information, which is of particular interest to equipment designers, application developers and system integrators, is provided in Section 5 of this *Catalog*. This supplementary material is referenced where useful in the Technical Notes.

Integrated Voice and Data Terminal Configurations for BRI Solutions

In many applications, the users benefit from integrated voice and data. Their phones and computers are closely coupled in an "integrated voice and data system", and both take advantage of ISDN.

With the variety of products available, the users can "package" their phone, personal computers and connection to ISDN in one of several ways. To demonstrate this flexibility, yet not exhaust the overwhelming number of possibilities, this document focuses on five typical packages. Most of the BRI guides in Sections 3.1 and 3.2 utilize one of the five packages, or configurations, shown below. Because PRI configurations are more complex, no similar packaging for PRI is used in the guides in Section 3.3.

The guides in the catalog are example solutions. Above most of the solution guides' configuration diagram, a list of configuration numbers appears. Because of space limitations, only the configuration number in bold and underlined (e.g., **2**) is fully explained in the guide. The other configuration numbers shown identify packaging alternatives for that solution, but other alternatives may exist.

Configuration 1   Personal computer (or workstation) equipped with an ISDN adapter

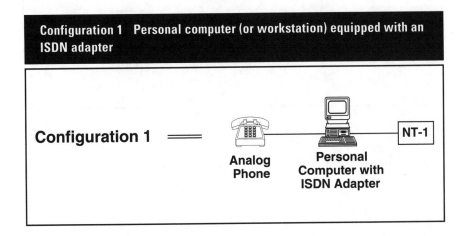

NOTE   Some suppliers allow a headset to be used instead of an analog phone. If the ISDN adapter is designed to power the analog phone (or headset) from the PC power supply, then turning off the PC will result in loss of phone service. See Section 5.1.8.5.

The following guides are illustrated using Configuration 1:

3.1.1	3.1.16	3.1.32
3.1.2	3.1.21	3.1.33
3.1.6	3.1.24	3.1.35

3.1.7	3.1.27
3.1.8	3.1.39
3.1.26	3.2.3

NOTE   Because of the previously described packaging alternatives, some guides which are illustrated in this document using other configurations may also be implemented using Configuration 1.

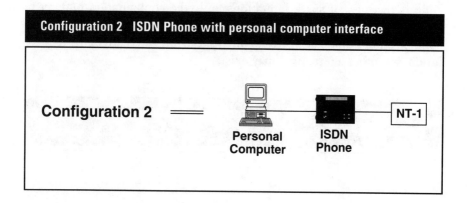

Configuration 2   ISDN Phone with personal computer interface

Configuration 2   ===   Personal Computer — ISDN Phone — NT-1

The following guides are illustrated using Configuration 2:

3.1.7	3.1.19
3.1.14	3.1.34
3.1.15	3.2.3

NOTE   Because of the previously described packaging alternatives, some guides which are illustrated in this document using other configurations may also be implemented using Configuration 2.

The following guides are illustrated using Configuration 3:

3.1.6	3.1.29
3.1.7	3.1.37
3.1.16	3.1.38
3.1.17	3.2.3
3.1.20	

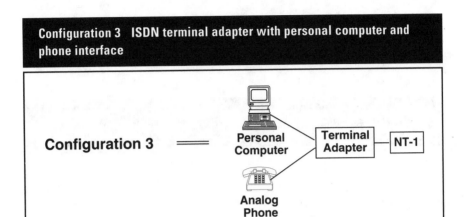

Configuration 3   ISDN terminal adapter with personal computer and phone interface

NOTE   Because of the previously described packaging alternatives, some guides which are illustrated in this document using other configurations may also be implemented using Configuration 3.

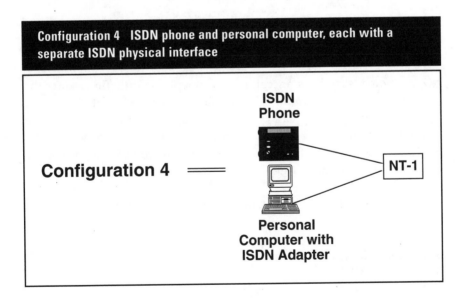

Configuration 4   ISDN phone and personal computer, each with a separate ISDN physical interface

The following guides are illustrated using Configuration 4:

3.1.12   3.2.4

NOTE   Because of the previously described packaging alternatives, some guides which are illustrated in this document using other configurations may also be implemented using Configuration 4.

Configuration 5   Personal computer (or workstation) with LAN interface and ISDN LAN bridge

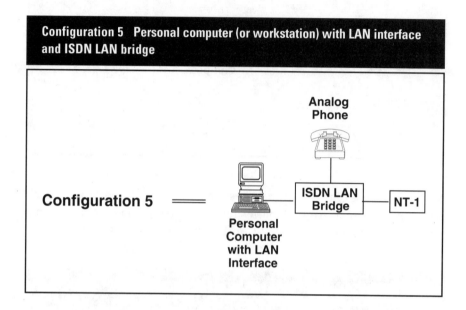

NOTE   Some suppliers integrate the telephone functions into the personal computer. Similarly, some suppliers provide all necessary LAN bridging and ISDN call control functionality on a single personal computer adapter card. An ISDN phone can also be plugged into the NT-1, as shown in Configuration 4. Potentially, routing functions can be part of the system as well.

The following guides are illustrated using Configuration 5:

3.1.3	3.1.8
3.1.4	3.1.22
3.1.5	3.1.25

NOTE   Because of the previously described packaging alternatives, some guides which are illustrated in this document using other configurations may also be implemented using Configuration 5.

3.1.22 High-Performance Telecommuting (INTERACTIVE Graphics and Text)

ISDN can provide a person who works at home or in a satellite office on-line access to the corporate computing environment with the ability to exchange large quantities of data at high speed. Examples include interactive graphics and desktop publishing. With data exchanged at rates of 64 or 128 Kbps, many applications will run almost as fast as they do at the main office.

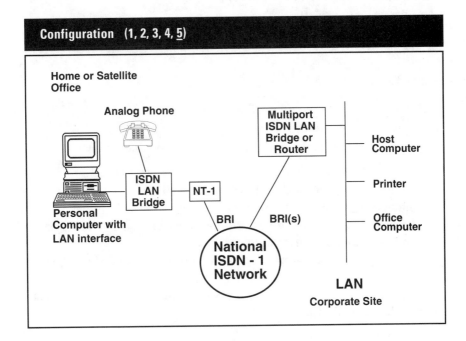

How It Works

The home computer functions just like one of the personal computers attached directly on the corporate network. The network operating system routes traffic to/from the remote personal computer without noticing the presence of ISDN. A local area network is limited by distance. To grow the network, bridges and routers can be used, which forward LAN datagrams between LAN segments, and learn addresses dynamically. ISDN LAN bridges function in pairs, with the two halves connected by two simultaneous circuit-data calls. LAN datagrams are forwarded between segments as necessary using circuit-data connections. ISDN LAN bridges and routers have a variety of different features, such as address screening for security and the ability to automatically dial (or hang-up) based on traffic.

Obtain Equipment with These Capabilities

Personal Computer with LAN Interface

- Applications compatible with network operating system and far end.
- LAN interface (e.g., Ethernet, token ring) compatible with far end.

ISDN LAN Bridge

- LAN bridge functions compatible with far end and local LAN (e.g., Ethernet or token ring).
- Address screening based on calling number or MAC address.
- B channel capabilities:
  - Simultaneous circuit-data calling on two B channels.
  - Simultaneous voice and circuit-data calling.
  - If using NI-1, support for two *directory numbers (DNs)* and *service profile ids (SPIDs)* will be needed.
  - Combine two 64 Kbps signals to/from the BRI into 128 Kbps signal in a way that is compatible with far end.
  - Support for the circuit-data features listed under "Network Interface to ISDN LAN Bridge."
- Physical interfaces:
  - Analog phone jack.
  - Local LAN (e.g., Ethernet or token ring).
  - RJ-45 connector to NT-1, or integrated NT-1.

Multiport ISDN LAN Bridge or Router

- LAN bridge or router functions compatible with far end and local LAN (e.g., Ethernet or token ring).
- Address screening based on calling number or MAC address.
- Multiple BRIs to meet network traffic requirements.

- B channel capabilities for each BRI:
  - Simultaneous circuit-data calling on two B channels.
  - If using NI-1, support for two *directory numbers (DNs)* and *service profile IDs (SPIDs)* will be needed.
  - Combine two 64 Kbps signals to/from the BRI into 128 Kbps signal in a way that is compatible with far end.
  - Support for the circuit-data features listed under "Network Interface to Multiport ISDN LAN Bridge or Router."
- Physical interfaces:
  - Local LAN (e.g., Ethernet or token ring).
  - RJ-45 connector to NT-1, or integrated NT-1.

Request These Capabilities From ISDN Service Provider

Network Interface to ISDN LAN Bridge
Network Services Required:
- One BRI (2B).
- One B channel for circuit-data calls, with circuit-data DN and SPID.
- One B channel for alternate voice and circuit-data calls. For NI-1, this requires both a voice DN and SPID and a circuit-data DN and SPID.
- Voice features:
  - None required.
- Circuit-data features:
  - Calling number identification services.

Subscription or Ordering Information:
- This interface is configured for simultaneous circuit-data calls and alternate voice and circuit-data calls (NIIG 15). Other NIIGs which have this functionality include 17, 25, and 27.
- Parameter groups for voice features:
  - None required.
- Parameter groups for circuit-data features:
  - A la carte: calling number identification services.

Network Interface to Multiport ISDN LAN Bridge or Router

Network Services Required:

- One or more BRI (2B).

For each BRI:

- Two B channels for circuit-data calls, with circuit-data DNs and SPIDs.
- Circuit-data features:
  - Calling number identification services

Subscription or Ordering Information:

- This interface is configured for two simultaneous circuit-data calls (NIIG 14). Other NIIGs which have this functionality include 15, 17, 24, 25, and 27.
- Parameter groups for circuit-data features:
  - A la carte: calling number identification services.

Technical Notes

- A Multiport LAN ISDN bridge or router can be replaced by multiple single port bridges or routers.
- Many multiport ISDN bridges and routers can utilize a PRI or multiple BRI lines for network access.
- Some ISDN LAN Bridges support data compression, so effective data throughput may be higher.
- The terminal configuration shown here uses a personal computer/work-station with a standalone ISDN LAN bridge. Some LAN adapter cards may have integrated ISDN LAN bridges.
- Dial-back options can improve security. When the person calls in, the corporate computer will refuse the call and then dial back, after verifying that access is permitted, for greater security. The performance tradeoff with dial back is added delay.
- For details on subscription and ordering information using *NIUF ISDN interface groups (NIIG)* and *NIUF parameter groups (NIPG)*, see Section 5.1.11.
- For detailed signaling flow diagrams for this application, see Sections 5.2.1.4 (Voice Call Setup), 5.2.1.5 (Circuit-Data Call Setup), and 5.2.1.6 (Voice and Circuit-Data Call Clearing).

Bibliography

This list of sources was used in the preparation of this book. To promote the text's readability, some detail has been sacrificed: there are no footnotes in the text that connect particular passages to specific sources. Furthermore, sources are listed first in the chapter where they first appear, rather than for every chapter in which they might have been cited.

1 Concepts and Perspectives of ISDN

Angus, Ian. *ISDN: A Manager's Guide to Today's Revolution in Business Telecommunications*. Pickering, Canada: Telemanagement Press, 1990.

Fritz, Jeff. *Sensible ISDN Data Applications*. Morgantown, WV: West Virginia University Press, 1992.

Goldstein, Fred R. *ISDN in Perspective*. Reading, MA: Addison-Wesley, 1992.

Havel, Bill; Rogers, Steve; and Zolnick, Doug. "North American ISDN Users' Forum Primer on ISDN." Presented at the NIUF, Gaithersburg, MD, 1991.

Heldman, Robert K. *Telecommunications Management Planning: ISDN Networks Products and Services*. Blue Ridge Summit, PA: TAB Books, 1987.

Heldman, Robert K. *ISDN In the Information Marketplace*. Blue Ridge Summit, PA: TAB Books, 1988.

Helgert, Herman J. *Integrated Services Digital Networks—Architectures, Protocols, Standards*. Reading, MA: Addison-Wesley, 1991.

Ronayne, John. *The Integrated Services Digital Network: From Concept to Application*. New York: John Wiley & Sons, 1988.

Rutkowski, Anthony M. *Integrated Services Digital Networks*. Norwood, MA: Artech House, 1985.

Stallings, William. *ISDN: An Introduction*. New York: MacMillan Publishing Co., 1989.

Sun Microsystems Computer Corporation. *ISDN Technology Technical White Paper*. Mountain View, CA: Sun Microsystems, 1992.

Verma, Pramode K. *ISDN Systems—Architecture, Technology and Applications*. Englewood Cliffs, NJ: Prentice Hall, 1990.

2   Demand Pull for ISDN

These four texts are highly recommended for further reading.

Bell, Daniel. *The Coming of the Post-Industrial Society*. New York: Basic Books, Inc., 1976. (An excellent but very academic book. It may help to start with Chapter 2, then go back to read the Introduction, Foreword, and Chapter 1.)

Drucker, Peter F. *The Age of Discontinuity*. New York: Harper & Row, 1969. (Perspective similar to Bell's book but much easier to read.)

Kranzberg, Melvin, and Gies, Joseph. *By the Sweat of Thy Brow*. New York: G. P. Putnam's Sons, 1975. (A highly readable and very entertaining book that chronicles the nature of work in the Western World. This book is a fast read.)

Shumacher, E. F. *Small Is Beautiful*. New York: Harper & Row, 1973. (Much more readable than the books by Bell and Drucker. Although it adds its own interesting perspective, it does not adequately cover the same territory.)

Many others have added, rehashed, or otherwise contributed to the idea of the postindustrial society. Some readers may prefer the more popular style of these sources.

Drucker, Peter F. *The New Realities*. New York: Harper & Row, 1989.

Naisbitt, John. *Megatrends*. New York: Warner Books, 1982.

Toffler, Alvin. *Future Shock*. New York: Random House, 1970.

———. The Third Wave. New York: William Morrow, 1980.

———. *PowerShift*. New York: Bantam Books, 1990.

Other sources of information include the following:

Berry, John M. "What's Slowing Job Growth? U.S. Workers' Efficiency." *Washington Post* (September 29, 1993): F1–F3.

Caldwell, Bruce. "New Vision Through Information." *Information Week* (16 December 1991): 30–34.

Curtice, Robert M. "Crossing Dysfunctional Boundaries." *Information Week* (9 September 1991): 56.

Ditto, Ken. "Fault Locators: When, Why, and How to Use Them." *Telephone Engineer and Management* (July 1, 1993): 29–32.

Gilder, George. "The Information Revolution." *The Executive Educator* (March 1993): 16–19.

Information Infrastructure Task Force. *The National Information Infrastructure: Agenda for Action*. Washington, D.C.: NTIA NII Office, 1993.

Knight, Robert M. "Computer-Integrated Manufacturing: IS Punches the Clock." *Information Week* (14 December 1992): 42–43.

Magnet, Myron. "Who's Winning the Information Revolution." *Fortune* (30 November 1992): 110–117.

McCarroll, Thomas. "What New Age?" *Time* (12 August 1991): 44–45.

Perez-Peña, Richard. "For Traffic-Weary Workers, an Office That's a Long Way from the Office." *New York Times* (7 January 1992).

Swoboda, Frank. "Losing a Numbers Game?" *Washington Post* (15 May 1994): H6.

Toffler, Alvin (interview). "Technology as Weaponry." *InformationWeek* (10 January 1994): 48–50.

"Virginia School Educates for the Computer Age." *Washington Post* (4 July 1991): VA6.

Wallace, David G., ed. *Business Week*. Special issue. "The Information Revolution: How Digital Technology is Changing the Way We Work and Live." (1994).

Wysocki, Bernard, Jr. "American Firms Send Office Work Abroad to Use Cheaper Labor." *Wall Street Journal* (14 August 1991).

Some people in our society are not enthusiastic about the introduction of technology into our workplaces or our lives. While some are simply neo-Luddites, who protest anything that is new or threatening, others quite appropriately warn against the dehumanizing aspects of technology and the alienation of workers. Examples of both follow.

Ellul, Jacques. *The Technological Society.* Translated by John Wilkinson. New York: Alfred A. Knopf, 1964.

Marcuse, Herbert. *One-Dimensional Man.* Boston: Beacon Press, 1964.

Teich, Albert H., ed. *Technology and Man's Future.* New York: St. Martin's Press, 1977.

3   What Is Information?

Campbell, Joe. *C Programmer's Guide to Serial Communications.* Indianapolis, IN: H. W. Sams, 1987. (The first four chapters in particular deal with interesting historical issues and describe ASCII issues in great detail.)

Ricotta, Frank J., Jr. "The Six Immutable Laws of Information." *Information Week* (19 July 1993): 63.

4   Supply Push for ISDN

ANSI T1.101-1987. *Synchronization Interface Standards for Digital Networks.*

ANSI T1.103-1987. *Digital Hierarchy—Synchronous DS3 Format Specification.*

ANSI T1.105-1988. *Digital Hierarchy—Optical Interface Rates and Formats Specifications.*

ANSI T1.106-1988. *Digital Hierarchy—Optical Interface Specifications (Single-Mode).*

AT&T Bell Laboratories, Technical Publication Department. *Engineering and Operations in the Bell System.* Murray Hill, NJ: AT&T Bell Laboratories, 1981–84.

Brooks, John. *Telephone: The First Hundred Years.* New York: Harper & Row, 1975.

Markoff, John. "Denser, Faster, Cheaper: The Microchip in the 21st Century." *New York Times* (29 December 1991).

Shanahan, Helen, and Milnes, Ian. "The Wonderful World of T-1 Frame Formats." *Telephone Engineer and Management* (15 April 1992): 40–43.

5 ISDN Network Services

Mason, Jim. "Caller ID Clues Lead to Arrests in Burglary." *Richmond Times-Dispatch* (14 August 1991).

Ramirez, Anthony. "The Pizza Version of Dialing '911': Each Call Is Routed to the Nearest Shop." *New York Times* (9 September 1991).

Rankin, Margaret. "Suspect Seized in I-295 Slaying." *Washington Times* (21 November 1991). (Caller ID enables officers to make arrest.)

SR-NWT-001937. *National ISDN-1*. Bellcore. Issue 1, February 1991; Revision 1 June 1993.

SR-NWT-2120. *National ISDN-2*. Bellcore. Issue 1, June 1992.

SR-NWT-002457. *National ISDN-3*. Bellcore. Issue 1, December 1993.

SR-NWT-002006. *National ISDN*. Bellcore. Issue 2, December 1993.

6 ISDN Protocols

ANSI T1.607-1990. *Digital Subscriber Signaling System No. 1—Layer 3 Signaling Specification for Circuit Switched Bearer Service*. American National Standards Institute, 1990.

FIPS 182. *Federal Information Processing Standard for Integrated Services Digital Network (ISDN)*. Washington, D.C.: NTIS, U.S. Department of Commerce, October 4, 1993.

TR-TSY-00861. *ISDN Layer 3 Protocol Details for the Support of Supplementary Services*. Bellcore. Issue 1, December 1988.

TR-TSY-000268. *ISDN Access Control Switching and Signaling Requirements*. Bellcore. Issue 3, May 1989.

TR-INS-000776. *Network Interface Description for ISDN Customer Access*. Bellcore. Issue 2, June 1991.

7   The Standards Process

American National Standards Institute. *1994 Catalog.* New York: American National Standards Institute, 1994. (See especially pages 86–89. Note: this catalog contains over 100 standards that might be considered to be ISDN or ISDN-related. They are not listed here.)

Cypser, R. J. *Communications for Cooperating Systems: OSI, SNA, and TCP/IP.* Reading, MA: Addison-Wesley, 1990.

Deitel, Harvey. *Operating Systems.* 2d ed. Reading, MA: Addison-Wesley, 1990.

European Telecommunications Standards Institute. ISDN Management and Coordination Committee. *Integrated Services Digital Network (ISDN) Standards Guide.* ETSI Technical Report 076. March 1993.

IEEE Communications Magazine. Special issue. "Standards: Their Global Impact." 32(1).

International Telephone Union—Telecommunications. *Catalogue of ITU-T Recommendations.* 1st ed. 1994. (Note: This document references all of the ITU-T recommendations in force. They are not listed here.)

Wilde, Candee. "Who Should Set Networking Standards?" Communications Week (3 June 1991): 51.

The following papers were given at the Americas Telecommunications Standards Symposium, April 13–15, 1992, in Orlando, Florida.

Committee T1. *Barriers and Facilitators to Interoperability from a Standards Development Organization's Point of View.*

Committee T1. *The Role of Standards in the Telecommunications Life Cycle Process.*

8   From Standards to Products

Evagora, Andreas. "Vendors Join ISDN-Standards Push." *Communications Week* (6 May 1991).

ISO 9646. *Information Processing Systems, OSI Conformance Testing Methodology and Framework.* Parts 1–5, 1989.

NIST. *Federal Information Processing Standard for Integrated Services Digital Network (ISDN).* Gaithersburg, MD: NIST, October 4, 1993.

NIST. *Overview of Integrated Services Digital Network Conformance Testing*. Special Publication. 823-1 Gaithersburg, MD: NIST, March 1992.

The following papers were given at the ISO/IEC Workshop on Worldwide Recognition of OSI Test Results, 6–8 May 1991 in Gaithersburg, Maryland.

Andrews, J. *Laboratory Accreditation.*

Davidson, Ian C. *An Overview of Conformance Testing.*

————. *An Overview of the Technical Level Feeders Forum Test Equivalence Methodology.*

The following papers were given at the Americas Telecommunications Standards Symposium, April 13–15, 1992, in Orlando, Florida.

Corporation for Open Systems International. *Base Standards to Interoperability—Need for an End-Goal Oriented Approach.*

Corporation for Open Systems International. *The Relevance of Standards to Market Requirements.*

Fraser, Leslie. *PICS and ATS.*

Hopkins, G. L. *Experience Using Standards Suggests New Techniques to Achieve Interoperability in a Multivendor Environment.*

Stokesberry, Dan. *Introduction to North American ISDN Users' Forum.*

9 The Users Speak Up

Commision of the European Communities. *European ISDN Users' Forum*. Report from the 6th Plenary Meeting. Amsterdam: 22–24 March 1993.

North American ISDN Users' Forum. *The North American ISDN Users' Forum*. Meeting 21, Vol. 3, Number 2, September 2, 1994.

Sammartino, Fred. "The ATM Forum: A Year in Review." *Data Communications* (October 1992): 123.

Stokesberry, Daniel P., and Hoffman, Dawn M. *North American ISDN Users' Forum Document Bibliography*. Gaithersburg, MD: NIUF, February, 1993.

10   How Might ISDN Be Used?

Aloia, Dick; Jacobson, Jake; andThompson, Matt, eds. *TRIP '92 PROFILES (Section 6)*. TRIP '92 ATLAS. Fairfax, VA: Corporation for Open Systems, 1992.

Bartholomew, Doug. "Production Line 'Ballet'." *Information Week* (20 July 1992): 22.

Brody, Alan. "Checking Out the Checkout Data." *Information Week* (14 December 1992): 34, 38.

Bulkeley, William M. "Computerizing Dull Meetings Is Touted As an Antidote to the Mouth that Bored." *Wall Street Journal* (23 January 1992).

Curtis, Terry. "Learning about Learning with ISDN." *The Executive Educator* (March 1993): 26–28.

DiCarlo, Lisa. "ATM and ISDN Make the Connection." *PC Week* (31 January 1994): 21.

Dziak, Michael. "Making Telecommuting Work" (15 October 1993): 52–55.

"Extending the School Day." *Communications Week* (27 May 1991): 40.

Fleming, Lee. "Computer Computing Is Catching On." *USA Today* (21 October 1991).

Fritz, Jeffrey. "Using ISDN to Access LANs." *Communications Week* (1 February 1993): 29.

Fujitsu Network Switching of America, Inc. "Pharmaceutical Firm Uses ISDN for Data Communication." *ISDN Insights* 4 (2): 1.

Fujitsu Network Switching of America, Inc. "State Uses ISDN for Call Coverage for Geographically Dispersed Offices." *ISDN Insights* 4 (2): 4.

Gawron, L. J.; Jackel, L. D.; Stenard, C. E.; and Lukas, F. X. "Scanned-Image Technologies Bring New Ways to Conduct Business." *AT&T Technology* 6 (4): 2–9.

Grzelakowski, Moe. "ISDN Centrex Goes to School." *Telephony* (25 October 1993).

"ISDN For School Net." *Communications Week* (6 May 1991): 10.

Lehman, H. Jane. "Office Telecommuting Goes Long-Distance." (26 March 1994): E1.

Mathews, Jay. "Checking Out Tomorrow's Offices." *Washington Post* (25 September 1993): F1.

McWilliams, Rex A. "Using ISDN." *Telephone Engineer & Management* (15 August 1991): 52, 54, 55.

Medina, Diane. "ISDN: The Meter Is Running." *Information Week* (29 July 1991).

Montgomery, Leland. "Paperless Claims: A Miracle Cure." *Finance World* (9 June 1992): 32.

Paul, Laren Gibbons. "Whiteboard Apps Aid Collaborators." *PC Week* (4 April 1994): 77.

Purvis, Andrew. "Healing by Wire." *Time* (18 May 1992).

Riedl, Richard E., and Strom, James L. "Making an Impact with ISDN." *The Executive Educator* (March 1993): 23–26.

Rooney, Paula. "Groupware Lets Users Cruise the Hallways for Colleages." *PC Week* (May 16, 1994): 31.

Ryan, Michael. "Go Anywhere! But Don't Leave Your Chair." *Parade Magazine* (21 March 1993): 18–19.

Shen, Fern. "U.S. Plans Telework Site in MD." *Washington Post* (29 December 1991).

Strom, James L. "In Education, Yesterday's Success Equals Tomorrow's Failures." *Optiv* (Fall 1992): 20–23.

Tebes, John. "Advanced Telecommunications in Health Care: Impact of the National ISDN Network on Health Care Delivery in the U.S." *Optiv* (Fall 1992): 24–26.

"Telecommuting with ISDN: Two Ideas Whose Time Has Come." *ISDN News* (23 October 1991): 1–3.

Teschler, Lee. "Technology Is Changing the Definition of the Workplace." *Industry Week* (16 September 1991).

Thyfault, Mary E. "Why Sit Alone at Your Desk?" *Information Week* (19 July 1993): 54.

Trotter, Andrew. "Wired for Learning." *The Executive Educator* (March 1993): 20–22.

Varanasi, Serge V. "ISDN Data Networking: Teleaction Services." *IEEE Communications Magazine* 32 (6): 25.

Wallace, Bob. "Domino's Delivers Using New Call Routing Service." *Network World* (August 12, 1991). (Note: this call management service uses the automatic number identification [ANI] of conventional telephony. Similar applications using ISDN make use of the CLID [calling line identification] number.)

11   Providing ISDN

Aloia, Dick. "Come to a Grand Opening." *Telephone Engineer & Management* (May 1, 1992):46.

Aloia, Dick; Jacobson, Jake; and Thompson, Matt, eds. *ISDN Tariffs, Deployment and Interconnection Plans (Section 5).* TRIP '92 ATLAS, Fairfax, VA: Corporation for Open Systems, 1992.

Cain, Roger. "How to Make ISDN BRI Available Now." *Telephone Engineer & Management* (15 May 1991).

Durr, Michael. "ISDN Reemerges." *LAN Magazine* (January 1994): 103–110.

Finneran, Micahel F. "Can the Telcos Develop a Market for ISDN?" *Business Communications Review* (November 1991): 45–49.

ISDN Users Forum for Development of New Technology (Japan). "Present Status of ISDN in Japan." Gaithersburg, MD: February 1994.

Machrone, Bill. "Today's Promising Technology Is Tomorrow's Broken Dream." *PC Week* (16 May 1994): 71.

Medina, Diane. "ISDN Trial: Hung Jury." *Information Week* (16 December 1991).

Metcalfe, Bob. "Microsoft's Plans Signal the Year of ISDN." *InforWorld* (4 April 1994).

North American ISDN Users' Forum. "ISDN Tariff Summary." Gaithersburg, MD: NIUF, June 1, 1993. (Summaries of tariffs provided by vendors throughout North America.)

Rogers, Dale T.; Nowicki, Jerry; Kawauchi, Takeshi; and Inoue, Osamu. "The Connectivity Factor." *Telephone Engineer & Management* (1 May 1992).

SR-NWT-002102. *ISDN Deployment Data.* Bellcore. Issue 5, November 1994.

Sweeney, Terry. "ISDNs Linked." *Communications Week* (August 26, 1991): 26–27. (Note: This paper was presented at the NIU Forum in June 1994.)

Thyfault, Mary E. "ISDN: Still a Leap of Faith?" *Information Week* (March 18, 1992): 34, 36.

Whitbread, Meg. "Leading Edge ISDN Strategies Waking Up the End User." *Interactive World* (April 6, 1992).

The Yankee Group. "ISDN: Ready, Willing, and Able." *Yankee Watch: Telecommunications* 8 (16).

The Yankee Group. "ISDN: The Walls of Resistance Finally Come Tumbling Down." *Yankee Watch: Telecommunications* 9 (3).

12   Implementing ISDN Services

Brown, Mark, and Hartley, Harry, eds. *ISDN Solutions Guide.* Fairfax, VA: Corporation for Open Systems International. In press.

Fritz, Jeff. "Using ISDN to Access LANS." *Communications Week* (1 February 1993): 29.

Fritz, Jeff. "Digital Remote Access." *Byte* (October 1994): 207.

Hobbs, Joseph J. "Enterprise Networking and National ISDN Synergy." *ConneXions* 7 (12): 2–17.

Immer, Dave. "Phone It In: Music Over ISDN for Individuals and Project Studios." *Mix* (February 1994): 89–97.

Kramer, Matt. "Whiteboards Getting Better." *PC Week* (7 February 1994): 21.

LaPier, David, ed. *A Catalog of National ISDN Solutions for Selected NIUF Applications.* 2d ed. Gaithersburg, MD: North American ISDN Users' Forum, February 11, 1994.

13   What Could Go Wrong?

Braue, Joseph. "Bush vs. Clinton: The Networking Angle." *Data Communications* (October 1992): 6.

Burger, Carolyn S. "Phone Companies Should be Able to Compete." *Delaware State News* (2 June 1991).

Casto, James E. "Caller ID—The Good More than Outweighs the Bad." (Huntington, WV) *Herald-Dispatch* (5 April 1992): D3

Cohen, Rachelle G. "Let's Make It Safe for Obscene Callers." *Boston Herald* (3 April 1992).

Dempsey, Paul Stephen. "Why Won't the Fat Lady Sing for Deregulation?" *Baltimore Sun* (13 September 1991).

Eby, Deborah. "Telecom Policy: Industry Still Waiting for Direction." *Telephone Engineer & Management* (15 October 1993): 15.

Fatemi, Erik. "Phone Calls Prove Costly for Thieves." *Vienna Sun Gazette* (May 3, 1990): 10.

Gilder, George. "Into the Telecosm." *Harvard Business Review* 69(2).

Grafstein, Laurence. "Free the Baby Bell Seven." *Wall Street Journal* (26 June 1992).

Hammer, Dianne. "Will a Federal Road not Taken Merge with the ISDN Freeway?" *Telephone Engineer & Management* (15 September 1992): 23–26.

Hammer, Dianne. "ISDN Emerges from Black Hole of Uncertainty." *America's Network* (15 April 1994): 42–45.

Handler, Gary. "The Importance of Time to Market." *Bellcore Digest of Technical Information* (December 1992): 2–4.

Hyatt, Josh. "Lotus Founder Launches Foundation." *Baltimore Sun* (13 April 1992): 10.

Keyworth, George A. "Telecommunications and Computing: The Unfulfilled Promise." *Forbes* (12 November 1990).

Killette, Kathleen. "NTIA Study: Telcos Need More Freedom." *Communications Week* (28 October 1991): 4.

Kretschmer, Ruth K. "Social Obligations Must Be Shared by New Entrants." *Telephone Engineer & Management* (15 April 1992): 56–58.

Lindstrom, Annie. "Bell Atlantic ISDN Delayed." *Communications Week* (1994) 55–58.

CCITT Draft Recommendation F.811. *Broadband Connection Oriented Bearer Service.* Study Group I, Geneva, December, 1991.

Masonly, Charles F. "Greene Giveth and Taketh Away." *Telephony* (5 August 1991).

Newton, Harry. "Between a Rock and a Hard Place." *Teleconnect* (August 1993): 8–11.

Noam, Eli M. "Telecom Privacy Policy Elements." *Transnational Data and Communications Report* (March 1990): 9–11, 12.

Northern Virginia Community College. "ISDN—Advanced Concepts." Loudon Campus Community Education (Spring 1994): 4.

Northern Virginia Community College. "ISDN—Introduction." Loudon Campus Community Education (Spring 1994): 4.

Obuchowski, Janice. *Comprehensive Study of the Domestic Telecommunications Infrastructure.* Washington, D.C.: National Telecommunications and Information Adminstration, U.S. Department of Commerce, 1990.

———. "Making an Office Without Walls: Industry Needs Freedom to Build Communications Infrastructure." *Washington Technology* (7 November 1991): 13.

Oxley, Michael (Rep., R-Ohio). "Letting Phone Companies into Other Services Will Speed Up a New Communications Network." *Roll Call* (9 April 1992): 22–23.

Richards, Bill. "Classified Rival Is Hampered by Newspapers." *Wall Street Journal* (27 May 1992): B1.

Sessions, William, and Goldman, Janlori. "Wiretap Preservation . . . and Reservations." *Washington Times* (24 May 1992): B3.

Slattery, Jim (Rep., D-Kansas). "It's Time to Let Phone Companies Produce and Sell Equipment." *Roll Call* (9 April 1992): 34–35.

"The Telecom Mess." *Washington Post* (June 7, 1991): A22.

"Untangle America's Telecoms." *The Economist* (August 3, 1991).

14 Broadband ISDN (BISDN)

Bylinsky, Gene. "The Marvels of 'Virtual Reality." *Fortune* (13 June 1991).

CCITT Recommendation I.121. *Broadband Aspects of ISDN.* Geneva, 1988 (blue books).

CCITT Draft Recommendations F.811. Broadband Connection Oriented Bearer Service. Study Group I, Geneva, December 1991.

CCITT Draft Recommendation F.812. *Broadband Connectionless Data Bearer Service.* Study Group I, Geneva, December, 1991.

CCITT Draft Recommendation I.150. *B-ISDN Asynchronous Transfer Mode Functional Characteristics.* Study Group XVIII, Geneva, February 1992.

CCITT Draft Recommendation I.211. *General Service Aspects of B-ISDN.* Study Group XVIII, Geneva, February 1992.

CCITT Draft Recommendation I.311. *B-ISDN General Network Aspects.* Study Group XVIII, Geneva, February 1992.

CCITT Draft Recommendation I.361. *B-ISDN ATM Layer Specification.* Study Group XVIII, Geneva, February 1992.

CCITT Draft Recommendation I.362. *B-ISDN ATM Adaptation Layer (AAL) Functional Description.* Study Group XVIII, Geneva, February 1992.

CCITT Draft Recommendation I.371. *Traffic Control and Resource Management in B-ISDN.* Study Group XVIII, Geneva, February 1992.

CCITT Draft Recommendation I.610. *OAM Principles of the B-ISDN Access.* Study Group XVIII, Geneva, February 1992.

CCITT Draft Recommendation I.413. *B-ISDN User-Network Interface.* Study Group XVIII, Geneva, February 1992.

CCITT Draft Recommendation I.cls. *Support of Broadband Connectionless Data Service on B-ISDN.* Study Group XVIII, Geneva, February 1992.

CCITT Draft Recommendation I.363. *B-ISDN ATM Adaptation Layer (AAL) Specification.* Study Group XVIII, Geneva, February 1992.

Chernicoff, David P. "Taking Some of the Mystery Out of an ATM Technology." *PC Week* (October 25, 1993): N1.

Halford, John. "Virtual Reality: Creating Your Own Values?" *The Plain Truth* (March 1994): 14–19.

Heolterhoff, Manuela. "High-Definition TV Gives Opera Brilliant New Focus." *Wall Street Journal* (11 September 1990): A20.

IEEE Communications Magazine. Special issue. "B-ISDN: High Performance Transport." 29 (9).

Kodama, Toshikazu, and Fukuda, Takeo. "Customer Premises Networks of the Future." *IEEE Communications Magazine* 32 (2): 96–98.

Parikh, Anand. "ATM: The Future of Networking." *Data Communications* (October 1992): 124–128.

Schatz, Willie. "Computing Without Boundaries." *Information Week* (3 August 1992): 22–24, 28.

Vickers, Richard. "The Development of ATM Standards and Technology: A Retrospective." *IEEE Micro* 13 (12): 62–73.

Glossary: Telecommunications Technology Pieces

What follows is a listing of technology "pieces" that the reader has already or likely will encounter while reading about or discussing ISDN. These pieces are listed here for two purposes: to describe what they are and to illustrate how they fit into the making of ISDN. Accordingly, the emphasis is explanatory rather than rigorous. You may encounter these terms in slightly different forms elsewhere.

Alliance for Telecommunications Industry Solutions (ATIS)
Formerly the Exchange Carriers Standards Association, but in 1993 it broadened its membership to include other organizations in the industry. It sponsors Committee T1, which writes ISDN standards for ANSI.

American National Standards Institute (ANSI)
Oversees standards for a wide variety of matters, including telecommunications. ISDN standards written by Committee T1 are published as ANSI specifications.

Analog signal
Used by pre-ISDN telephone systems. Electrical signals on telephone transmission media follow the same patterns as the varying sound pressures of the voice signals that are created when you speak.

Asynchronous transfer mode (ATM)

Sometimes referred to as a fast-packet method. This is a relatively recent technology based on a synchronous stream of cells. Each cell is of fixed length and contains a header in addition to the user-data part. The header is used to route and associate individual cells with calls. If a particular call needs a lot of bandwidth at any point in time, a large fraction of the cells are allocated to that call. If at a particular time very little bandwidth is required, a very small fraction of the cells are used for that particular call (and are available for other simultaneous calls). It therefore has certain aspects of packet-mode service and certain aspects of circuit-mode service. It is planned to be used for providing BISDN services.

Automatic call distributor (ACD)

Equipment used to support large quantities of incoming calls (for example, a catalog-ordering or product-support "help desk"). Usually an incoming caller will hear a recording such as "please wait for the next available agent." It is important to be able to route a high volume of incoming calls to the proper person for answering in order to collect better statistics and offer better service.

Basic rate access (BRA); basic rate interface (BRI)

Access and interface (to) ISDN service. A combination of a single 16 Kbps D channel and 0, 1, or 2 64 Kbps B channels. Often referred to as 2B + D, which is the maximum configuration.

B channel

A 64 Kbps bearer channel (the "bearer" of information). It is the bandwidth or portion of bandwidth allocated to transporting user-information from end to end.

Bearer service

User-information being transmitted to another user. It could be data, voice, images, or whatever else the user wishes to send (digitally, of course) on ISDN.

Bell Communications Research (Bellcore)

The research arm of the Regional Bell Operating Companies (formerly the telephone companies of the Bell System). It was created during divestiture when the Bell System was dissolved. The Bell Laboratories spawned both Bellcore and the present AT&T Bell Laboratories. A

great deal of research and planning for the entire telephone industry
is done by Bellcore.

Binary 8-bit zero suppression (B8ZS)

A coding method to produce 64 Kbps "clear" transmission. It solves
the problem of meeting the requirement of some carrier systems to
avoid carrying the line-signal value of zero. (Some digital 1 values,
found in all nonzero values, are needed in order for the carrier system
to stay synchronized). When a line-signal value of zero is encountered, a substitute value is inserted. This substitute value, which contains enough digital 1s to maintain synchronization, is removed at the
far end and the line signal value of zero is reinserted.

Bit robbing

A technique to signal in-band on digital facilities. By "robbing" from
the speech path a few line-signal bits for signaling purposes, limited
amounts of pre-ISDN telephony signaling information is conveyed
across digital facilities. The remaining line-signal bits are adequate
to recreate the electrical analog signal (and ultimately, the original
sound).

Bonding

Concatenating two or more B channels to form a single channel with
bandwidth larger than 64 Kbps. Two methods (multilink PPP, and the
bonding specification) are implemented entirely outside of the ISDN network by establishing multiple B channel circuit-switched calls. The
associations are made in the user equipment. A third method (multi-
rate services) allows a user to request multiple B channels be associated within the network. Sometimes "bonding" is referred to as
inverse multiplexing, since multiplexing has traditionally involved
deriving smaller channels from larger ones.

Broadband Integrated Services Digital Network (BISDN)

The next generation of ISDN, at higher speeds (greater than 1.5 Mbps).
Some newer technology constructs are contained (for example, ATM).

Broadband services

Services that operate at speeds exceeding the primary rate of ISDN
(1.5 Mbps).

Calling line ID (CLID)

The information element in DSS1 protocol (the access protocol for
ISDN) that contains the telephone number of the telephone from

which the person is calling. The number is the same as the calling party number, which appears in a different protocol (SS7 protocol).

Calling party number (CPN)

The information element in the SS7 protocol (the network protocol) that contains the telephone number of the telephone from which the person is calling. The number is the same as the calling line ID, which appears in the ISDN access protocol (DSS1).

Central office (CO)

Another way of saying telephone (network) switch. Literally, it is the building, cabling, and equipment, including the switch, but generally it is used to mean the network switch.

Circuit-mode bearer service

For both data and speech, a connection is established and maintained for the duration of the call. Unsuccessful attempts are "blocked." During the call, the entire (speech or constant bit-rate data) bandwidth is allocated to the connection between the two users. When the call is finished, the network resources (switches and trunks) are released for the next user.

Committee T1

The first committee established by ECSA (now ATIS) to write standards for the North American telecommunications industry.

Common channel signaling (CCS)

Signaling System 7 is an example of this. In earlier network protocols, the signaling was part of the circuit being established. In ISDN and future telephony network protocols, the signaling is separated from the circuits being established.

Compression

Expressing the original information in fewer bits. When transporting data, an $n:1$ compression ratio allows sending n times as much data per second as would otherwise be possible. To compress data, the sending side must compute the compression algorithm prior to transmission, and the receiving side must compute the inverse algorithm (decode) it so that the user obtains the original information.

Conformance (testing, criteria, certification, recognition)

Testing insures that a product complies with protocol specifications. *Criteria* is the test itself; testing is the process of determining whether

a product complies. *Certification* is testimony that a product passed
the test. *Recognition* is where the certification is appropriate (for
example, a certification issued by one government may or may not
be recognized by another). Passing conformance tests indicates a
likelihood that ISDN equipment will interoperate with other equipment that have also passed conformance tests.

Connection-less service

Used when packets or frames are sent to their destination individually,
without establishing a connection per se. This is done by including
destination information in the header of each packet or frame. For
some types of bursty computer traffic, this is more efficient than
connection-oriented service.

Connection-oriented service

Provided by telephone service today. A call is established (started),
conversation ensues, and then the call is ended (torn down, dis-
established, cleared). in packet-mode services, a logical channel
is established, then a series of packets are transmitted to the receiver,
and then the logical channel is cleared.

Constant bit rate (CBR)

A data service where the bits are conveyed regularly in time (following
a timing source or clock just as members of a marching band follow
the beat of the drummer).

Corporation for Open Systems (COS)

A member-driven organization that promotes open systems and connectivity. Sponsors of the TRIP '92, and ISDN Solutions '94 conferences.
Home of the ISDN Executive Council, which was instrumental in obtaining industry support of National ISDN-1 in 1991.

Customer-provided equipment (CPE)

Also end-user equipment. Equipment that is owned by the ISDN
customer (end user). It is outside the ISDN network and sometimes
referred to as a terminal, sometimes a telephone, and is often a PC.
The U.S. govern-ment declares the NT1—the device that terminates
the ISDN line at the end user's building—to be CPE. End users need to
purchase, install, and maintain their NT1. In other countries, governments declare it part of the ISDN network and include it in the price
of ISDN service.

Cyclical redundancy check (CRC)

A value computed by examining a packet or frame of user data. The bits that represent the user data are treated as one binary number. An algorithm (using a polynomial) is used to compute the CRC value, which is then appended to the user data. When the entire packet or frame is received, the user data is examined, and a new CRC is computed, using the same user-data bits and the same algorithm. Not surprisingly, the same CRC should be computed. If no difference is observed when the two CRCs are compared, the received data is considered accurate. (Actually there is an extremely small possibility that it is not. Mathematicians write whole volumes on this subject.) If the two CRCs are found to be different, the received data is presumed to be in error. Typically, the receiver will then request a retransmission from the sender.

D channel

The separate (out-of-band) channel for signaling between the user and the ISDN network. Protocols for these signaling packets is described in DSS1. The D channel can also be used as a bearer channel for X.25 packet service. (These bearer packets are identified to be different from signaling packets, and are separated from them.) In a BRI, the D channel is 16 Kbps; in a PRI, it is 64 Kbps.

Digital signaling rates (DS*n*)

A hierarchical system for transmission rates. A DS0 is 64 Kbps (same as a B channel). A DS1 is 1.5 Mbps (same as a PRI).

Digital Subscriber Signaling System 1 (DSS1)

A user-network protocol. Often it is casually expressed as Q.931 access protocol; however, this is only the layer-3 protocol. DSS1 is a suite of protocols that includes the layers 1, 2, and 3 protocols *and* protocols for accessing supplementary services.

Digital Subscriber Signaling System 2 (DSS2)

A user-network protocol for BISDN.

End office

A telephone network switch (central office) at the user-edge of the network. It is attached to and serves end users via local loops. Other switches (offices) in the network, such as tandem offices, don't directly serve (provide local loops to) end users.

Enterprise Network Data Interconnectivity Family (ENDIF) (in NIUF)

In this group of applications, ISDN LAN adapter vendors are working for interoperability, using IETF PPP procedures.

Euro-ISDN

The European implementation of ISDN. In some ways, it differs from NISDN-1. Users can, however, call from the United States to Europe and complete ISDN calls. It is more questionable whether they can carry their end-user equipment from the United States and use it effectively in Europe.

European ISDN Users' Forum (EIUF)

A European forum for end users.

Fast-packet services (FPS)

Packet services at speeds in excess of 1.5 Mbps. ATM is currently the most discussed. Other services are also available.

Feeder cable

Houses the subscriber loop closer to the serving central office. It is a larger cable, which typically contains hundreds of copper wires or fiber strands inside metal and plastic sheaths.

Flat-rate

A pricing plan independent of usage.

Frame

A layer-2 (in the OSI model) construct. In a bitstream, bits have meaning depending upon their position and relative position. The receiver must know "when to start counting" in the bitstream. Typically, a flag (a specified and unique pattern of bits) is transmitted periodically for this purpose. Bits between flags are called frames. A frame has meaning only between two end points, such as between the end user and the network (layer 2 of ISDN signaling) or between the end user and the distant end user (such as when conveying data via a packet-mode bearer service).

Frame relay

An ISDN bearer service, similar to packet service. Unlike packet service, however, only parts of layer 2 (frames, not packets) are defined. It is a streamlined, less functional packet-mode service. For example, there are no error-correction procedures in frame relay, but there are such procedures in other packet mode services. For transmission media having very low error rates (for example, fiber systems), it may be more efficient to use frame relay service (more throughput, faster response times).

High-definition television (HDTV)

A digital television signal capable of producing pictures much superior to today's television signal. It has greater resolution and the same aspect ratio (height and width) as a movie screen. It requires a large (about 150 Mbps) digital bandwidth.

High-density wave division multiplexing

A method of carrying more signals over a single fiber-optic strand. Current fiber-optic signals use one light source; by using sources of different colors, a great deal more capacity can be derived from the same strand. This can potentially greatly reduce transmission costs.

Implementation agreement

A document that implementors can use to create interoperable products without any other document or information. This means that everything the document intends to cover must be explicit and clearly covered.

In-band signaling

Signaling over the channel used to carry user information. In pre-ISDN telephony, voice circuits used signaling over the same facilities as for the voice service itself. For example, touch tone signals convey the called number to the network, and you can hear them over the same channel that you and the other person use to speak.

Information element

Part of a signaling message. For example, when an ISDN call is initiated, a SETup message is transferred across the user-network interface. One of the information elements in that message is the telephone number.

Information society

A society that relies on information as a key ingredient for success and well-being.

Initializing terminals

Sometimes called self-initializing terminals. An ISDN terminal that can generate its own terminal identification number. This makes it easier for the network and the terminal to agree on the number to use. The other possible scheme is to have permanent ID numbers in each terminal; however, this leads to the possibility of nonunique identification in situations where uniqueness is needed or desired.

Integrated access
Being able to access all services by a single method (such as ISDN signaling over a basic rate interface).

Interexchange carrier (IC, IEC, or IXC); also InterLATA carrier
The network-service provider that the U.S. government allows to carry telephone traffic outside of a local access transport area (LATA). (The United States is divided into 161 LATAs.)

Interfaces
A specification that defines the various protocol levels at a particular reference point. For example, at the "U" reference point, the interface at layer 1 uses a 2B1Q line code. (The other levels are also described; the physical layer contains plug and jack details.)

International Standards Organization (ISO)
An international organization known for producing the OSI seven-layer model and for other data communications standards.

International Telegraph and Telephone Consultative Committee
Now called the ITU-T, or the International Telephone Union—Telecommunications Sector. This is the standards group that produces the I series of ISDN recommendations.

Internet
A worldwide "network of networks" used by government, education, and business. It provides the closest thing we have to a universal e-mail service. The desire to access some of the higher bandwidth capabilities of the Internet (especially using the Mosaic software program) has driven interest in ISDN access.

Internet Engineering Task Force (IETF)
A group that works out procedures for operating the Internet and similar data communications networks. These procedures are called requests for comments (RFCs).

Interoperable
Two pieces of equipment are interoperable if they work together in expected ways. End-user ISDN terminals are interoperable with the network if they can obtain services, and they are interoperable with other ISDN terminals if they can achieve the intended purposes, such as sending faxes or accessing LANs from distant locations.

ISDN user part (ISUP)

Part of the SS7 specification. Its main function is to perform the network signaling tasks necessary to set up basic calls (in ISDN and in conventional telephony).

ITU-T

The telecommunications sector of the International Telephone Union; formerly the CCITT. ITU writes international standards for ISDN, mostly in Geneva.

Key systems

Telephone equipment with extra buttons that allows users to obtain more functionality than with regular telephones. These buttons (or keys) light up in ways that show the user which lines are in use, on hold, and so on.

Line termination (LT)

Electronics at the ISDN network side of the user-network interface, that complements the electronics equipment (NT1) at the user side of the interface. In combination, the two pieces of equipment provide the high-speed digital line signals needed for basic rate ISDN access.

Link access procedure (LAPD)

Link access procedure (layer 2) establishes a connection between the user and the network. This procedure (on the D channel) is required to provide a link for the user to signal to the network. This concept (the "core aspects of LAPD") has been extended to the bearer channel to provide an end-to-end link, over which higher-layer (even proprietary) protocols might operate. This is the essence of the frame relay service.

Local access transport area (LATA)

The United States is divided into 161 parcels, each of which is a LATA. Local exchange carriers provide service within the LATA. Some carriers provide service within and between LATAs, but the 7 regional Bell operating companies are prohibited by the U.S. government from offering service between LATAs.

Local area network (LAN)

A method to connect various data equipment within a small, local, geographical area. Although a variety of methods and procedures exist, a common implementation is a client-server architecture using an Ethernet-like protocol.

Local exchange carrier (LEC)

A network service provider offering services to end users within a LATA.

Local loop (or loop)

The pair of copper wires that connects the end user to the telephone network. These same wires are used to provide ISDN service but need the addition of the NT1 at the end-user location and the LT at the network location.

Mass customization

The process of producing goods or services that are customized to the tastes or requirements of the user but at mass-production costs. Often, this means significantly less than mass-production quantities, and sometimes it means a quantity of one. Achieving this desirable combination of production cost and customized goods or services usually involves computer-based systems, tools, or machines.

Message-oriented signaling

Messages used to convey signaling information. For example, a SETup message to establish a call, rather than sensing current over a loop to see if a subscriber has gone off-hook to place a telephone call.

Metropolitan area network (MAN)

Conceptually similar to LANs, these networks connect various data equipment at high speeds and over a larger geographic area (a town or city), using appropriate technologies such as ATM.

Modem (MOdulator/DEModulator)

Used in pre-ISDN telephony for sending data signals over an analog channel. It encodes digital signals into tones. Newer modems have, surprisingly, been able to send increasingly larger amounts of data over analog circuits. Nevertheless, they are becoming inadequate in our information society.

Multilink

Many links. Used in the context of point-to-point protocol. A procedure to route data packets over many links to obtain increased bandwidth. For example, two B channels on a single BRI for 128 Kbps.

Narrowband ISDN (NISDN)

A term for ISDN used by broadband enthusiasts to distinguish it from Broadband ISDN (BISDN).

National ISDN 1 (NISDN-1 or NI-1)

An agreement among service providers and vendors to jointly provide the first phase of a standards-based ISDN. Vendors agree to manufacture products that are consistent with a particular collection of Bellcore Technical References (based on ANSI and ITU-T specifications). Service providers agree to buy and deploy this equipment; users benefit by being able to plan on using a widely deployed, standard ISDN.

NI-2, NI-3, and so on

Subsequent phases of National ISDN. Each higher number adds more ISDN capabilities (and occurs later in time). While no particular time frame separates each subsequent phase, 12 to 18 months would probably be required for development, deployment, and agreements.

North American ISDN Users' Forum (NIUF)

Forum for ISDN users in North America.

North American Numbering Plan (NANP)

The numbering plan for the United States, Canada, Mexico, and the rest of North America. It's the familiar area code followed by the local 7-digit telephone number. (In the future, more digits are planned to meet the growing demand for new telephone numbers.)

NT1

Network terminating equipment; electronics at the ISDN user side of the user-network interface that complements the line termination (LT) electronics equipment at the network side of the interface. In combination, the two pieces of equipment provide the high-speed digital line signals needed for basic rate ISDN access. End users must purchase this equipment; it cannot be provided as part of the basic ISDN service in the United States. (in many other parts of the world, the NT1 comes as part of the ISDN service and is included in the tariff prices to the end user.)

NT2

Network terminating equipment, on the customer side of an NT1. PBXs are a typical example of an implementation of an NT2.

Out-of-band signaling

Requesting services, establishing circuits, and other signaling functions is sent by way of messages over a separate signaling channel, rather than within the channel that carries information from one user to the other. ISDN uses out-of-band signaling; but, more significantly, the signaling over that separate channel consists of messages rather than simple stimuli.

Packet

A layer-3 construct (in the OSI model). A grouping of bits that constitute part of a particular connection or call. Packets can be of variable length and are created when there is a need to transfer information. During other periods of time, the available channel bandwidth can be used for other connections. A series of packets is related to a particular connection by examining codes in the header of each packet. (The header is a well-identified group of bits which appears at the beginning of each packet.)

Pair

A pair of wires (in telephony, called the tip and ring, from the parts of a jack inserted into a cordboard). A subscriber loop is a pair of wires from the user to the serving central office. Two wires are used, rather than one, because the line signal is "balanced" with respect to ground to mitigate electrical interference.

Permanent virtual circuit (PVC)

A logical connection established by arrangement with the telephone company or network provider (as opposed to a circuit switched connection, which is established at the time of call setup).

Plain old telephone service (POTS)

A convenient way to contrast "regular" telephone service with any of the advanced new services being described.

Point-to-point protocol (PPP)

Defined by the IETF. Provides efficient data transfer processes using ISDN. Especially popular in remote access to LAN applications.

Portability

An end-user's ISDN terminal equipment is said to be completely portable if the end user can remove it from its working location and reinsert it into another location for that or any other ISDN network. Achieving portability is a matter of degree—the more the better.

Postindustrial society

Current and future society that relies on information rather than industrial production to produce wealth and success.

Powering

ISDN end user equipment is powered locally, like a television or radio. This requires that end users plan whether and how they wish to power their ISDN systems during power failures.

Primary rate access (PRA); primary rate interface (PRI)

Access to and interface for ISDN, using a 1.5 Mbps access connection. This provides 23 B channels (64 Kbps each) and 1 D channel (also at 64 Kbps). It is also available as 24 B channels (all at 64 Kbps). Still other configurations provide for the aggregating of B channels for channels capable of transporting user information at 64 Kbps times the number of B channels in the aggregate.

Protocol

A set of rules that define how equipment interoperates with like equipment. In ISDN, message-oriented protocols are protocols in which messages are exchanged, and procedures are followed as a result of the message exchange.

Protocol implementation conformance statements (PICS); PICS proformas

A formal method to allow implementors to express the degree and the way their equipment conforms to a standard.

Public utilities commission (PUC); public services commission (PSC)

Governmental organizations (usually for a state) that regulate telephone companies (and power companies and sometimes taxi service as well). The FCC regulates some aspects, and the local regulatory bodies regulate other aspects.

Quantizing

Analog to digital conversion, by assigning a range (from the continuous analog values) to a discrete number.

Rate adaptation

A technique to allow two pieces of data equipment to interoperate, even though they operate at dissimilar rates. For ISDN in the United States, rate adaptation is done mostly using V.120 and, in other parts of the world, often by V.110.

Rate cap

Regulatory construct of more recent origin than "rate of return" (next entry). Protects the consumer by capping rates, but rewards good management by allowing increasing rewards for good management.

Rate of return

Regulatory construct that sets prices to constrain profitability to be a fair (compared to other industries) ratio of earnings to capital. Although this method has merit, it is criticized because it distorts the risk-reward incentives to offer new telephony service and because it doesn't reward success as well as other constructs (such as full competition).

Real time

The notion of needing and using information "now" (in real time) rather than at some time in the past or future.

Re-engineering

Rethinking how to run a business, without being limited by how it operates today. The benefit is being able to stop performing work that doesn't really add value to the company or its customers, thus avoiding costs without affecting the product. Often associated with computer-based information systems or computer integrated manufacturing systems to produce more efficiently or effectively.

Reference point

A spot in a topological model (a model that shows how the pieces form a whole). Each spot of interest (that is, any spot that might need to be referred to in discussion or writing) is identified. Examples include the S reference point and the U reference point. These particular points are also interfaces.

Regional Bell Operating Company (RBOC)

One of the local exchange carriers that were divested as part of the settlement of the antitrust case against the Bell System. By the terms of the modified final judgment (MFJ) of that settlement (and among other constraints), RBOCs could not offer long-distance telephone service (between LATAs) or manufacture equipment.

Request for Comment (RFC)

An IETF "standard" by another name.

Resolving comments

Process intended to maximize satisfaction and support of standards when they are adopted. A "no" vote is accompanied by proposed wording changes that are then discussed. Attempts are made to propose new wording acceptable to everyone. When successful, the new wording adopted in the approved standard is supported by all participants.

Service profile identification (SPID)

An alphanumeric string (value) that uniquely identifies the services capabilities in an ISDN terminal. It is actually a label identifier that points to a particular location in central office memory where the relevant details are stored.

Signaling System 7 (SS7)

Common channel signaling system that performs network signaling functions. Among other things, it will be used to establish ISDN call connections. SS7 usually refers to the ANSI specification, which differs from the CCITT specification (known as CCS 7).

64 Kbps clear channel capability (64 CCC)

A transmission channel that carries 64 Kbps of transmission capacity without constraint. That is, the user can send any combination of ones or zeroes. This has historically been difficult to achieve because traditional DS1 rates and formats used "bit robbing" of the channel to provide inband signaling. Using common channel signaling (for example, SS7) allows the bits that would otherwise be robbed for signaling to be used for line signal values. Many carrier systems also require B8ZS or some similar scheme to maintain system synchronization.

Standard

Generally, for an ISDN standard, written documents agreed to by others. For most standards bodies covered in this book, this involves a lot of very formal practices, including written letter ballots used in voting. De facto standards (not done in standards bodies) are often donated by industry leaders (or, from a different perspective, imposed on industry by those who dominate it).

Subscriber loop

The pair of copper wires that connect the end user to the telephone network. These same wires are used to provide ISDN service but need the addition of the NT1 at the end-user location and the LT at the network location.

Supplementary service

"Acts" on a bearer service. For example, call forwarding "acts" on incoming circuit-switched calls.

Switched virtual circuit (SVC)

A logical connection established at the time of call setup. Generally used in the context of data circuits, where only a portion of the available channel bandwidth is associated with a particular SVC.

Switching, switch

Switching is the act of connecting two or more lines or trunks (or logical channels). A *switch* is the equipment that performs that function. In the telephone network (and ISDN), each subscriber has a dedicated loop to the nearest telephone switch. All of the switches have access (can switch and connect the loop) to trunks. A call from one user to another consists of a loop at each end of the connection, with some number of switched trunks in between.

Synchronous

A constant bit rate where the timing is derived from a central time source, often by synchronizing with the line signal being received.

Systems integrators

Providers of whole solutions using technologies from a variety of different sources.

Tariff

A rate-and-availability schedule for telephone and ISDN services from regulated network-service providers. Also, any general terms and conditions of service. It must be filed with and approved by a regulatory body in order to become effective (in force).

TE1, or terminal equipment (ISDN)

Connects to an ISDN network. It could be an ISDN telephone, a personal computer capable of working with an ISDN network, or any other device capable of performing the user-network protocol.

TE2, or terminal equipment (non-ISDN)

Connects to some non-ISDN or pre-ISDN network. To be used with an ISDN, a terminal adapter must be used with a TE2. The combination of a TE2 and a TA is functionally equivalent to a TE1.

Technical Reference (TR)

Detailed specifications (from Bellcore) that define various interfaces, protocols, and requirements. A set of these TRs are identified in order to define the contents of NI-1.

Telephone user part (TUP)

Part of CCS 7 (the CCITT specification). It does not appear in the ANSI version of SS7. Its main function is to provide basic call connection within the network. Later versions of CCS 7 for ISDN will include ISUP.

Terminal adapter (TA)

Adapts a non-ISDN terminal to be used at an ISDN interface. (See TE2.)

TRanscontinental ISDN Project '92(TRIP '92)

Conferences held in November 1992. Over 150 sites around the world displayed ISDN products and services. Many of these sites were hosted by ISDN users, showing how they actually used ISDN. Others, such as the Reston, Virginia site, contained exhibits of equipment and presentations from a variety of users and vendors. The key value of TRIP '92 was that it inaugurated the National ISDN network, which uses specifications conforming to the Bellcore TRs (which, in turn, were based on ANSI and ITU-T standards). Previously, ISDN was provided in a variety of vendor-specific methods.

Transmission

To send and receive signals that convey information from one device (for example, a telephone or telephone switch) to another. In ISDN, all transmission is digital.

Two bits 1 quartenary (2B1Q)

A line code at layer 1 for basic rate ISDN at the "U" interface. Two bits of data value (2B) are mapped into one of four line values (1Q, or one quartenary). This coding scheme allows a single pair of copper cable (of lengths up to about 3 miles) to carry 160 Kbps of information in both directions and at the same time.

Uninterruptible power supply (UPS)

Equipment that provides continuous electrical power, even when commercial power fails. Since ISDN terminals are not powered from the telephone line (as traditional phones are), they need commercial power to operate. To continue using ISDN during power failures, a battery back-up or UPS is needed. Typical UPS-protected ISDN terminal equipment receives operating power from a battery, which in turn continuously receives rectified commercial power to keep itself charged. When commercial power fails, the battery continues to supply the ISDN equipment until the battery is drained. Telephone-switching machines are powered this way, using a string (often tens) of batteries that look much like automobile batteries. For extended outages, a diesel generator stationed right at the telephone switch can continuously operate the battery charger and switch.

Usage-sensitive

Prices for services, such as ISDN circuit-switched data, that are billed by the time that they are actually in use.

Virtual office

Coined to broaden the idea (beyond "work-at-home") that your office can be wherever you are. In addition to working at home, you can have your office in a hotel room, an airport terminal, or any other location. ISDN is one of the key ingredients of a virtual office.

Virtual reality

A re-creation of something that is so real that it seems to actually *be* real. In virtual reality, one sees pictures, hears sounds, and may also be physically moved or jostled. Physical interactions with the virtual-reality environment are made possible with devices, such as goggles and gloves with sensors that allow the user to "touch" and "move" things.

Wide area network (WAN)

Generally, connecting LANs together. Connectivity, implicitly in a data environment. Technologies for doing this include packet networks, pre-ISDN networks, and ISDN networks. In exchange for extending into wide areas, the user encounters longer response times and slower transmission. ISDN currently offers the best solution to connecting LANs to wider areas, especially now that it is being widely deployed.

Wiring

Generally, inside (a building). For ISDN, some of the older wiring will not be sufficient and will have to be altered or replaced. Often, this is not necessary, but the user should consider the possibility.

Workstations

Allow end-user knowledge workers to gain access and provide information to others. Examples include PCs (of all types), terminals (for example, X-Windows), and other higher-powered devices (more traditionally considered to be workstations and are often found in engineering environments).

X.25

The CCITT recommendation that describes protocol for packet-mode services.

Zero-byte time slot interchange (ZBTSI)

An alternate method to B8ZS for allowing 64 Kbps unrestricted user data (i.e., allowing all zeros in the user data). It is not as generally accepted as 8BZS.

Index